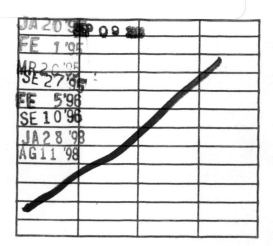

SEE NO EVIL

Blind Devotion and Bloodshed in David Koresh's Holy War

Tim Madigan

The Summit Group
Fort Worth Texas

Published by The Summit Group
1227 West Magnolia
Fort Worth, Texas 76104

Publisher's Cataloging in Publication
(*Prepared by Quality Books Inc.*)

Madigan, Timothy.
    See no evil: blind devotion and bloodshed in David Koresh's
holy war / by Tim Madigan.
    p. cm.
    ISBN 1-56530-063-7

1. Koresh, David. 2. Christian sects—Texas.   I. Title.

BX9998.K67M33 1993   289.9'09764'284
                                       QBI93-678

Cover Design by Amber Brown
Book Design by Sean Walker

For Catherine, now and always.

CONTENTS

FOREWORD

For more than a decade, I have crisscrossed the country as a cult deprogrammer, confronting destructive cults and fanatical religious groups in every corner of the nation. In hundreds of cases, I have seen firsthand the suffering and broken lives they engender. Yet it so often seemed as if the American people were indifferent to the dangers posed by these extremists flourishing within our society. When warnings were sounded about cults, few listened.

Today, people throughout the United States and the world have been shocked into reality. As we watched Mount Carmel burn to the ground near Waco, horrified by the terrible loss of life, we jointly witnessed fanaticism's ultimate handiwork. One cult leader, David Koresh, controlled his followers to their deaths.

There are thousands of destructive cult groups operating in this country in every state. They have penetrated virtually every metropolitan area, even finding their way into small towns and isolated communities. No matter where we go, no matter what we do, we can not hide from this problem. How will we face it? Will we attempt to learn from the tragedy at Waco? It is my hope that this book will increase and stimulate the process of education about cults and destructive religious groups—enlightenment that hopefully will save others from sharing in the Branch Davidians' awful fate.

First, America must take a long, hard look at Vernon Howell, later known to the world as David Koresh, because among cult leaders, he is not atypical. It seems they are all the same. As I travel the country and delve into different destructive cults, I meet the same cult leader over and over again. Only the names are different. They are self-obsessed, egomaniacal, sociopathic and heartless individuals with no regard whatsoever for their followers. They seek only their personal aggrandizement, financial well-being and physical pleasure. Such leaders exercise total control over their followers. The personalities of those adherents have been dismantled by systematic brainwashing to the point where the leader's desires become their own. Cult victims and fanatical followers of radical sects are deceived, lied to, manipulated and ultimately exploited. They number in the millions.

We would all like to believe that only crazy people from bizarre families or those with deep personal problems join destructive cults. This is a convenient form of denial, not the truth. The Waco Branch Davidians came from many socioeconomic, educational, ethnic and national backgrounds. David Koresh recruited from around the world and from every strata of society. Some of his followers sought greater meaning in life, others had become disenchanted with our society's materialism. David Koresh seemingly offered a sense of belonging to those from broken homes, or seemed to provide his followers with direction and great spiritual insight. For many

Davidians, his fraud never became apparent.

Once recruited, there was one main reason Koresh's followers stayed: they stopped thinking critically for themselves. Through a process of manipulation, they fell under the control of an absolute, authoritarian leader. They were isolated from the outside world, cut off from any other frame of reference. Even their families and old friends often were discredited. Again, the mind-control methods of David Koresh are typical of many cult leaders.

What can be learned from the tragedy at Mount Carmel? What are the warning signs? A prospective member of an unknown sect or religious group should be wary if the group's leader is accountable to no one. He or she should think twice if members are not allowed to question; if isolation and spiritual elitism are promoted by an ethnocentric theology; if independent thinking is discouraged or described as rebellion against God; if the only truth is the leader's truth; or if the leader is above "man's law" and accountable only to "God." In destructive cults, that deity most often speaks exclusively through their leader, who may ignore all civil authority and reject accountability to anyone.

The Waco Branch Davidians are a wake-up call to America. Destructive cults are no longer a distant reality in the jungles of Guyana, but have come home to claim scores of victims in the heartland of the country. Meanwhile, other violent cults continue to proliferate across the American landscape. White supremacist churches, apocalyptic Bible-based cults and other fanatical groups in all shapes and sizes are waiting to explode on the American scene at any time.

Everyone must be aware of the dangers posed by these groups. But it is also time for government and law enforcement agencies, and child protection services to enforce the law. Destructive cults should not be allowed to hide behind the walls of separation of church and state. All Americans are responsible to the same laws of reasonable conduct. That includes so-called religious organizations which illegally stockpile weapons, abuse children and sexually exploit their members in the name of God. Mount Carmel represents the consequences of a nation "looking the other way."

Where will the next Waco be? Who will be the next David Koresh? If we don't heed the tragic lessons of the Branch Davidians and their leader, it will only be a matter of time before we find out.

> *Rick Ross*
> Phoenix
> April 25, 1993

PREFACE

My challenge was to produce against a four-week dead-line a book that might somehow explain David Koresh and the tragedy of Mount Carmel. As I sit now, I can see the futility of that task. The mystery of Koresh can not be unraveled in four weeks. It could not be unraveled in four years. The man who has consumed my every waking moment, seven days a week since early March, is clearly one whose evil defies diagnoses or explanation.

What follows instead are signposts from David Koresh's journey into madness, from the youngster whose boyish picture still sits on the living room mantel in his grandmother's home, to the cult leader who condemned his followers to death in a tragic inferno.

To a large extent, *See No Evil* also is the story of those left behind, anguished relatives from around the world who were completely mystified by Koresh's power over their loved ones. In dozens of interviews over the last month, I grew to know many of them personally, and by extension, their family members who had surrendered mind, body and soul to the guitar-playing, ninth-grade dropout who claimed to be God. Many of these relatives believed those who followed Koresh had ceased to live, long before the Mount Carmel fire of April 19, 1993. Perhaps that is the greatest tragedy of all.

I owe a tremendous debt to many people, without whose support, assistance and encouragement this book would not have been possible. My editors at the *Fort Worth Star-Telegram*; Mike Blackman, Mary Jo Meisner, Ken Bunting, Roland Lindsey, Gary Hardee, Joe Stebbins, Barry Shlachter, Ernie Makovy, Jim Peipert and Raul Reyes, were unceasing with their assistance and patience.

I leaned heavily on the *Star-Telegram*'s reporting staff during the research and writing of the book, friends and colleagues who provided Fort Worth readers with distinguished coverage of one of the biggest stories of our generation. Reporters Kathy Sanders, Jack Douglas, Jr., Hollace Weiner, Thomas Korosec, Jim Jones, Tim Sullivan, Frank Perkins, Stefani Gammage Kopenec, Mede Nix, John Gonzalez, Michael Whiteley, Stan Jones and Bob Mahlburg were never too busy meeting their own deadlines to help me with mine.

This project was undertaken on the advice of two good friends, *Star-Telegram* authors Larry Swindell and Jerry Flemmons. There were times in the last month that I cursed them both. I'm glad I listened now. Without their shared expertise and constant support, the book never would have been written. I also thank Jeff Guinn and Sam Hudson for their friendship and encouragement.

Summit Group managing editor Mike Towle was unceasingly patient and supportive throughout the project.

In the course of my research, I was deeply honored by those who trusted me so fully with the details of their private anguish. My heart goes out now to Samuel Henry and Lloyd Hardial in Manchester, England. Erline Clark also lost much on that fiery day in Texas. She was kind, gracious and open with me during an extended Sunday afternoon in March. She and her family have my deepest condolences. Andy Leamon was unsparing with his time, recollections and feelings about his childhood companion. I must also thank Bob Lott, Charlie Seraphin, Denise Wilkerson and the players of Rif Raf for their significant contributions to this book.

No one was more generous or shed more light into the dark mystery of David Koresh than Rick Ross. His knowledge of Koresh and the Branch Davidians is unequaled, and though in wide demand during the stand-off at Mount Carmel, Rick was always available to answer my questions and share his wisdom. He graciously consented to write the foreword for this book. I now consider him a friend and am hopelessly in his debt.

I thank my parents, Myke and Lois in Crookston, Minnesota, for a lifetime of love. I thank my dear friend and mentor Norval Kneten. Norval is a beacon.

My greatest gratitude, however, is reserved for those who sleep under my roof. Catherine is a wife of boundless love and beauty, who is also the best editor I know. She worked tirelessly on this project. It was a team effort in every respect. I am very proud of what we accomplished together in so short a time.

Melanie, our daughter, sustained us with her love and

cheerful assistance. Many times it was her smile and cool head that kept her parents from losing theirs. Finally I thank Catherine, Melanie, and little Patrick for constantly reminding me during my journey into the madness of David Koresh that the world is a truly wonderful place after all.

ABOUT THE AUTHOR

Tim Madigan, thirty-five, is a reporter for the *Fort Worth* (Texas) *Star-Telegram*. A native of Crookston, Minnesota, he studied journalism at the University of North Dakota and has worked at several newspapers, including the *Odessa* (Texas) *American* and the *Chicago Tribune*. Madigan has won several awards for his reporting and writing during a thirteen-year career as a newspaper reporter. This is his first book. Madigan, his wife Catherine McMahon, daughter Melanie and son Patrick, live in Arlington, Texas.

1

SAMUEL HENRY'S LAMENT

Samuel Henry felt the blood drain from his face as his wife spoke, unable to believe what he was hearing. It was a Sunday evening in their Manchester, England home. The next morning, Zilla Henry said, she and the children were leaving for America to seek salvation in the teachings of the man named Vernon Howell.

Her husband felt faint, speechless at first.

"You've got to be joking," Samuel cried finally. "Let's pray about this. Let's talk about this."

But his wife's bags were packed, as were the children's.

"It's too late now," Zilla, Samuel's wife of thirty years, said calmly on that spring evening in 1990. "This man is the Christ."

It would be Samuel Henry's final humiliation, the ultimate defeat by an American whom Henry had come to regard as the incarnation of Satan. When that devil was done, all Henry would have left was a large, empty house full of bittersweet memories.

The middle-aged building contractor would often think back to the time he added rooms to the couple's two-story brick home on Coleridge Road to keep pace with the needs of their growing family. There were five children and Zilla, a quiet nurse who taught Sabbath Day classes at their Seventh-day Adventist[1] church.

The children, three girls and two boys, were well-mannered and talented, praised for their performances at church-sponsored music recitals. Their home seemed among the most popular in Manchester, with the comings and goings of the Henry offspring and their many friends; with the frequent meetings held by church elders there; with the Henry family tradition of gathering around the piano to sing hymns.

That was before the devil came.

Samuel Henry's oldest child was the first to fall. Diana Henry was twenty-three years old in 1988 when a boy-friend introduced her to Vernon Howell. Howell was a guitar-playing Yank, a pleasant-looking young man with curly, shoulder-length blond hair and wire-rimmed glasses. But neither Howell's music nor his appearance could account for the spell he cast. His power apparently derived from his riveting interpretation of the Book of Revelation, consisting of apocalyptic prophecies that gushed from his mouth in marathon Bible sessions held at a small church college near London. Howell had come to seek souls and to speak obliquely of a Great Light, a light that Diana Henry saw as the path to salvation.

She had been a prudent and circumspect young woman until then, a devout Seventh-day Adventist like her parents. Her father described her as highly intelli-

---

[1]Church authorities use "Seventh-day Adventist" as standard form, although *Random House Webster's Collegiate Dictionary* (1991) prefers Seventh-Day or seventh-day when referring to Adventists.

gent, a recent college graduate with degrees in both psychology and sociology. She worked for a London welfare agency while planning eventually to continue her studies in graduate school. But her father noticed a change the minute she called him from London after meeting the "great man."

"Daddy, listen!" Diana Henry cried. "Listen!"

Samuel Henry listened, but skeptically. He was deeply religious and well-versed in the Bible. As his daughter continued speaking on the telephone that day, it became clear to him that Vernon Howell's teachings made no sense. His daughter refused to be dissuaded and would not heed her father's warnings about false prophets.

It was at Diana's urging that the rest of the family traveled 180 miles to London to meet Howell for themselves—even Zilla, who was curious about her oldest daughter's new passion. Only Samuel remained behind.

Like dominoes they tumbled. Diana Henry was first, abandoning her school plans and traveling to America to a desolate place on the plains of Texas called Mount Carmel, where Howell had promised her and other British friends that his full message would be revealed.

Samuel himself followed in 1989, desperate to learn more about the self-proclaimed prophet who had come to possess such influence over his family. When he arrived at the place near Waco he found a cluster of tumble-down bungalows without indoor plumbing, scores of adoring adherents like his daughter, and Howell, the leader of the sect known as the Branch Davidians.

Samuel resisted the Davidian leader's earnest attempts to mystify him with scatter-shot rantings from the Bible, scoffing at Howell's absurd claims that he alone could unravel the apocalyptic mysteries contained therein. To

Samuel, the Bible's message was simple, not mysterious—love God and love man—and he told Howell so to his face as the two sat together inside a building at Mount Carmel, located about ten miles northeast of Waco in central Texas.

"Jesus did say there will be false Christs and false prophets," Samuel admonished the younger man.

"I am one of those," Howell replied sarcastically, growing angry.

"Well stated," the British father said with equal sarcasm.

Henry had heard all he needed by then. He left Mount Carmel within an hour and was dropped off by his daughter at a Waco bus station. A few days later, he returned to England, determined to save the rest of his family.

"This man is evil," he told his wife when he had returned from America.

But like Diana, neither Zilla nor the rest of the children would listen. Samuel pleaded. He begged. He tried to bribe one son with a car to keep him from leaving. Then came Zilla's shocking news that night in 1990, and eventually they were all gone to that dreadful place overseas.

On Coleridge Road, the house they left behind seemed to echo when Samuel Henry returned from work each night. Twice in the months after his family departed, he pulled his van from the road, overtaken by his sorrow, unable to drive. What could possibly be worse than this? he sometimes wondered.

He was soon to learn. At 6:00 a.m., Monday, March 1, 1993, Henry was jolted awake by a ringing telephone. It was a friend calling from London.

"Brother Henry, have you been listening to the news?" the friend asked.

"What news?"

"You haven't heard what's happening in Waco?"

Later that night, watching the television news at the home of another friend, Henry saw for himself. The scene seemed a true-crime dramatization so popular on American television. Only what he saw was real—dozens of federal agents, dressed for combat in helmets and dark blue uniforms with the letters ATF emblazoned in white on their backs. They fired shot after shot at the beige-colored buildings of Mount Carmel in an attack that had taken place the day before.

His wife and children were behind those bullet-pierced walls, Samuel Henry knew. They had lost their souls to Vernon Howell, the man now known to the world as David Koresh, and now seemed condemned to lose their lives as well.

Before that grim day in March, Henry felt he had wept as much as any man could. He rose from his chair to walk outside when he could watch no more, tears washing down his cheeks once again.

The weekend news had been dominated by Friday's bombing of the World Trade Center in New York, an engrossing story of death, intrigue and heroism, with undertones of religious fanaticism. But within hours of a Sunday morning bloodbath far away in the Texas countryside, the madness at Manhattan's twin towers would be supplanted on television screens by the dimpled visage of a self-proclaimed prophet.

You couldn't escape David Koresh, not in the immediate aftermath of the furious shootout between the Branch

Davidians and federal agents, nor in the long siege that would follow. There was Koresh on the national news, night after night after night, the same film clip running again and again, the one that showed the unshaven cult leader, curly hair dangling to his shoulders, a Bible in one hand, gesturing wildly with the other, preaching to a few dozen of his flock who looked on, transfixed.

He would command the front pages of every newspaper from the *New York Times* to the *Los Angeles Times* to the London tabloids. His face would adorn the covers of *Time*, *Newsweek* and *People*. He would gobble up air time on Phil and Oprah, "48 Hours," "Dateline," "Nightline," "Prime-Time Live," Leno and "Saturday Night Live." One night in March, Dolly Parton told David Letterman about being holed up with her band in a tour bus during a New York blizzard.

"I felt like that David Koresh," Parton quipped.

"Weekend Update" anchor Kevin Nealon offered this news flash during a March episode of "Saturday Night Live."

"This just in," Nealon said. "David Koresh has admitted he's not really Jesus, but actually is a disgruntled postal employee."

Koresh, remarkably enough, had in a violent spasm become one of the world's most recognizable faces, no small feat for someone born to a fifteen-year-old single mother in Houston thirty-three years earlier; for a boy shuttled between grandparents for most of his early years; for a person whose later talents consisted chiefly of playing the guitar and memorizing large chunks of the Bible.

It was the latter gift that Koresh, who changed his name in 1990, used as a young adult to badger irritated relatives at family reunions, to pester co-workers on construction sites and to buttonhole fellow church members. His preaching was unending. No one could be sure what his message meant. There was a passage from Revelation here, Psalms there, with some Daniel occasionally thrown in. But he was at it constantly, an irrepressible young man, not only weird, but tiresome.

"Shut up, Vernon," people would say. "Just shut up."

Yet history records that one man's fool is another man's prophet, and people would soon listen to Vernon Howell. In the early 1980s, shortly before his incessant preaching got him thrown out of a Seventh-day Adventist church in the town of Tyler, a friend introduced him to an obscure and until then peace-loving sect living in the country near Waco.

The Branch Davidians, who had splintered from the Seventh-day Adventist church decades before, were led by an elderly woman named Lois Roden. To her, Vernon Howell's skill with the Scripture made him a prophet, divinely inspired, not a kook, a view perhaps colored by the fact that Roden, in her late sixties, reportedly took the handsome young newcomer into her bed.

Howell had finally found what he most craved. The Davidians followed Lois Roden's lead and actually listened to him. They were no rubes, either, drawn as they were from the Harvard Law Class of 1977, the U.S. Postal Service, professions of engineering, nursing, the ordained Christian clergy. They were young and old, rich and poor, eventually coming to share one bond: membership in Vernon Howell's adoring congregation.

They sat spellbound at the feet of the young man with the amazing capacity for reciting Scripture, sometimes for fifteen hours straight. The followers felt inferior at his insight. Only a prophet could know so much, they thought, listening approvingly as the ninth-grade dropout eventually declared himself the son of God, the Lamb described in Revelation who would unlock the mysteries of the seven seals and, therefore, the end of time.

They listened as he cranked out rock music as lead singer and guitarist of his band "Messiah," often at noisy 3:00 a.m. jam sessions at Mount Carmel when others tried to sleep.

They watched as he methodically claimed the females of his flock for himself, including the wives of his closest advisors and girls as young as twelve. His harem became biblically ordained, according to Howell, because it was written only the Lamb possessed the Godly seed.

"Howell is obsessed with sex," former cult member Marc Breault would write in a 1989 court affidavit. "I have often witnessed Howell giving Bible studies, if you can call them that, in which literally hours were spent describing sex, sexual acts and sexual preferences in graphic detail. Little children were also forced to listen."

Later, on national television a young woman named Robyn Bunds, who was a member of Howell's concubine before escaping the cult, put it very simply.

"We were having babies for God," said Bunds, who bore Howell a son.

It was, as one cult expert later described it, "a sexual psychopath's dream."

The Davidians also stood by as he beat their children. They acquiesced as he took their money and material goods—hundreds of thousands of dollars as well as houses, boats and cars.

And they followed as Howell led them down the road to war, to Armageddon. Mount Carmel was transformed from a pastoral complex of small houses into an interconnected fortress, replete with a four-story guard tower and underground firing range. Believers, women and children included, braced for the imminent apocalypse. A gun was assigned to every man. Target practice included enough firepower to stop a small army.

A 1987 gun battle for cult leadership at Mount Carmel with Lois Roden's son hinted ominously of Vernon Howell's intentions. After the shootout, which left George Roden wounded and Howell under arrest for attempted murder, authorities confiscated shotguns, rifles, and box upon box of ammunition.

"I haven't seen ammunition like this since Vietnam," one sheriff's deputy said then.

In one of the most bizarre trials in Waco history, in which the decayed corpse of an old woman was a key piece of evidence, jurors were unable to reach a verdict on the attempted-murder charges against Howell. The charges were dismissed, thus removing the final obstacle to his absolute control of the Davidians.

He would continue adding to an arsenal that once seemed destined for overseas targets. Koresh taught that the apocalyptic battle would take place in Israel. In 1987, Jimbo Ward, the lead singer of a Waco rock band, had a strange conversation with a member of the Davidians who also was the bass player for Koresh's rock group.

"He said they were training, getting guns and stuff, because they were going to take back the Holy Land," Ward said he was told.

Ward thought that was funny.

"Man, there's a bunch of other countries wanting to beat you to it," Ward replied.

As years passed, Howell spoke of a threat closer to home. In 1990, he changed his name to Koresh, which is

Hebrew for Cyrus, the Old Testament ruler who delivered the promised people from Babylonia. The Babylonians soon would come again, he insisted, but not from other lands. He suggested it would be agents of the U.S. government who would storm the Mount Carmel gates.

The stockpiles grew. Mount Carmel fortifications continued. Armed guards were posted at the compound around the clock. One terrified newspaper delivery man came under fire early one morning by mistake, according to a man who left the cult.

By 1992, the sect that had lived quietly for decades ten miles northeast of Waco began to attract the attention of outsiders. A nine-month investigation by the *Waco Tribune-Herald* detailed Koresh's more untoward sexual proclivities. At the same time, agents of the federal Bureau of Alcohol, Tobacco and Firearms were monitoring the flow of thousands of dollars of weapons into the compound. Included were parts for turning legal rifles into illegal machine guns and material for the manufacture of explosives. Former members spoke of night vision equipment at the compound. One delivery man saw grenade hulls after a case bound for the Davidians reportedly fell open by accident. Reports to federal agents indicated Koresh sought access to anti-tank weapons.

Then, shortly before 10:00 a.m. on February 28, 1993, one David Koresh prophecy came true.

Designed as a modern-day Trojan Horse ruse, more than 100 heavily armed ATF agents in full battle armor loaded into the rear of two red and white gooseneck cattle trailers. The plan, rehearsed by elite ATF teams for months, was to catch David Koresh after a morning Bible study when his guns would be locked away and while he napped. Two warrants would be served, one for Koresh's arrest for federal weapon's violations, the other to search the compound.

The small convoy set out from a Waco staging area about 9:30 a.m. on Sunday, February 28. They drove out Loop 340 from town, turned left onto Farm-to-Market-Road 2491 for the winding trip past grazing goats and trailer homes. Farm houses and black cattle speckled the rolling land.

But their arrival at the Branch Davidian compound was the worst-kept secret in Waco. Waiting in the mist on the cold, gray morning were *Waco Tribune-Herald* reporters and photographers, their seven-part series on Koresh, "The Sinful Messiah," having begun the day before. A local television crew was waiting, too. They expected a show of government muscle. What they saw was a Branch Davidian ambush.

Agents rushing from trailers toward the buildings were greeted by gunfire, hundreds of shots recklessly blasted through walls, floors and ceilings by Koresh's followers, some of them reportedly dressed in black and wearing black ski masks. The agents had underestimated the ferocity of their foes.

What would become excruciatingly familiar television footage captured one agent on the compound roof being blasted through a wall, wood splinters flying, bullets lodging in a protective vest, before he managed to scurry down a ladder to safety.

Rifles were fired at agents from every available window, or so it seemed. Davidians sniped from the watch tower, apparently armed with a .50-caliber machine gun powerful enough to take down armored vehicles from a mile away. Two of three government helicopters hovering nearby were hit and forced to land. One agent fell wounded and continued to take fire from the Davidians as he lay exposed and helpless.

By the time Koresh agreed to a cease-fire by telephone forty-five minutes later, four ATF agents were dead or dying. Sixteen others were wounded, at least two by hand grenade fragments. Davidians also suffered casualties, but exactly how many, no one outside of the compound could immediately be sure. Koresh told authorities he was wounded.

The scene afterward was reminiscent of Vietnam after a losing firefight—dazed agents, carrying their wounded, some of them weeping, plodding in retreat across open fields. The wounded were carried away in cars or on the hoods of trucks. It would become the bloodiest day in the federal bureau's history, the worst since two ATF agents were killed in a shootout with Pretty Boy Floyd six decades before. One Waco newspaper reporter, shaken himself after witnessing the battle, approached the retreating officers for an interview. An agent half-pleadingly ordered him away.

"Can't you see we've been through it?" the agent said.

A media city of satellite dishes and television cameras sprouted on the prairie within hours, reporters settling in for what would become a long stand-off with the hundreds of federal agents. They would be bit players in a bizarre drama, a drama in which David Koresh alone held the spotlight. In the stand-off's opening hours, he would take to the airwaves of North Texas radio stations to personally introduce the world to his version of the seven seals of Revelation.

The questions raised by the day's bloody events tumbled one upon another. Why had the raid been so badly botched? Who tipped Koresh to the attack? But the questions concerning Koresh himself were more troubling. In an instant, the Branch Davidians had become the most famous of an estimated 5,000 cults in America, and the world would wonder what motivated its leader. How could he command such devotion and loyalty from his followers, even unto death?

These were not criminals inside the compound walls, at least not until now. Not warriors, but people like Samuel Henry's children, unusual perhaps, only in their deep quest for meaning in life, a quest that at least initially, David Koresh had fulfilled. Was no one safe?

Outsiders decried the mind control techniques of a man with an undoubted genius for using the Bible as a tool for manipulation. Yet David Koresh was scarcely the first. There were eerie parallels between Koresh and the Reverend Jim Jones fifteen years earlier. Jones, an ordained minister and San Francisco public official, was a godlike figure to his followers, too, people who were drawn from a similarly wide spectrum of American life. Jones also demanded their obedience, their sex, their money. Then on November 18, 1978, after he had moved his cult to the jungles of Guyana in South America, he authored one of civilization's darkest days.

"Everyone has to die," Jones said as more than 900 people either committed suicide or were murdered. "If you love me as I love you, we must all die or be destroyed from the outside."

Around the world, loved ones of the thirty-eight children, forty-nine women and forty-eight men inside the Branch Davidian compound feared David Koresh's followers would meet the same end, or would be led into an apocalyptic shootout that would end in mass death.

Seventh-day Adventist Pastor Lloyd Antonio was among the Manchester churchmen who tried to warn the Henrys and others about Koresh and his teachings. Now he could only wait.

"Many of us feel that it's going to be another Jonestown," Antonio said early in the siege. "That's why we've been so worried and praying so hard about this."

In the Los Angeles suburb of LaVerne, California, Robyn Bunds requested police protection, fearing she was on a Davidian hit list reserved for members who had fled the cult.

Further south, in a suburb of San Diego, cement worker Andy Leamon watched news reports of the stand-off with his wife. The name David Koresh meant nothing, but then the cult leader's face flashed across the screen, and Leamon shot to his feet.

"Babe, that's my cousin!" Leamon said.

Twenty-five years earlier the two relatives had been best friends. The same age, they idled away childhood days together with adventures in the country. Andy Leamon watched Vernon Howell change.

"Vernon was always the type wanting to be a leader or he was always wanting to get people to listen to him," Andy Leamon said as the siege at Mount Carmel continued. "I guess he's succeeded. He's got the whole world listening to him now."

2

MAKING OF A MESSIAH

His grandfather called him Sputnik for the Russian satellite launched about the time he was born. The nickname seemed appropriate. Vernon Howell was a rocket-propelled youngster who loved to fish, play with animals, work with his hands and more than occasionally partake of childish mischief.

There was just one thing that seemed strange about Vernon back then, something his grandmother, Erline Clark, didn't fully realize until years later, when her grandson had become known throughout the world as David Koresh.

From the time he was a young boy, no more than four or five years old, Vernon loved church, his grandmother remembered. Erline remembered how her own children would fuss and fidget in church, climbing all over the pews as kids that age often do. But Vernon sat quietly, devoutly, transfixed by the sermons, belting out the hymns. He paid close attention when his grandmother read Bible stories to him, tales the other kids thought woefully boring.

Such was the one vivid thread that would traverse the years of his growing up, a childhood that would be studied three decades later by those hoping to make sense of the tragedy at Mount Carmel. What possibly could have spawned the religious and sexual obsessions of the Waco cult leader? Could the acute cravings to lead, the pathological desire to be heard, be explained by events of his childhood?

It would be said that David Koresh was the ultimate cynic, the consummate manipulator who used the Bible only as a tool to obtain adoration, sex, money, and power—an assertion that could be supported by bountiful evidence. Yet it was also true that in his childhood, something about the Bible moved him deeply and genuinely. His mother would later tell reporters of finding her son secluded in a family barn as a boy, lost in prayer, or kneeling at his bedside, weeping and praying. He memorized the New Testament by the time he was twelve.

Relatives spoke of a boy who loved guitars, engines and romping through the rural fields of North Texas. But eventually, Vernon Howell's religious devotion turned to obsession, and to bizarre behavior that got him fired from a job and booted from church. Eventually, the Bible became a weapon that in Koresh's hands would ruin many lives and destroy countless others.

Vernon Wayne Howell was born August 17, 1959, in a Houston hospital. Bonnie Clark woke her mother at seven o'clock that morning, telling Erline Clark that her baby was about to come. The child, named after his maternal grandfather, was delivered two hours later. Vernon's father was absent for the birth, and it would be up to his grandfather to pay the hospital bills. Bonnie Clark's own feelings about Vernon Howell's arrival were understandably mixed, Bonnie's mother remembered later.

"She was as happy as someone in her situation could be," Erline Clark said.

It was indeed a tough spot for the dark-haired, fifteen-year-old girl who most often kept her feelings to herself. She was a girl caught up in a tumultuous love affair with someone older, but he was not much more than a boy himself.

Bobby Howell and Bonnie Clark met through friends. They had been dating for about a year when Bonnie became pregnant. Howell was nineteen or twenty at the time, Erline Clark remembered, a raffish jack-of-all-trades who worked odd jobs as a mechanic and carpenter. Relatives remember Bobby Howell as a handsome young man, six-feet tall with blond hair, never at a loss for female companionship. His son, Vernon, later would bear a striking physical resemblance to his father.

His young parents came close to marriage on several occasions after Vernon was born. Bobby and Bonnie would decide to wed, but one or the other would back out. Once, Bobby brought Bonnie to the courthouse to purchase a wedding license. They were told they needed birth certificates. By the time they mailed away for them, the wedding was off again.

The stormy romance lasted for almost two years after Vernon's birth. Bonnie and the baby lived with Bobby's mother most of that time. Then Bobby Howell took up with another woman, a woman he eventually would marry, and Bonnie left with Vernon for good. She and the baby moved back in with her mother.

Erline Clark remembered seeing Bobby Howell with his son on only one other occasion, three years later. Bonnie, who had recently married, was planning to move from Houston to Dallas.

"He came to my house before we moved to Dallas," Erline Clark said. "He came and gave Vernon a $20 bill. I guess that was the only one he gave him."

Erline, who raised Vernon for several years after his parents split up, had two younger children of her own, so the grandchild fit right in, a typical kid with ready-made playmates and something of a knack for mischief.

One day, Vernon filled his grandmother's gas tank with water. Another time, after he busted out a headlight of his grandfather's car with a hammer, he came frightened to Erline.

"Grampa's going to whip me," Vernon said.

But it was hard to stay mad at a little boy who was so well-behaved in church.

"He just really had a big interest in it," Erline Clark remembered years later. "He would just listen to the stories and the songs, and be real happy. He was just always anxious to go."

Andy Leamon heard the theories about where David Koresh went bad and why. He listened to the incessant news coverage from Mount Carmel like everyone else. But none of it made any sense. Leamon would know better than most. He was the same age as Koresh, grew up side by side with him, though his companion was named Vernon Howell then. Vernon's childhood seemed no worse than his own, and Leamon had turned out all right.

Why would Howell's life be any different?

"I've heard people say that he was a lonely child," Leamon said one night as his cousin remained holed up at Mount Carmel, surrounded by federal agents. "But I can't really see where that's true because his mom and dad were good to him. And he had me. We were buddies."

After the shootout at Mount Carmel, Leamon thought plenty about those years spent with Vernon Howell. Some days, it was all he could think about. They knew each other from the time they were five years old until they were young adults. Roy Haldeman, the brother of Leamon's mother, moved his family to Dallas in 1964 after he and Bonnie were married. The new family settled in the suburb of Richardson. Leamon lived in the nearby suburb of Plano, and the two families got together often. He and Vernon hit it off immediately, meeting many days after school and on weekends.

"He was the only friend I had," Leamon said. "We were the best of pals."

They grew up in an era that preceded the arrival of urban sprawl that eventually engulfed Dallas' northern suburbs. It was a time before the Kmarts and convenience stores, shopping centers and subdivisions replaced the endless fields of maize that were a country kid's ideal romping grounds.

Vernon was just a normal boy then, a guy who enjoyed the same activities as his cousin. They took the shotguns down when parents would allow and headed for the fields, shooting at anything that moved, birds mostly, though nothing they aimed at ever dropped because neither boy could hit the broad side of a barn.

Other days they would set out together in the morning and wouldn't return until night, hiking the fields, wading the streams, investigating abandoned farm buildings, peering down country wells. When they were probably ten or eleven, Vernon found something that would apparently trigger an enduring passion for rock music, a passion that would accompany him to Mount Carmel years later.

That day, the boys were poking around an abandoned barn and Vernon came across an old, beat-up guitar missing most of its strings. He seemed fascinated by the instrument, Leamon remembered.

"He was happy he found it," Leamon said. "We carried it home. He was trying to play it on the way home. When we got back, his mother bought him some strings and he started playing every day. He just liked it. He taught himself to play and he got pretty darn good at it, too."

Leamon and Vernon also shared a profound ambivalence toward schoolwork. Vernon's mother would one day tell reporters that her son suffered from dyslexia as a child, the disability apparently among the reasons he never attended a full year of school past the ninth grade. Andy Leamon, however, attributed Vernon's academic struggles more to disinterest.

"Neither one of us did worth a crap in school," Leamon remembered. "He could read and write and everything. He just didn't have no interest in it, just like me. Neither one of us were worried about what happened in school until report cards came out, and we'd come home with bad cards and get our asses beat."

It started about the time the two became teenagers. Leamon watched as Vernon began to change from a trusted companion and friend to a tiresome religious fanatic who was more than a little weird. One of the first hints came when they were about twelve and Leamon smuggled a pack of cigarettes out into the country. He begged Howell to join him in a puff, to be grown up and cool. Leamon was pointedly rebuffed.

"He told me right off the bat I was going to hell for smoking cigarettes," Leamon said.

While the interests of most boys his age turned to the Dallas Cowboys, Vernon began to pester adults with strange questions, especially for one so young.

"Who is the leader of the Jews?"

"What's the difference between the Old Testament and New Testament?"

"What's the difference between Baptists and Catholics?"

Adults heard the boy reciting large chunks of the New Testament aloud by the time he was thirteen. The incessant preaching started a few years later, non-stop biblical harangues to anyone who would lend half an ear. If there was a slack moment in any conversation, Vernon stepped in with verse. The slightest hint of interest energized him. His odd evangelism even carried over to the construction sites where Vernon and Leamon worked together.

"He just claimed he knew when the end of the world was going to come," Leamon said. "He was seventeen when I heard him say he thought he was the Messiah.

"If you didn't listen to him, you were going to hell," he continued. "If you smoked or drank or cursed you were going to hell. Then we'd all get off work and he'd drink beer with us. That kind of sums it up right there."

When he was about twenty, Leamon recalled, Vernon Howell's preaching ultimately cost him a job. While working on a construction crew that was putting up a Dallas office building, Vernon constantly badgered co-workers about the Bible despite repeated warnings from his boss to desist. The boss finally could take no more and Vernon was canned.

Leamon saw his cousin for the last time about a year later. Relatives had gathered for a family reunion at a Dallas lake and Vernon was there. But if anything, he was more obnoxious than before, hounding relatives at every turn with his notions on the Book of Revelation and the keys to salvation. Leamon took it upon himself to tell his cousin that enough was enough.

"Knock it off," he told Vernon. "Quit your preaching. Let it go for a while."

Vernon became angry, and the boyhood companions came to blows. The fight ended after a few minutes, Leamon remembered, with his cousin on the ground holding his nose, silenced, but only for the moment.

In subsequent years, Leamon kept up with his cousin through the rumors among relatives. Some said Vernon had moved to California, still preaching, though reports indicated he had found some sort of following. Leamon had no idea of his cousin's Mount Carmel flock until news reports of the shootout in Waco.

"I love the guy, kinda, I guess," Leamon would say one night after the shootout. "But I don't think what's going down now is right. I don't think it's right at all."

To people at the Seventh-day Adventist church in Tyler, the curly-haired young man was weird at best, blasphemous at worst. They were introduced to him as a younger boy, probably around thirteen, when he briefly was living with his grandmother and attending church school in the city of 70,000 people, world famous for its roses. No one at the Tyler church noticed anything particularly unusual about him then.

It was different when he reappeared in 1979. He came back with his grandmother to a Wednesday night church seminar on current events and the thirteenth chapter of Revelation, that was presented by a Dallas evangelist.

"Then I stood on the sand of the sea. And I saw a beast rising up out of the sea, having seven heads and ten horns, and on his horns ten crowns, and on his heads a blasphemous name," the chapter begins.

Vernon had no comment on the beast that night, or at least none that people could remember. But he would not go unnoticed for long. He made plans to join the church, spending several weeks of study at the arm of a clergyman. The day Vernon was scheduled to be baptized, however, he showed up late for the service, almost missing it altogether. What happened after he got there, people in attendance likely will never forget.

Howell picked up a guitar that happened to be sitting at hand, and started to play music sounding suspiciously like rock and roll. The young man's behavior sent others into a prayerful tizzy. Howell concluded his impromptu concert, settled down, and was baptized on schedule.

Unstable is a word people used to describe him then. Howell's life indeed seemed to be in flux, his family moving around the Dallas area several times. Then in 1977, Roy and Bonnie Haldeman moved to a place in the country near Tyler, just down the road from the house where Bonnie's parents, Vernon and Erline Clark, lived.

Vernon Howell, seventeen at the time and not permanently enrolled in school, was not encouraged to continue living with his parents, Erline Clark said.

"I think they had some problems in the home," Howell's grandmother said. "They kind of wanted him to move out."

So he drifted back and forth between his parents, grandparents and other families who might put him up for a night or two. He worked odd jobs as a carpenter and carpet layer, but never seemed to keep one for very long. He preferred fishing with his grandfather in the bountiful East Texas lakes, or riding motorcycles, or breaking down old cars and getting them running again, something for which he enjoyed an obvious knack. He honed his skills on the guitar and made sporadic trips to California, apparently attempting to get a music career started, relatives said.

He was seventeen when he set out to find Bobby Howell.

"Vernon never knew he existed until he was seventeen," Erline Clark said. "His mother never spoke about him. He just wanted to get to know his people. He went down to Houston to look his daddy up."

News reports years later recounted Vernon Howell's hunt through the Houston telephone directory, finally finding someone who knew the whereabouts of his father. Hugs and tears punctuated the reunion between father and son, relatives later recounted. But Bobby Howell apparently was turned off by one part of his long-lost offspring's personality.

"I told him I didn't want to talk religion," Bobby Howell told a Houston television station. "The time I'd seen him before, he preached at me the whole time."

If Vernon Howell wanted to endear himself to fellow members of the Seventh-day Adventist church in Tyler, he went to some lengths not to show it. He wore long hair and favored blue jeans, a personal appearance that was rather an anathema to the button-down members of the conservative congregation, Erline Clark said.

His romantic designs on the pastor's daughter didn't help, either. Not long after joining the church, Vernon told Pastor L. Hartley Berlin that God had given Berlin's daughter, Sandy, to him, Berlin's wife later told the *Waco Tribune-Herald*.

"He felt that God wanted him to marry her," the wife said. The pastor had a different interpretation of God's will and barred Vernon from seeing his daughter.

It was the young man's consistently overbearing behavior that riled church members the most. He seemed exceptionally intelligent, and claimed a much better grasp of the Bible than most people his age. But Howell never knew when it was appropriate to display his unusual biblical knowledge, and when it was time to listen.

He frequently would interrupt prayer meetings and Bible studies to gratuitously offer his own theological slant. Before services on Saturday, the Seventh-day Adventists' Sabbath, he buttonholed church members outside, or in church halls, pestering them to listen. It seemed as if he was trying to take over the church, to convert the whole group to his way of thinking, though what exactly he believed was hard to decipher from his rambling evangelical style.

"He thought he knew more than anybody else," a church member said. "He wanted people to listen to him. He wanted the spotlight."

His stunt at the 11:00 a.m. service on a Sabbath day in 1982 was the last straw. During the service, the pastor asked if those in attendance wished to give witness to the Lord. According to tradition, it was an invitation for church members to publicly, and briefly, stand up in the congregation and attest to their faith.

Vernon Howell rose, but instead of offering his witness from where he stood, he strode to the front of the church, took over the pulpit from the dumbstruck pastor, and wouldn't give it back. He preached for ten minutes, rambling on from one book of the Bible to another, as was his habit. He preached for twenty minutes as people fidgeted in their pews. Some left, disgusted. It was forty-five minutes before Howell surrendered the pulpit. A short while later, church elders voted to "disfellowship" the strange young man, the church euphemism for kicking him out. The pastor gave Howell the news.

"He took it very gracefully," a church member said. "He knew it was time to move on."

It may have been some consolation that by that time, there was a place for Vernon Howell to go, a place near the Central Texas town of Waco. He had been traveling back and forth between Tyler and Mount Carmel for two years by then, having learned of the Branch Davidians in 1980 through a Tyler church friend.

The friend was an older woman with sons about Howell's age. She pitied the young man who seemed so troubled that he often would break out in tears during Sabbath services. The woman and her husband hired Howell for odd carpentry jobs on their farm near Tyler, and occasionally put him up for the night. Some days he would disappear for hours into the woods with his Bible.

All her life, meanwhile, the woman had heard about the Branch Davidians, a group that had broken away from her church and was living in a place called Mount Carmel a few hours drive to the south. As a little girl she knew a boy who was now a member of the Branch

Davidians. While she had no intention of joining the sect herself, her curiosity finally got the best of her. She planned to make a visit and offered to take Vernon Howell along for the ride.

Howell's friend didn't say much after they arrived that day in 1980 at the little hamlet in the country. She just listened as Vernon did all the talking. Within a few hours they were headed back to Tyler. She didn't think much about the trip at the time, didn't think of it much at all until that bloody Sunday morning thirteen years later.

3

VERNON HOWELL TAKES CHARGE

The charge against him was attempted murder, but during the 1988 trial at the McClennan County Courthouse in Waco, Vernon Howell's gentle manner and engaging smile made him seem more saint than sinner.

During breaks in the court proceedings, Howell hovered close to wife Rachel, a blonde woman who worked as a check-out girl at a local supermarket. Rachel was fourteen years old, Howell twenty-four, when he married her four years earlier. Recesses also found Howell coddling his two children, Cyrus and Star, or speaking consolingly to the many elderly women concerned with his legal predicament. Vernon Howell, quite simply, was ministering to his Branch Davidian flock.

The Davidians crowded the third-floor courtroom each day of the ten-day trial. The women wore straight hair, no makeup and dressed in stern, floor-length dresses. As the testimony proceeded, adults quietly distributed school lessons to their Davidian youngsters, who dutifully passed them down the rows of a courtroom that prosecutors grumbled had been turned into a kindergarten.

The trial was a circus in most other respects as well. At one point, the decaying corpse of what had been an elderly woman was hefted up the courthouse steps, purportedly a key piece of evidence for the defense in one of the strangest judicial proceedings ever held in Waco.

Sometimes lost amid the folly was the fact that on November 3, 1987, Howell and seven of his followers, dressed in camouflage fatigues and heavily armed, snuck into Mount Carmel and shot it out with the compound's current proprietor, George Roden. Roden was Howell's chief rival for leadership of the biblical sect. Amid all the side shows, it became increasingly difficult to remember who was on trial, and for what.

Then came that extraordinary moment, a snippet from Howell's own testimony that abruptly snapped things back into perspective. Prosecutors asked the defendant to demonstrate his version of the shooting that wounded Roden. Howell was quite happy to oblige. Stepping from the witness stand, he took hold of an unloaded weapon and walked confidently to within inches of the lawyers who were attempting to send him to prison. He bent to one knee, leaned over the prosecution's table and aimed at the witness chair.

"Let's say George Roden was sitting in the witness chair," Howell said, still aiming.

"Pow!" he yelled.

"Pow!"

"Pow!"

His voice reverberated throughout the courtroom, startling twenty-six-year-old prosecutor Denise Wilkerson and nearly jolting her out of her chair. These were not the actions of a man of God, Wilkerson thought then. To her, despite the appearances, this man was a criminal who knew his way around weapons and took obvious delight in using them.

Howell, twenty-eight years old at the time, had enjoyed a brief, and rather improbable turn as leader of the people living quietly in and around Waco since the 1930s. Now, if the group were to survive, someone else would have to take charge of its legacy. Vernon Howell, the humble shepherd, was going to prison, Wilkerson believed. She would have bet on it.

Like Vernon Howell, William Miller seemed an unlikely conduit for the word of God. Miller was simply a Baptist farmer who had fought as a militia lieutenant in the War of 1812. Eventually, however, he would begin speaking to anyone who would listen about his biblical discovery from the Book of Daniel. Something Miller discovered there convinced him that Christ would come again in the year 1843. He was determined that others should have the benefit of his insight. By 1839, his proclamation of the coming "Advent" would in fact become the focus of a robust movement that included widespread distribution of literature and high-spirited revivals across New England and western New York.

"As word of the imminent millennium spread, the crowds at these meetings grew larger and larger, and the excitement more and more intense," Frances FitzGerald wrote in her 1986 book, *Cities on a Hill*. "By 1843, it was estimated that some fifty thousand people were convinced the Day was coming, while perhaps a million people across the country from New England to the frontier waited with skeptical attention. As the day Miller had appointed approached, hundreds of people gave up their worldly occupations to preach the good news; some sold their property and in the end went up to the tops of hills to watch for Christ's coming."

Alas, civilization survived past that appointed date, and the faithful did not take their disappointment well, storming Adventist meeting places, casting Miller out, and in general leaving for other spiritual disciplines.

A scattering of Adventists survived, however, "some maintaining that Miller had simply made an error in reckoning, others that Christ had come on the appointed day, but not materially, in the flesh," FitzGerald wrote.

Eventually, a prophet named Ellen G. White gathered up the remnants of Miller's movement into what would become the Seventh-day Adventist church.

Over the decades, the growing church would draw its members from all walks of life, yet its practices put it somewhat outside mainstream Christianity. Seventh-day Adventists observed the Sabbath on Saturday, the seventh day of the week rather than the first. They advocated a vegetarian diet, and strictly proscribed the use of alcohol, tobacco and the nonmedical use of drugs.

But while Seventh-day Adventist theology focused on the Book of Revelation and the church continued to proclaim the imminent return of Christ, they had learned an important lesson from Miller's misfortune. Where the Second Coming was concerned, they didn't attempt to set a date.

Among those attracted to the strict new religion was a stocky, taciturn Bulgarian immigrant named Victor Houteff. Houteff had emigrated to the United States while in his early twenties, first working in the hotel and grocery businesses in Rockford, Illinois. Several years later, he joined the prosperity-seeking migration heading westward to California.

After his arrival, Houteff became disenchanted with the church he had joined in 1919, believing its members had strayed from the strict teachings of the Bible, and were becoming too worldly and materialistic. His was not a popular view among church members, who banished Houteff from Seventh-day Adventism in the 1930s, sending him off in search of a place from which to promulgate his beliefs. His search eventually led to the plains of Texas.

"He was looking at the Bible and saw that the New Israel would be in the middle of the land," said Baylor University historian Bill Pitts. "He looked and saw Texas as the middle of the land."

Others, however, say Houteff's reasoning was more prosaic.

"He went to Texas more or less as a centralized location to equalize mailing costs and equalize travel distances for members from both coasts who wanted to come and visit," said Jeriel Bingham, whose father edited several of Houteff's religious publications. "In Texas at the time, land was cheap."

In any event, Houteff and about seventy followers settled on a few hundred scenic acres along the Brazos River just west of Waco, a place they called Mount Carmel. They set up printing presses to disseminate the leader's call for a purer Christianity, the kind he thought necessary for entrance into the imminent kingdom. Houteff's preoccupation with the Second Coming was reflected by a mosaic on the floor of one of his buildings, a sundial which purportedly depicted the timing of the end of the world.

Houteff, however, never suggested a date himself. His wife, Florence, who succeeded her husband as Davidian leader after his death in 1955, was less circumspect. Shortly after Houteff's death, Florence Houteff took advantage of a lucrative real estate market and sold the property on the Brazos, moving Mount Carmel to a remote spot in the country ten miles northeast of Waco.

From that location, Houteff's widow offered a faintly familiar prediction: The Adventists would be purified on Easter Sunday, April 22, 1959. Believers interpreted her statement as a euphemism for the Second Coming, and responded much as Miller's adherents did in the debacle more than a century before. About 800 people from across the country sold homes and belongings, and came to Mount Carmel. Some of them donned white robes that fateful Sunday to await the apocalypse, according to news reports of the time.

If indeed Florence Houteff's prophecy came true, and the world ended on Easter, it would be the biggest news to come out of Waco since the tornado hit town six years earlier, killing 114 people.

Whether by coincidence or design, Victor Houteff could not have picked a more fitting Texas city in which to locate his little group of fundamentalists. Cynics would always point out the multitude of sin in Waco, a city on the plains ninety miles south of Dallas that would ultimately grow to a population of more than 100,000. But all in all, a more God-fearing place could not be found in the Lone Star State: Jerusalem on the Brazos, it would sometimes be called.

Its piety originated with Dr. Rufus C. Burleson, who moved to town in the 1860s and established a highly regarded Baptist institution of higher learning. The school attracted children from the best button-down Baptist families in the state, from El Paso to Tyler. Burleson's graduates tended to settle in Waco, lending a conservative religious cast to the place. In the broad spectrum of the faithful, Baptists read their Bibles literally, and otherwise played life fairly close to the vest.

The town's devout disposition was further ensured in 1886, when Baylor University, another Baptist school, merged with Burleson's institution, creating what would ultimately be the largest Baptist secondary school in the world. The piety would be long lasting. A century later, when *Playboy* Magazine came to town hunting subjects for its "Girls of the Southwest Conference" pictorial, University President Abner McCall threatened to expel any student who posed. He ended up barring one senior from graduation exercises.

Yet the town's religious flavor also was the source of great irony and no small amount of contradiction. Texas, from the earliest days of its frontier, would always be a fertile breeding ground for temptation.

Waco, named for the Indian tribe that lived at that location along the Brazos for centuries, would be a popular stopover on the Chisholm Trail. For almost twenty-five years, beginning about the time professor Burleson set up shop, massive cattle herds thundered through town one after another, cutting a huge, dusty rut from South Texas, through San Antonio, Austin, Waco, north to Fort Worth, and on into Oklahoma and the northern plains.

The cowboys who drove those cows were restless and thirsty when they got to town. Waco city directories of the time listed between thirty-five and forty saloons. They also listed the names of twenty-seven women who described themselves as actresses. Many of them lived together in houses in what was known as the red-light district.

No one, perhaps, took greater delight in Waco's contradictions (he would call it hypocrisy) than newspaper editor William Cowper Brann, whose 1890s publication, the *Iconoclast*, took regular swipes at the Baptists.

"He had no quarrel with the Baptists," Waco historian Roger Conger is fond of saying today. "In his opinion, they just weren't held under water long enough."

Brann pointed out, among other things, that the home of Baylor University also had the state's only registered red-light district. On one occasion, as Baylor officials squabbled about naming a new president, Brann wondered about the ruckus over a job "which pays a salary about one-half of that enjoyed by a good whiskey salesman."

For his reward, Brann took a fatal bullet where his suspenders crossed in the back, a shot fired by the outraged father of a Baylor student.

Four decades later, Victor Houteff added another twist to Waco's religious heritage, moving his printing presses there. Florence Houteff livened things up a bit herself with her prophecy the same year a boy named Vernon Howell was born. The record shows that Easter 1959 came and went without incident. Civilization plodded forward, once again in defiance of the prophecy. After three weeks or so, the assembled throng began to disperse from Mount Carmel, bemoaning what became known as "The Great Disappointment."

Florence Houteff, her credibility as a prophet destroyed, eventually surrendered Davidian leadership to a member of the sect named Ben Roden, who died in 1978, and was succeeded in turn by his wife. Lois Roden remained the incumbent Davidian prophet into the early 1980s, when a good-looking, guitar-playing, scripture-spouting young man named Vernon Howell came to Mount Carmel from Tyler, looking for a place to fit in.

At first, Denise Wilkerson was sure the call was some kind of a joke. Halloween Day, after all, was the perfect time to pull this kind of morbid prank. But after a few minutes on the telephone, the McClennan County prosecutor realized sheriff's Deputy Elijah Dickerson was serious. He had several Branch Davidians in his office, he said, and they wanted to file charges for corpse abuse.

The call was too bizarre not to be true. According to the Davidians, George Roden had dug up the body of an old woman named Anna Hughes, who had been dead and buried at Mount Carmel since 1968. Roden challenged Vernon Howell to a contest that would settle the question of leadership of the Davidians once and for all. Whomever could raise Hughes from the dead, Roden proposed, would be the rightful heir to the legacy of Victor Houteff.

Lois Roden's son already had gone to some trouble to prepare for that macabre duel, which Howell wisely declined. David Jones saw it for himself. Jones, a Waco area mailman, was among those in Dickerson's office that day. During a recent visit to Mount Carmel, he said, the old woman's coffin was sitting in the chapel, draped in the flag of the Star of David.

Wilkerson was flabbergasted.

"We're going to need something more," she told the deputy. "For all we know, it could be an empty coffin. Can you get a photograph of the corpse?"

"Yeah, that's no problem," the Davidians said when the deputy relayed Wilkerson's question, and the group filed out.

Unbeknownst to McClennan County authorities, it was only the latest twist in a bizarre power struggle that had gone on virtually from the time Vernon Howell set foot on Davidian property.

On that Halloween Day in 1987, Howell and most of the Davidians were living in exile. Men, women and children, young and old, were huddled deep in the pine woods of East Texas near the appropriately named village of Palestine. George Roden had run Howell and most of his followers off Mount Carmel in 1985.

The Davidians were forced to take shelter in crude plywood huts under the towering pines, huts with curtains for doors that were just large enough for a bed or a set of bunks and a kerosene heater. Children were taught in a school bus parked on the twenty acres that relatives said had been purchased by Howell. Visitors later would witness women preparing vegetarian meals in a central building where communal dining and Bible studies took place.

The animosity between Howell and George Roden had been brewing for years. It began, according to the *Waco Tribune-Herald*, when Lois Roden took pity on Howell after hearing him tell group members he was concerned about his problem with excessive masturbation. The young man and older woman became lovers, with Howell claiming to his followers several years later that Lois Roden actually became pregnant in fulfillment of Isaiah, the eighth chapter:

"And I went unto the prophetess; and she conceived, and bare a son. Then the Lord said to me, 'Call his name Maher-Shalal-Hash-Baz.'"

Lois Roden suffered a miscarriage as punishment for giving church money to her children, Howell later explained. Her control over the sect seemed to be waning in any event, because members were offended at her proclamation that the Holy Spirit was feminine. Yet the alternative, George Roden, seemed an ill-suited successor. Many at Mount Carmel thought Roden, a bearish, bearded man, was simply crazy, a belief borne out later in court.

"I have a charitable organization. I'm a minister. I'm a presidential candidate. I'm a truck driver," George Roden would testify. "I guess I'm a jack-of-all-trades."

Howell willingly stepped into the power vacuum. He began intimating that the old woman was losing her inspiration, former cult members said. He also suggested that Lois Roden get rid of her son. When a member of her flock approached Lois with a question, she replied with a sigh: "Ask Vernon. He seems to be in charge."

By the time Lois Roden died in 1986, Howell enjoyed the loyalties of most at Mount Carmel, winning them over with what seemed to be a divinely inspired knowledge of the Bible. He began referring to himself as the Lamb of God from Revelation. He alone could reveal the mystery of the seven seals, and ultimately redeem his followers after the apocalypse, he claimed.

"He was developing this incredible ability to recite verse that seemed to back up his power and seemed to dumbfound his followers," said Mark Bunds, the son of a longtime Davidian, and later one of Howell's adherents.

"Most really hated to admit that they didn't understand what he was saying."

George Roden, however, was not impressed. Roden accused Howell of raping his mother. He believed the newcomer had taken away his birthright to the Davidian leadership. Roden began appearing around the compound at Mount Carmel armed with a pistol or an Uzi machine gun, and finally ordered most of the Davidians away from their thirty-year home.

Hitchhikers and assorted hangers-on replaced the men, women and children at Mount Carmel and the village of seventeen little bungalows, a chapel and administration building fell into sorry disrepair. Yet Roden continued nursing his desire to lead the sect, and in 1987 concocted his sure-fire plan to wrest back control. In his mind, the corpse of Anna Hughes would be the test.

At 3:00 a.m. on November 3, 1987, the eight intruders, all heavily armed and dressed in camouflage gear, snuck into Mount Carmel to gather the crucial piece of evidence, a photograph of what was left of Anna Hughes. Vernon Howell and his followers would be disappointed. Unbeknownst to the Davidian strike team, the woman's body had been moved by Roden from the chapel into a mechanic's shed.

The team lingered unseen for hours at the place by then renamed Rodenville. Later, in midafternoon, they moved in, walking from house to house, identifying themselves as sheriff's deputies who were on the property to serve a warrant.

"They told the hitchhikers that there was going to be trouble and that they better leave," Denise Wilkerson said.

George Roden, upon learning of his unexpected visitors, armed himself with an Uzi and stepped outside to see Howell and three of his men advancing toward him.

"Is that you, Vernon?" Roden shouted from a distance. "Who are you? What do you want?"

Although the question of who fired the first shot would be the topic of future debate, there would be little doubt as to who held the munitions advantage. Roden, suffering a minor wound to his hand, fell pinned behind the stump of a large tree where investigators later counted more than fifteen bullet holes. The one-sided battle went on for twenty minutes. When sheriff's deputies arrived, Howell and his followers calmly laid down their weapons: five assault rifles, two assault shotguns, two .22-caliber rifles and thousands of rounds of ammunition.

Six months later, Branch Davidians crowded the third-floor courtroom as Howell and his seven followers stood trial for attempted murder. Much had changed during the interim. George Roden no longer ruled at Mount Carmel. The Davidians quickly returned from exile, a cheering busload arriving from Palestine within hours after Roden's arrest for filing an obscene legal motion.

The trial in Waco became a study in contrasts between the sinister, seemingly demented Roden, and the handsome young prophet accused of attempting to kill him. Roden often lapsed into profanity from the witness stand. He admitted he had tried to resurrect Anna Hughes from the dead, not once but on three occasions.

Howell was as charming as Roden was offensive, quietly impressive in the hold he had on his people. While Roden raged out of control, Howell showed great restraint on the witness stand, obeying admonitions from his attorney, Gary Coker, to stick to the matter at hand and refrain from meandering biblical references. Howell magnanimously assumed full responsibility for the shooting, saying his followers merely fired into the air. The leader himself argued that he didn't actually fire at Roden, either, but at the tree that Roden cowered behind.

Howell could claim the moral high ground for another reason. In the battle with George Roden, he only wanted to rescue his people from the squalor of Palestine and return them to what was their rightful home.

"The jury loved him," Denise Wilkerson said later.

Yet Wilkerson experienced another side to the man, an eerie dimension that the jurors apparently missed. As the trial unfolded, the Branch Davidian leader began to surreptitiously pass her notes, a highly unusual practice for a defendant. Each cryptic message referred to a biblical passage that Wilkerson later would reference. One note instructed her to read a verse from the twenty-fourth chapter of the Book of Samuel.

"Know and see that there is neither evil nor rebellion in my hand, and I have not sinned against you," Wilkerson read. "Yet you hunt my life to take it."

But it was the corpse of Anna Hughes that best illustrated the trial's insanity. After twenty years in the ground, the body consisted of little more than some bones and a few thatches of hair. Howell and his followers insisted the remains comprised a crucial piece of evidence that jurors must be allowed to see.

Hughes's coffin arrived at the McClennan County Courthouse in a green van. Defendants serving as pallbearers hoisted the 500-pound coffin inside the eighty-year-old red granite courthouse. When the coffin proved too large for the elevator, the men hauled it up a flight of stairs to the second floor, depositing it just off the courthouse rotunda. Visitors were free to come by and gawk.

The coffin didn't sit for long. Presiding Judge Herman Fitts quickly denied a defense motion to have the jurors view Hughes's remains, and the muscle-sore defendants rose once again, returned to the second floor, loaded the coffin onto their shoulders and walked it out of the courthouse and down the street, leading a procession of news photographers and Branch Davidian members.

The jurors were not completely deprived of a glimpse of Hughes's remains. To preserve the dead woman's dignity, Howell and his followers tied a pink ribbon around her neckbone, then joined around the open casket for a group photograph that later was submitted as evidence.

"They posed in the picture with her," Wilkerson said. "Some of them would line up behind the casket and point into the box. It was so bizarre. I can't believe we lost that case because I thought the jury would think that these guys were absolutely looney tunes."

Instead, two jurors hugged Howell after acquitting all seven of his followers. Howell himself fared almost as well. Jurors announced they could not reach a verdict on the leader, deadlocking at a 9-3 vote of not guilty.

"The state didn't prove a thing," juror Sid Berry told reporters. "I don't think they should retry Vernon. He's not guilty of attempted murder. Look at him."

The shepherd himself expressed relief that his followers had been spared.

"I don't care if I go to prison," Howell told reporters then. "I just didn't want these men to go. If I go, I'll convert the prison. The decision is in God's hands. Who knows the minds of men? I'll wait on God."

Then he invited jury members to join him and his followers for an ice cream social at Mount Carmel.

McClennan County prosecutors chose not to retry

Vernon Howell for attempted murder, a decision based in part on George Roden's deteriorating mental condition. A short time after his release on the contempt charge, Roden moved to the West Texas town of Odessa, where he was arrested for killing a man. A jury there found Roden not guilty by reason of insanity.

Denise Wilkerson had not seen the last of Vernon Howell, however. Colleagues, in fact, began to joke that she was about to become the Davidian's next convert. On three occasions, Howell and two followers showed up in the prosecutor's office for impromptu chats.

"Denise, it concerns me that someone of your intelligence can believe that I would be capable of trying to kill someone," Howell told her on one of the visits. "It concerns me because I'm not that kind of person. It bothers me that anybody would think that way of me."

Howell invited her to visit Mount Carmel.

"I want you to have the opportunity to get to know us better," he said.

"I believe in the jury system," Wilkerson told Howell. "But this time I think the jury was wrong."

The prosecutor often remembered Howell's demonstration of the shooting in court that day, the strange notes, the arsenal that deputies seized, an arsenal returned to Howell when his case was closed. To Wilkerson, Victor Houteff's heir was a dangerous man. An important opportunity to diffuse a ticking bomb had been lost.

"We knew Vernon Howell was going to be dangerous," Wilkerson said years later. "He was building an arsenal. We didn't know where next his animosities might be focused. But even then, it was obvious they were preparing for a battle with someone."

4

THE LAMB GATHERS HIS FLOCK

The church that had spurned him ultimately would be
Vernon Howell's prey. Howell knew the ways of the
Seventh-day Adventists, knew their vulnerabilities, their
theology, their customs. When his power at Mount Carmel
was secure, he would haunt their pews to the far corners
of the earth. If he indeed was the Lamb of God, his message must not be confined to one state, even one country.

By 1988, Howell had become a rich man at the expense
of his followers. Hundreds of thousands of dollars were
poured in his lap. Surely he could afford the sightseeing
trip to Israel, a chance for the prophet to wander among
the shrines of the Holy Land he had come to know so well
from the Bible. It was the kind of journey that would
further validate Howell in the eyes of his followers.

The excursions to Britain and Australia were different. They were working trips, recruiting missions to English-speaking countries rich with Seventh-day Adventists
to add to his flock. Howell packed his Bible, his guitar and
enough blue jeans to last him for a trip's duration. He
rarely returned empty-handed.

From Manchester to Melbourne, his methods were the same. A willing host would offer a living room. Small groups would assemble. Some would think him a nut, of course, and quietly excuse themselves. But others would be dazzled by Howell's preaching and his guitar. Oliver Gyarfas was one such devotee.

Gyarfas would sit and listen to Howell for days given the chance. Howell was the prophet he was waiting for. Gyarfas, an unemployed Seventh-day Adventist in Melbourne, Australia's second largest city, first heard Howell's message on a cassette tape sent to Australia in 1985 by Branch Davidians in America.

"We could not make out much because he was so far ahead of us in Scripture," Gyarfas remembered years later.

In 1986, Howell made the first of three trips to Australia, where Gyarfas finally met him and heard firsthand the message that would change his life. In his marathon Bible study sessions, Howell insisted that he alone bore the message of the Seventh Angel of the Book of Revelation, and thus knew how the world would end.

"I wasn't taken with him so much as a man," Gyarfas said years later. "I realized this guy was inspired. He was sent by God. I was fully convinced he was sent by God. I still am."

Gyarfas was so impressed he allowed his daughter, Aisha, who was ten years old in 1986, to marry a Branch Davidian cult member a few years later and move to America. Oliver Gyarfas, Jr., was eighteen when he joined his sister at Mount Carmel in 1992. Their father left the Seventh-day Adventist church and made two pilgrimages to the settlement on the Texas plains where Aussie accents by now were abundant.

None of Vernon Howell's recruiting missions was more fruitful than those to the United Kingdom. By February 1993, more than thirty of the Queen's subjects were holed up inside Mount Carmel with their new monarch, the man by then known as David Koresh. Each of them, in one way or another, could trace their conversions to a serpentine chain of events that began at Newbold College in the summer of 1988.

Hugh Dunton had scarcely set down his briefcase that morning when his secretary approached with what seemed a matter of utmost urgency.

"You really ought to hear what's going on," she told the Newbold College librarian.

Dunton had been away for several days at the British and Irish Conference for Mission Studies and thus had missed the origins of the uproar on the normally sedate campus of 350 students. His name was Vernon Howell, Dunton was told, a mysterious visitor from America who had appropriated a campus living room for the headquarters of a very curious brand of evangelism. Rumors of his preaching swirled about the Seventh-day Adventist school near Windsor Castle like no gossip had for years.

It wasn't just what Howell was saying that created such a stir—he claimed to have the answer for every biblical mystery—but the way he was saying it. Howell cracked his Bible in early morning and wouldn't close it again until well past midnight. Then, in midverse, this pleasant-looking, if a bit unkempt visitor would grab his guitar and serenade his listeners with rock music. Each day, twelve to fifteen listeners from the college took up sofas, chairs and the floor to listen, many for the duration.

So Newbold had a new celebrity by the time Dunton returned, and the faculty was becoming concerned. Howell had taken advantage of local hospitality to gain a significant following, one that included many Newbold students studying for the ministry. Just what was being taught on their property, Newbold officials increasingly wondered. What were their students being exposed to? After speaking with his secretary, Dunton consulted with the Newbold principal, who asked him to check out Howell's sessions and report back.

Newbold officials had been warned of course. Only a few weeks before, Steve Schneider appeared on campus, requesting that college officials grant Howell access to the school's students. Schneider was no stranger to the school, having enrolled in 1972 as a candidate for the ministry from the United States. He was booted out the next year, after being caught "legless" on several occasions. In America, Schneider's condition was known as drunkenness.

Many years later, disenchanted with his continuing inability to find a ministry in the Seventh-day Adventist church, Schneider hooked up with Howell, someone with a few axes to grind in that regard as well. Schneider, who also possessed a daunting command of the Bible, soon became the Branch Davidian leader's chief lieutenant, his advance man in the worldwide quest for souls.

It was in that role that Schneider returned to Britain and the scene of earlier humiliation, and though denied by the Newbold administrators, he successfully put the word out among students. A man would soon come, Schneider told them, with a message from the Bible unlike anything the Brits had ever heard.

Howell showed up a few weeks later, finding a sedate country place of abundant trees, flowers and old brick buildings set around a verdant commons. Despite the school's conservative reputation as a training ground for Seventh-day Adventist ministers, Howell also discovered a plentiful supply of open minds.

He was inconspicuous at first, befriending a Newbold cook who lived in a campus bungalow. The cook allowed Howell to pitch a tent in his garden and use his living room for what was understood to be a series of intimate, brief Bible studies. The cook was mistaken on both counts. Students and community members filled the living room from the moment Howell began to speak. The sessions went on nearly around the clock.

It was shortly before noon, several days into Howell's visit, when Dunton set out on a five-minute walk across campus to where Howell held forth. A door of the bungalow was wedged open and Dunton let himself in, taking a vacant seat only a few feet from the speaker who commanded the middle of the room. Howell was casually dressed and unshaven. He gripped a Bible in one hand and continuously gestured with the other. His guitar sat within reach. Howell ignored Dunton when the faculty member entered, focusing instead on other listeners who sat without questioning, without moving, some of them without breathing, it seemed to Dunton.

"There was no fidgeting or looking at watches," Dunton remembered later. "He definitely had the attention of his audience."

Dunton had been determined to give Howell the benefit of the doubt. He tried to listen with an open mind. But he soon became puzzled at the allure of Howell's rambling monologue. It seemed to lead nowhere, made no point and was riddled with biblical interpretation of dubious quality. Howell's Bible was open to Zechariah when Dunton sat down, a book from the Old Testament that was written in highly symbolic language, problematic for the most learned theologians. Howell, however, claimed to have Zechariah figured out.

"For I will gather all the nations to battle against Jerusalem," Howell read from the fourteenth chapter. "The city shall be taken, the houses rifled, and the women ravished."

"You know what rifle is?" Howell asked his audience. "The city will be rifled means the city will be shot up."

Dunton was almost amused.

"In that day, rifle meant to 'go through,'" Dunton said later. "He had taken the word 'rifled' and applied it to modern weaponry. That was the level of his expression."

Sexual innuendo also laced Howell's teaching. Once, Howell suggested that damned souls would be sodomized by biblical giants. He seized upon a passage from the Song of Solomon, using it as his description of paradise where "There are sixty queens and eighty concubines and virgins without number."

Dunton heard enough within an hour, leaving as silently as he had come. He was troubled as he began his walk back across campus. Howell's preaching was rubbish, he was sure. But Dunton saw how quietly, almost reverently, those in the living room had listened. It occurred to him that the visitor was attempting to brainwash his listeners with babble, hour upon hour, hobbling their ability to think critically.

"A man holding meetings for that length of time is not how a true man of God operates," Dunton thought. "The Lord didn't have long meetings, day after day after day."

But what actual danger could Howell present? In a few days he would be gone and campus life would return to normal. The cook who befriended Howell later was scolded for his indiscretion, and promised never to make such an accommodation again. To toss Howell off campus now, however, might only add to his mystique, Dunton thought, making him out to be a martyr.

It would be some time before Newbold officials would learn that Howell had stood trial for attempted murder only a few weeks before his visit. Only later did they learn he would turn his cult into a harem. Only later did they learn that Howell had ignited a chain reaction in their midst, that Newbold graduate John McBean had been swept under Howell's spell during that 1988 visit. McBean would sway his London girlfriend, Diana Henry. Henry in turn led her family into Howell's flock, and ultimately, friends from back home in Manchester, like Sandra Hardial.

Only later did Newbold officials realize that Vernon Howell's time on campus had been a very fruitful visit indeed.

Perhaps it was the weather that lured her away. That made as much sense to Lloyd Hardial as anything. Manchester was a smoky industrial city of derelict textile mills and food processing plants, oil refineries and dye manufacturers, a dank and grimy place made more insufferable by the weather of northwest England. A chill wind blew incessantly from the Irish Sea. Most days were wet and gray. By contrast, Lloyd's sister would often say how much she enjoyed the hot, sunny days of her new home in the Texas countryside. There must have been more to it, of course. No one just dropped everything—career, family, friends—for a change in climate. But Lloyd Hardial had utterly no clue what it was.

Lloyd and Sandra Hardial had grown up together. Lloyd was only a year older than his sister, the only children of a Manchester mechanical engineer and a nurse. He knew Sandra as a smart, outgoing, athletic person who enjoyed everything from reading poetry to bowling. She took annual ski trips to the Alps. Sandra had graduated from college and landed a good job in the housing department of the Manchester City Council, where she was regarded as popular and dependable. If she was unfulfilled, if Sandra was searching for something more in life, her brother had no hint.

After a childhood in which she was indifferent to religion, she joined a Seventh-day Adventist church. But her attendance at services was sporadic. She hardly seemed a zealot.

Lloyd also had come to enjoy the friends Sandra had met at her new church. He often would accompany his sister when she and the Henry offspring went bowling. The five children of Samuel and Zilla Henry were all roughly Sandra's age. Sandra occasionally dated Samuel's oldest son, Stephen Henry, who seemed a thoroughly decent bloke. There certainly was nothing about the family that gave Lloyd cause for concern.

But it was undoubtedly the Henrys who introduced Sandra to the guitar-playing prophet from America. In 1990, Sandra would have a chance to hear the teachings of Vernon Howell relayed by his right-hand man. Diana Henry had made the arrangements for Steve Schneider's visit. For three days he held forth in a Manchester living room and Sandra Hardial would join the Henrys to welcome him.

The local clergy were much less enthused. They had heard the bizarre reports out of Newbold College after Howell's visit there two years before. They couldn't prevent Schneider from coming, but they would be prepared. When Schneider spoke , Lloyd Antonio and other Seventh-day Adventist ministers would be there to listen.

"Very aggressive. Very arrogant. Very persistent," Antonio said later of Schneider. "While myself and other ministers were present, he didn't present the things that were bizarre. After we left, the weird teachings were shared with the young people, things about Armageddon and so forth."

Later, the ministers mounted a campaign against Schneider, and by extension, Howell, from their pulpits. They held Bible studies and distributed literature among the young people, attempting to demonstrate the folly of Branch Davidian teaching. The ministers won a small victory. At their urging, Schneider's host refused to entertain him for a third night.

The American, apparently with Diana Henry's assistance, quickly found another living room for the final session of what again would prove to be a fruitful trip. Soon after Schneider departed, Sandra Hardial joined about a dozen others on a two-week trip to the place in Texas he had so glowingly described. For many, it also was the first meeting with the young prophet, who by then had changed his name to David Koresh.

Sandra described her trip enthusiastically but obliquely when she returned, telling her brother of the daily Bible studies and the abundant sunshine. The name of Vernon Howell never came up between them, then or later.

"She felt it was a good break," Lloyd said.

Lloyd noticed subtle changes in his sister in the following months. Sandra spent more time with her Bible and began to collect religious literature. Otherwise she seemed the same; outgoing and upbeat. Colleagues noticed no change at work. And if Sandra had undergone a conversion, she wouldn't have shared it with her brother in any event. The two talked about everything else, but Sandra knew of Lloyd's profound disdain for religion and knew he would not have tolerated talk of a new light had she even bothered to raise it.

Not until March 1992 did Lloyd learn of the depth of Sandra's new passion. The two had planned to meet in Jamaica for a vacation, with Lloyd to arrive first and Sandra a week later. Sandra never showed. When her worried brother called relatives in Manchester, he was stunned to learn why. Sandra was traveling all right, but to a different destination. She had quit her job without notice, and gone off to live at Mount Carmel, leaving only an address, a telephone number and a note behind.

"She said that she felt that there was something she needed to find out for herself," Lloyd said.

Lloyd eventually recovered from his shock. In the year after Sandra left, he and Sandra spoke often on the telephone and wrote to each other frequently. Sandra routinely promised to come home soon, but never said when. Otherwise, she seemed the same person Lloyd had grown up with. There was no hint of distress.

On Monday morning, March 1, 1993, Lloyd noticed the large photograph of a wounded federal agent on the front page of his morning newspaper. He glanced to the account of the shootout with the Branch Davidian sect and his heart sank when he saw the dateline: Waco, Texas.

Only a few weeks before, he had talked to his sister on her twenty-seventh birthday. Now, after recovering his senses, Lloyd dialed that number again. A recorded message informed him that the line had been disconnected.

Samuel Henry moved to Manchester from Jamaica in 1958, lured to the new land at the age of twenty-two by the promise of a better life. He had done well for himself, made a good living as a builder. But Samuel believed his children would be the ultimate fulfillment of the immigrant's dream.

He and Zilla were married on December 1, 1963, a few years after church friends introduced him to the quiet nurse who had just arrived from Trinidad. Samuel Henry ultimately would become an elder at the couple's Seventh-day Adventist church. Zilla taught Sabbath Day classes and served as a church officer.

Diana was born on New Year's Day 1965, the first of the couple's five children to arrive over the next eight years. To their father, all were exemplary children. Diana earned two college degrees and planned to attend graduate school. Stephen worked alongside his father. Paulina and Vanessa, the youngest, both were planning to attend college. Phillip seemed the brightest of all. He was a brilliant boy who planned to study medicine. When the devil came, Samuel was sure Phillip would recognize the nonsense. But he seemed taken with Vernon Howell like all the others. He, like they, would not or could not explain the attraction.

Samuel pleaded with his youngest son to come to his senses. He offered to buy him a new car if he stayed in

Britain and continued his studies. On another occasion, he promised to buy back the plane ticket Phillip had purchased for America. His son refused to listen.

"You must go see for yourself," Phillip said calmly, just like the rest.

But Samuel had seen. While visiting friends in Florida in 1989, he decided on the spur of the moment to find this place called Mount Carmel. The bus trip across the south took nearly two days. It was early evening when he pulled into a Waco bus station and was hugged by Diana who had come to greet him. As a friend drove them into the country, Diana talked nonstop about her new life, and the man whom she said had thousands of followers around the world. She insisted that her father join them for a late-night Bible study, where he could meet Vernon Howell.

"Diana, I'm dead tired," Samuel said. "The only thing I can study right now is a bed."

What Samuel saw when they arrived more resembled the poverty of his native Jamaica than the paradise Diana had described. Mount Carmel was just a small cluster of crumbling bungalows without toilets or running water. But his bed in Diana's quarters was comfortable and at the time that was all he cared about. He quickly fell into a deep sleep and was angry when Diana shook him at ten o'clock.

"Please, daddy," Diana said. "Come to study."

"Not over my dead body," her father replied.

In the morning, Diana brought him oat porridge for breakfast. After eating, Samuel strolled to a larger building where people seemed to congregate. He found Vernon Howell sitting there. Samuel introduced himself and attempted to make small talk, telling Howell how much he enjoyed the United States.

"You could live here in Texas, and the authorities would never find you," Howell assured him.

As they spoke, Diana Henry and several other women walked silently by holding Bibles. Their leader started in on his newest visitor. Howell bragged of spiritual discernment no other man possessed. He quoted from the fourth chapter of Revelation: "Immediately I was in the Spirit, and behold, a throne set in heaven, and One sat on the throne."

"I've got something better for you," Howell told Samuel. "See yourself in the kingdom around the throne. Until you hear what I have to say, you don't know anything."

This man must think I'm a fool or something, Samuel thought. Finally he could listen no more. "Look," he said. "I was led to the Seventh-day Adventist church by God and I am going to die in that church."

Howell sprang to his feet, wild-eyed, suddenly screaming at his startled guest.

"I could whip you!" Howell said. "I could whip you, you hypocrite!"

Samuel stood and walked away to find his daughter. His visit was over. Diana wept when he told her he must leave. Spurning the prophet meant the soul of her father would be lost forever. But to Samuel, it was Diana who was lost. As he boarded the bus back to Florida, sadness hung like a rock over his heart. Yet he learned what he had come to find out. He had learned of Vernon Howell's evil.

But he was the only one who would see. He would never forget the Sunday night in 1990 when Zilla called him upstairs, saying she and the rest of the children would be leaving the next day to join Diana.

Zilla traveled back and forth for awhile after that. When she returned from Mount Carmel, she looked thin. Her mind was a world away. She moved from his bed.

"If the minds don't go together, the bodies can't either," she told her husband.

She worked two nursing jobs, one at a hospital, another in a private home, and though she never said, Samuel knew the money was being given to Howell. At home she spent her time reading the Bible, mostly Revelation and Isaiah. Religion was the only subject she would discuss with her husband.

Zilla left England for the last time in March 1992, apparently traveling with Sandra Hardial. Samuel's letters to his wife and children were never answered. He telephoned Mount Carmel, pleading with his family to return home, but often would end up speaking to Vernon Howell.

"Brother Henry," Howell would say. "How good it is to hear from you. Why don't you come and join us?"

Samuel Henry spoke with his wife only a few weeks before the shootout. After three years, he was filing for a divorce. Property matters in England needed discussion. Gloom replaced his desperation, a dark sense of foreboding that Henry would express in a letter sent to his family.

"This man is another Jim Jones," Samuel Henry wrote. "The Davidians are headed down the path of destruction."

5

JONESTOWN REVISITED

Their names became almost synonymous after the deadly events at Mount Carmel. Like the Reverend Jim Jones of the Peoples Temple, a spasm of violence vaulted David Koresh to international fame, placing him next to Jones on a short list of the century's most destructive cult leaders. And as the Texas stand-off continued, the world feared Koresh's legacy would resemble Jones in another tragic respect: the mass death of his followers.

"Many of us feel that it's going to be another Jonestown," Reverend Lloyd Antonio, a Seventh-day Adventist pastor in Manchester, England, said a few days after the Waco shootout. "That's why we've been so worried and we're praying so hard."

The parallels between them were indeed inescapable, the differences seeming more a matter of degree and personal style. Both Jones and Koresh, for example, seemed to draw their inspiration from the Bible, at least initially. Both enjoyed absolute authority and demanded unquestioning loyalty from their followers. Both isolated their acolytes from friends, family members and outside information in remote compounds. Both Jones and Koresh grew rich from the earnings, belongings and life savings of their converts. Both cult leaders stockpiled weapons and began to exhibit increasingly violent tendencies. Both fostered notions of ultimate confrontation with the outside world, using their paranoia to keep the followers in line. Jones and Koresh precluded cult members from having sexual relationships, while satiating their own voracious sexual appetites, bragging about their conquests.

Above all, perhaps, they shared an acute megalomania that ultimately made their prophecies self-fulfilling.

The parallels extended to their childhoods as well. Like Koresh, Jones found comfort in church at an unusually early age, spiritual salve for a profound sense of alienation he felt growing up. It was a childhood of contradictions. Jones was born May 13, 1931, in Lynn, Indiana, a small community where casket making was the major industry. Early on he displayed a love of the Bible and compassion for animals of all kinds. Strays often found a home with the boy who on one occasion performed a candlelight funeral service for a dead mouse, whose remains reposed in a matchbox.

Yet the young Jones could also be mean-spirited and vulgar, sometimes greeting neighbors with, "Good morning, you son of a bitch." As an adult, he bragged of filling one detested preacher's Bible with manure and urinating in a holy water receptacle of a Catholic church: "They didn't know they were anointing themselves with my pee."

Jones nonetheless aspired to the ministry. At age eighteen, the dark-haired and handsome young man married Marceline Baldwin, a nurse he had met while working as an orderly at a hospital. The couple moved to Indianapolis, where Jones attended night school and ultimately founded his own church. The Christian Assembly of God featured his spectacular faith-healing ministry and head-quartered an impressive array of social services that distributed food to the poor and helped the jobless find work.

In Indianapolis, a hotbed of the Ku Klux Klan, Jones also developed twin passions that would dominate the rest of his life: racial integration and socialism. He and his wife adopted black and Korean children, and Jones frequently railed from the pulpit against racism in the 1950s when racial tensions in America were coming to a boil. In 1961, his passion led the mayor of Indianapolis to appoint Jones the first full-time director of the city's human rights commission.

By then, Jones had long been a devout communist, viewing a socialist system as a preferable alternative to the vast economic inequities of American capitalism. His political beliefs were not explicit in his preaching until the following decade, when it became obvious that socialism, not the Bible, was the driving ideal of the Peoples Temple, as Jones's church eventually came to be called.

In the mid-1960s, apparently weary of the intolerance of Indianapolis, Jones moved his church, by then officially affiliated with the Disciples of Christ, to northern California. Jones was ordained a Disciples of Christ minister in 1964. Like Koresh years later, Jones continued to freely appropriate biblical verses, twisting them to support his vision of a new socialist order.

In California, Jones quickly made a name for himself as an altruist and political activist. He purchased an old synagogue in San Francisco's inner city and opened an infirmary, a day-care center, a carpentry shop and kitchens for feeding the neighborhood poor. The operation was powerful testament to his commitment to the admonitions of Christ in the twenty-fifth chapter of the book of Matthew, verses that adorned the Peoples Temple letterhead.

"For I was hungered and ye gave me meat;
I was thirsty and ye gave me drink;
I was a stranger and ye took me in;
Naked and ye clothed me;
I was in prison and ye came unto me."

His deeds scarcely went unnoticed. In 1975, one religious magazine named Jones one of the nation's 100 outstanding clergymen. The next year, he received a Los Angeles newspaper's humanitarian-of-the-year award.

"Pastor Jones...has been largely responsible for the establishment of a large congregation of everyday human beings from all walks of life, binding them together in a truly extraordinary commitment to human service," a regional president of the Disciples of Christ wrote in 1975. "The ministries of this pastor and his congregation are staggering in scope and effectiveness."

According to some estimates, Jones's congregation had grown to nearly 5,000 members, 80 percent of them black, people whom the leader routinely enlisted for liberal political causes. His list of political contacts included California Governor Jerry Brown and San Francisco Mayor George Moscone, who appointed Jones to the city's housing authority in 1976. Jones's political heft earned him an invitation aboard the private plane of Vice-President Walter Mondale, and a handwritten thank-you note from Rosalynn Carter.

But unknown to most at the time, behind the impressive facade, was a man started on the downhill cycle towards dementia, a progression that began about the time he arrived in California, according to later reports.

He began to proclaim himself to his followers as the embodiment of God. His people had been placed in bondage by an evil deity Jones called the Sky God.

"The savior had arrived to rescue them from the works of the Sky God. He would heal them, raise them from the dead, open their blinded eyes, get them out of jail, give them a home, take care of them when they were lonely," wrote David Chidester in his 1988 book, *Salvation and Suicide*. "He declared himself as the living manifestation of a God that was Principle, that was Love, that was Socialism."

As with David Koresh years later, Jones supported his claim to divinity by quotations from the Bible.

"I am just like you," Jones said, "flesh of your flesh, bone of your bone, very much God, but very much human."

Jones often noted that no one in his congregation had died since 1959 and claimed to have the power to resurrect them in any event. He was not above grotesque trickery, claiming bloody chicken gizzards were really cancers he had drawn from the bodies of the ill. Followers began to call him "Dad." In the meantime, Jones helped himself to a fortune from the earnings and savings of his flock. He banned sex among Peoples Temple members, but indulged his own voracious bisexual appetites. He once bragged of having sex with fourteen women and two men on the same day. Though supposedly opposed to homosexual activity, Jones said he had sex with men to connect them symbolically with himself.

Jones became increasingly obsessed with suicide, both to escape his tormentors and as a means to further his political philosophy. In 1973, while his civic and political popularity was still on the rise, Jones called associates into his home to discuss the desertion of eight cult members who fled because of the sex ban.

"Something terrible has happened," Jones said. "Eight people have defected. In order to keep our apostolic socialism, we should all kill ourselves and leave a note saying that because of harassment, a socialist group cannot exist at this time."

The suicide plan was scotched on that occasion, but to Jones, the evil forces had begun to close in, and the ultimate confrontation was nearing. Indeed, for the first time, there were public accusations that the Peoples Temple was something other than an oasis of love for those in need. A 1973 series by the *San Francisco Examiner* chronicled Jones's messianic pretensions, reporting his claims that he had raised forty-three people from the dead, and called into question the temple's authoritarian structure. Four years later, other stories documented the use of violence to ensure the obedience of his followers.

Jones's response was to flee, leasing 3,000 acres in Guyana, an English-speaking country on the northern coast of South America that Jones had visited while briefly living in Brazil fifteen years earlier, and one sympathetic with his socialist inclinations. Fifteen of his acolytes arrived in March 1974 to begin clearing the dense jungle and breaking ground for the village that would be called Jonestown. A year later, the settlement had grown to fifty residents who continued hacking away the jungle, built houses, and otherwise laid the groundwork for the Peoples Temple Agricultural Project.

In 1977, with the publication of other negative stories about Jones and his church, the exodus to Jonestown greatly intensified. Jones was already in Guyana by August 1977, when an article in *New West* magazine quoted several former members accusing the cult of financial improprieties, physical coercion, and questionable involvement in San Francisco politics. The leader decided it was time to move the temple to its promised land. On August 3, 1977, Jones radioed his resignation to the San Francisco Housing Authority and never returned to the United States.

A month later, the Jonestown population had swollen to almost 1,000, and an impressive village sprang up virtually overnight. Three-quarters of the Jonestown residents were black, approximately two-thirds were women. There were 300 children and 150 senior citizens living in a community that soon included a nursery, schools, adult education programs, medical services and a variety of entertainments.

"Jonestown was designed as a Utopia on earth, a socialist paradise in the jungle where racism, sexism, ageism, classism would be eliminated, and people who had been deprived, discriminated against, and persecuted in America could live in peace and freedom," Chidester wrote.

But in jungle isolation, where dependence on the leader was magnified, Jones's messianic notions calcified further. Dictates of his communist Utopia demanded even greater selflessness from his followers. His paranoia at what he considered to be a conspiracy of former members, the news media and the federal government grew. Jones refined his notions of revolutionary suicide—what he considered an attempt to maintain human dignity by fighting the forces of oppression with death. The specter of mass suicide also was a potent control device for main-

65

taining loyalty and cohesion among the cult. Jones said the defection of even one member could trigger the deaths of everyone left behind.

In July 1978, Jones exhorted his followers to write him letters about their feelings toward the world, their place in it, about life and death. The dark missives that resulted, printed later in *Time* magazine, were testament to his hold on their souls. Those with money condemned themselves as elitists. To many of his nearly illiterate followers, death seemed preferable to corruption by a world their leader taught was evil. Some examples[2]:

"I have two children now. They both mean so much to me. I want to give them security, but I also know I need them to be a security for me. I know I needed someone to share my life with because it seemed to be so lonely at times. It's the fault of too selfish parent. I know if they must die for Socialism it will be a most honorable death because dying for Peace, Justice, Freedom for all is worth the struggle."—C. Wilhite.

"I don't respect Dad the way I should. I respect Dad out of fear of getting in trouble, rather than respecting him for what he is, a Marxist Leninist."—Eugene Smith.

"I waisted money buying cars and trucks, and I waisted money buying candy and soda pop, hamburgers, clothing that I didn't need. And I waist

---

[2]Each excerpt is reprinted here as originally published, to include grammatical and spelling errors.

money buying gasoline and oil, waste money paying telephone bills, now Dad after hearing your teaching about how the tax off these above items help to keep our sisters and brothers in slavement I feel very guilty. Oh yes, I bought beear, whisky, cigars, cigarettes by the carton and I feel guilt."— Gabriel Thomas.

"My Feeling for Father & this cause is a very happy one I can not think of anything that I would or could be happier with. Father is wonderful, clean, straight forward & Supernatural. I play no sexual games to jealous to play sexual games. I am not afraid to die but would like to die for a reason."—Rose Shelton.

"Another fault is that I miss soda, candy, pie, etc., which I shouldn't miss at all. That way I can prevent this is on agricultural Sunday work extra hard and I think everyone else should to because this produces more. Not only for sweet stuff do we only work but to make our community more advance."— Lisa Rodriquez, age 12.

"I used to think why was I born, why do people have to die, every time I think about it I cried. Now I'm ready to die for this cause."—Burnelle Wilson.

"How I feel about dying—It feels like being alone. I would like to stay around a little longer."— Syda Turner.

"I feel very lonely but I am satisfied with the fact that I am over the hill, 29 yrs. old. I think the best use of sex at this time is to further the cause of Communism. Most days I wish I would vanish into thin air. Death is something I look forward to. My only objection is being away from people I care about and someone I'll miss, that's you."— Maureen Talley

In the end, Guyana's distance could not keep the worldly forces at bay. The final confrontation ultimately would come with the United States government, not with law enforcement as in Waco, but with a congressman from California. Leo Ryan, a liberal Democrat, walked into a powder keg unaware he was holding a match.

For more than a year, Ryan had fielded reports that Jones populated his new South American colony by coercion. Constituents worried about family members living with Jones in the rain forest. The congressman decided to travel to Jonestown to investigate. In November 1978, Ryan, Jones's attorney Mark Lane, eight journalists and several relatives of temple members set out for South America.

After arriving in the Guyanan capital of Georgetown, Ryan held a press conference challenging the tax-exempt status of the Peoples Temple, stating "there is a posturing of religious belief, but I'm not sure it exists." He also raised questions about violations of social security laws, finance laws and passport regulations. He threatened to initiate full-scale congressional hearings if he and his party were not admitted into the village.

On November 17, Ryan and his party arrived in a chartered aircraft at an airstrip six miles from Jonestown, then drove across bad roads on a flatbed trailer to reach the settlement. After a confrontational beginning to the visit, the outsiders' arrival seemed cause for celebration among Jonestown residents and the leader himself. The party was met by Jones's wife and given several extensive tours of the compound, including the central pavilion used as both a school and an assembly hall, the newly completed saw mill, the 10,000-volume library and nursery where mosquito netting protected peacefully sleeping infants. In the evening, Ryan and his party were the guests of honor at a music-filled celebration.

"From what I've seen, there are a lot of people here who think this is the best thing that has happened in their whole lives," Ryan told cheering Jonestown residents and an applauding Jim Jones.

But the truth could not be contained. The next day, distress began to filter out to members of the visiting party. Some temple members surreptitiously slipped notes to Ryan's party begging to leave with them. Eventually, fourteen members came forward to say they wanted to defect.

"Anyone is free to come and go," Jones said assuringly to the congressman. "I want to hug them before they leave."

His mood quickly darkened, however.

"They will try to destroy us," he said after learning of the defectors' intentions. "They always do."

As Ryan spoke with Jones about the defectors, the congressman was attacked by a knife-wielding Jonestown security officer. Though uninjured, the incident proved a precursor of what was soon to come. Later that day, as Ryan's party, swollen by the Peoples Temple defectors, attempted to leave in two aircraft, a trailer pulled into the airstrip. Three men on the vehicle grabbed weapons and began firing. Inside one of the planes, a Jones follower posing as a defector opened fire with a handgun. When the shooting stopped, Ryan, three journalists and one defector were dead and nine others were wounded. The world would not know it for several days, but the death toll had only begun. One of the century's darkest moments was at hand.

Until 6:00 p.m. on November 18, 1978, the white night exercises had been loyalty tests. Every few weeks, it seemed, Jonestown residents were summoned from their beds by loudspeakers and ordered to drink what was described as poison.

"We were told we would be tortured by mercenaries if we were taken alive," former Peoples Temple member Deborah Blakely wrote in an affidavit to the Justice Department. "Everyone, including the children, would line up. As we passed through the line, we were given a small glass of red liquid to drink. We were told that the liquid contained poison and that we would die within forty-five minutes. We all did as we were told. When the time came when we should have dropped dead, Reverend Jones explained that the poison was not real and that we had just been through a loyalty test. He warned us that the time was not far off when it would become necessary for us to die by our own hands."

Following Ryan's departure, Jones again summoned his followers to the pavilion for the final white night.

"When fourteen of his people decided to go out with Ryan, Jim Jones went mad," Charles Garry, another of

Jones's attorneys, later told reporters. "He thought it was a repudiation of his work. I tried to tell him that fourteen out of 1,200 was damn good, but Jones was desolate."

A psychopathic ego had been fatally ruptured by the defections. Yet to most of his people, Jones was still "Dad," the God who now was calling them to strike a blow for socialism.

"Jones had served as the example, expression, and manifestation of this superhuman, Divine Socialism, the exemplary model through which they had sought their salvation, and it was now his will that they lay down their lives in protest against the dehumanizing conditions of the world," Chidester wrote.

In the end, most submitted to the final white night willingly. Those who didn't were compelled to do so at gunpoint. One woman told Jones she had a right to do what she wanted with her own life. "Guards with guns and bows and arrows pressed in on her, and Jones tried to make her understand that she had to do it," survivor Stanley Clayton said later. About that time the henchman from the airstrip had returned in the truck and rushed up to Jones.

"(Jones) announced that Ryan was dead and we had to do what we had to do," Clayton said. "He told the nurses to hurry with the potion. He told them to take care of the babies. He said any survivors would be castrated and tortured by the Guyanese Army.

"The nurses started taking the babies from the mothers. Jones kept saying, 'Hurry! Hurry!' But the people were not responding. The guards then moved in and started pulling people, trying to get them to take the potion. It was dark by now. I went around to each of the guards, embraced them and told them, 'I'll see you later.'

I skipped out to the bushes. All the time I kept saying to myself, I can't believe this. Jim Jones is mad."

Babies and children died first in the madness that Clayton left behind. Parents squirted potassium cyanide and potassium chloride onto the tongues of infants. Adults and older children sipped the poison, sweetened by purple Kool-Aid, from a metal vat placed in the center of the pavilion. Witnesses later described some families calmly wandering off together to die.

"They were all crying, but it wasn't like they were afraid," survivor Odell Rhodes said later. "They were talking about how they were going to see each other on the other side. It wasn't like they were going to die at all. It was more like moving day—when somebody moves out of the neighborhood and everybody's crying, not because where they're going is so bad, but more because they're sad to be leaving one another."

Another survivor portrayed a more wrenching scene in which "babies were screaming, children were screaming, and there was mass confusion."

One elderly man, Grover Davis, jumped into a ditch when the suicides were ordered by Jones and pretended to be dead until everyone had left. "Because I didn't want to die," Davis explained later. Another of the temple's elderly, a woman in her seventies, was ill and slept through the entire poison-taking ritual.

"I thought everybody had run off," she said. "I started crying and wailing, 'Why did they leave me? Why did they leave me?'"

Jones viewed the destruction of his people from a wicker chair set above the fray, exhorting his followers with promises that they would "meet in another place." Jones, forty-seven years old, died of a self-inflicted gunshot wound to the head. He had not swallowed any of his poison, an autopsy showed.

A few days later, *Time* magazine correspondent Donald Neff was among the first to fly into the death scene, one about to be scorched into the memory of a generation.

"The large central building was ringed by bright colors," Neff said of the appearance of Jonestown from the air. "It looked like a parking lot filled with cars. When the plane dipped lower, the cars turned out to be bodies. Scores of bodies—hundreds of bodies—wearing red dresses, blue T-shirts, green blouses, pink slacks, children's polka-dotted jumpers. Couples with their arms around each other, children holding parents. Nothing moved."

On the ground the horror grew more vivid.

"The first of the bodies was a man by himself, face down, his features bloated, his torso puffed into balloon shape," Neff reported. "Then more bodies, lying in a yard. Grotesque in their swollenness, but looking relaxed as though comforted in their family togetherness. Nearly all of them were on their faces, eerie figures of slumber. I turned a corner, and the whole mass of bodies came into view. The smell was overpowering, the sight unworldly. There were no signs of violence. No blood. Only a few bodies showed the gruesome signs of cyanide rictus. Outside there were three dead dogs, poisoned. Down the road in a large cage was 'Mr. Muggs,' the commune's pet gorilla. He had been shot. In a tree-shaded area was Jones's home, a three-room bungalow. Bodies were scattered all over the three rooms, some on the beds, others on the floor. The quiet was broken only by the meowing of a cat beyond the porch."

Authorities eventually counted 914 bodies that were loaded into body bags by soldiers and flown back to the

United States on Air Force cargo planes. A stunned world struggled to comprehend one of history's largest collective acts of self-destruction. Those who had crossed paths with Jones, including politicians like Governor Brown and Mayor Moscone, took pains to distance themselves from the man who had become the personification of evil.

The Unification Church of Reverend Sun Myung Moon, another target of the anticult movement, declared it had no association to the Peoples Temple which "was not religion—it was not even a cult. It was a Marxist commune rooted in the demonic philosophy of Communism."

In a newspaper column written in the aftermath of the Jonestown tragedy, Reverend Billy Graham cited Christ's warnings of false prophets contained in the twenty-fourth chapter of Matthew. Ironically, it was the subsequent chapter of the same New Testament book that once had adorned the Peoples Temple letterhead: "For I was hungry and ye gave me meat..."

"One may speak of the Jones situation as that of a cult, but it would be a sad mistake to identify it in any way with Christianity. It is true that he came from a religious background, but what he did and how he thought can have no relationship to the views and teachings of any legitimate form of historic Christianity," Graham wrote. "We have witnessed a false messiah who used the cloak of religion to cover a confused mind filled with a mixture of pseudo-religion, political ambition, sensual lust, financial dishonesty, and apparently, even murder.... Apparently Mr. Jones was a slave of a diabolical supernatural power from which he refused to be set free."

It was *Time* magazine essayist Lance Morrow who succeeded better than most in putting Jonestown in perspective.

"Religion and insanity occupy adjacent territories in the mind," Morrow wrote. "Historically, cults have kept up a traffic between the two."

Somewhere, Jim Jones had crossed that line into the darkness, a departure that would not occur again so dramatically until David Koresh crossed over himself, more than a decade later.

6

RICK ROSS TAKES ONE BACK

By all appearances, Bill[3] had it made. He was an intelligent, highly trained and well-paid professional in his thirties. He was tall and Hollywood handsome, with piercing blue eyes and light brown hair; the kind of guy who caused heads to turn. Who would have guessed he hadn't had a date in four years or that he turned over his salary to a self-proclaimed prophet in Texas?

By that summer day in 1992, Bill's life had begun falling apart. He was exhausted, overly thin and overcome with anxiety as he sat across from a short, boyish-looking man named Rick Ross in that house in Santa Barbara. Ross had brought his Bible to their meeting, stacks of literature, videos on cults and this troubling suggestion: Maybe David Koresh wasn't God after all.

For the first time, Bill had begun to have some doubts himself. He had begun to notice chinks in the spiritual armor of Koresh, the man for whom he had sworn off sex,

---

[3]"Bill" is not his real name. His name has been changed and his surname deleted for the purpose of confidentiality.

the man to whom he turned over his money. But those doubts came at a high price—terror that gripped his soul, took his breath away. Bill was sure he was betraying God just by sitting there talking to Rick Ross. David Koresh had opened the book of life and given Bill the secret, or so Koresh said. Those like Bill who knew the truth and rejected it would be condemned to burn in the Lake of Fire for eternity. That's what Koresh taught his followers. Who wouldn't be anxious? What if the Branch Davidian leader was right?

Yet Bill listened that July morning, even as his heart raced and he felt like fleeing. He and Ross were sequestered in a home in California, safe from Koresh for the moment, far from Mount Carmel, the place that had been Bill's home off and on for four years. And Ross was beginning to make sense. What indeed if David Koresh wasn't God? What if he was just a psycho who used the Bible to get rich and get laid? What if David Koresh, beneath the Lamb's clothing, was really just a ninth grade dropout named Vern?

The radical Pentecostals had infiltrated the nursing staff at the Jewish retirement home, and Rick Ross's grandmother, Anna Tucker, was among their targets. Anna, deeply religious and intensely proud of her Jewish heritage, had survived the religious pogroms of Eastern Europe at the turn of the century. Now, eighty years later, she was confronted by religious persecution of another stripe. A nurse approached and began preaching fire and brimstone Christianity, warning Anna she would burn in hell if she didn't convert.

Ross had worked as a loan officer after high school and was running a family salvage operation when his distraught grandmother called that day in 1982 to tell him about the incident. Ambivalent to religion before then, Ross was outraged. He complained to the director of the nursing home, and insisted on conducting a personal investigation. A subsequent conversation with one of the Pentecostal leaders would change his life: "God has judged the Jewish people through the Holocaust," Ross was told.

"That really offended me," Ross said years later. "That was my first exposure to radical religionists. After that, one thing led to another."

His experience at his grandmother's nursing home inspired Ross to write a brochure for Jewish groups in Phoenix called *What in God's Name is Going on in Arizona?* The publication received wide notice. A short time later he was appointed to national committees of Jewish organizations that dealt with religious persecution and cults. Ross began hearing stories about brainwashing and mind control. He started building files on Bible-based cults, and embarked on his own exhaustive study of Scripture to determine how it was being manipulated.

Ross left the salvage business, taking a staff position at a Jewish social service agency in Phoenix where he worked with people caught up in destructive religious groups or cults. When confronted with the truth, Ross found, most agreed to leave the group or at least re-evaluate their decisions to join. His career as a deprogrammer had begun.

In 1986, he left the social service agency for private practice, charging $500 a day plus expenses for services he discovered were in great demand. The former salvage company executive soon became a national celebrity of sorts, making the national television circuit. He appeared on Geraldo, Sally Jesse Raphael, Oprah and Donahue. He was featured on the news show "48 Hours" on three occasions.

Television producers weren't the only ones calling his Phoenix office, listed in the local yellow pages under "cult deprogrammers." Mothers and fathers called Ross about their children. Sisters called about brothers. Children called about parents, wives about husbands, husbands about wives. They were disparate people who shared a profound, often desperate concern for loved ones who had fallen into Bible-based cults, cults that seemed to be proliferating across North America. Most of his clients had been normal people seeking love or truth during confusing times, or relief from anxiety or depression. By fate or circumstance, a cult recruiter had come along at the moment they had reached the bottom. Ross had seen it happen over and over again. In this day and age, no one was really safe.

"We all have vulnerabilities," Ross said. "Most people don't want to admit that."

The 1980s would indeed be boom times for his fledgling profession. Ross, who worked exclusively with members of Bible-based cults, was consulted by more than 2,000 families. He performed close to 300 deprogrammings, his work taking him from Toronto to Dallas, Los Angeles to Washington, D.C., from Montana to Miami. Clients ranged from children as young as five to people in their nineties, and came from all walks of life.

Ross was successful in eight of ten cases, his clients agreeing to sever cultish bonds that had made them virtual captives. Contrary to popular belief, he used neither smoke nor mirrors; no hocus-pocus or exorcisms. Instead, the forty-year-old with thinning brown hair armed himself with information and logic. Given time, Ross learned, truth usually triumphed over fear and evil.

With a few exceptions, his dealings with cult members were voluntary, the result of family members pleading with loved ones to listen to another side. While the names and locations changed, Ross found cult tactics largely the same. He diagrammed their recruiting tactics, the sleep or food deprivation, the mind control. He discussed with the cult member why loved ones were concerned. Perhaps most importantly, he demonstrated how cult leaders invariably manipulated the Bible to their own ends. At best, cult leaders were victims of their own religious delusions. At worst, they used the Bible as a means of extortion. To Rick Ross, there could be no better example of the latter than David Koresh.

Ross first learned about Koresh and the Waco Davidians in 1989 from the relatives of cult members. One young man suffered a nervous breakdown while a Waco Davidian, his parents said. Koresh had him loaded onto a plane and flown home, where he was dumped in a heap on his parents' doorstep by a Koresh acolyte. The children of another family called, frantic because their parents had turned over $300,000 to Koresh after joining his cult.

Ross encountered the handiwork of David Koresh firsthand in 1992. It started with a phone call from Bill's brother and sister. Until then, they said they had stayed out of Bill's business, even when he abruptly set off on a strange new life. Bill met Steve Schneider while vacationing on a Hawaii beach seven years before, and at Schneider's urging converted to the Seventh-day Adventist church. Schneider became Bill's trusted spiritual advisor. When Schneider joined the Davidians, Bill followed.

Bill's job allowed him to come and go as he pleased. He began to divide his time between California and the compound in Waco. His family was concerned, but Bill seemed happy, and he still maintained a life apart from the cult.

Then, in early 1992, something about him changed. Bill's family later learned that Koresh had begun preaching about an imminent apocalypse. The world likely would end in June, Koresh said. While visiting his family in May, Bill spoke of quitting his job, severing all ties to the outside world and moving to Mount Carmel. With his life spinning out of control, Bill's siblings could stay silent no longer. They had heard about Ross and pleaded with Bill to talk with him.

"It can't hurt," the siblings told Bill. "You know you're free to do whatever you want to do."

Less than an hour before he was to leave his brother's home and return to Mount Carmel, Bill reluctantly agreed. Ross talked quickly when the phone call came. He had many seeds to plant, and not much time. Ross spoke generically about how cults operated, asking Bill to notice if anything sounded familiar. Was there an absolute authority figure not accountable to anyone? Were members required to conform completely to the leader's dictates? Was outside information filtered through the leader? Was there an "us against them" mentality? Were those outside the cult dismissed and berated? Lastly, Ross asked Bill, did the leader's claims from the Bible ultimately lead to his own aggrandizement, power and control?

"I don't know if that's true," Bill said. "I'll look and see if that's true, but it doesn't seem that way to me. Maybe

I'll call you again."

Bill called two months later. He had begun to see the patterns of Mount Carmel for himself, he told Ross. There were disturbing similarities. Too many prophecies remained unfulfilled or served only to benefit the prophet. Bill agreed to meet with Ross in California.

The lessons of Jonestown apparently were short-lived. By the time David Koresh's Davidians opened fire on that dreary Sunday morning in Texas, as many as 5,000 cults existed across the United States, ranging in size from twelve or fifteen members to millions. Most came with a familiar pathology, starting with a self-professed leader with or without messianic pretensions, who promised to impart special knowledge in return for total obedience.

"If you don't like the word cult," said Margaret Thaler Singer, a University of California at Berkeley psychologist and one of the nation's leading experts on the topic, "try closed, intense groups in which there is an intense commitment to the leader."

The definition should have inspired chills after Jonestown. Yet cults continued to thrive after the nightmare in Guyana, as they had periodically throughout history. Cults were lingering proof of the lengths human souls would travel in the search for meaning, and the willingness of others to take full advantage for themselves.

Cults had flourished for centuries during periods of great change and dislocation. They thrived after the Fall of Rome for example, after the French Revolution and during the Industrial Revolution, times in which life

seemed to lose its compass. To many, with the materialism, greed and continuing disintegration of the family,
that seemed to describe the decade of the 1980s.

"Today more than ever, people search for meaning
and purpose in life. They realize that material goods and
the pursuit of pleasure have not brought happiness," cult
experts James and Marcia Rudin wrote in their 1980 book,
Prison or Paradise, The New Religious Cults. "At this point
the cults appear on the scene offering singleness of purpose. In a decadent society they preach a radiant, tran-
scendent ideal, a meaningful way of life that is not merely
a continuation of consumerism and conspicuous con-
sumption. 'No, that's not all there is,' declares the cult
recruiter. 'Our group offers meaning in life, goals to aim
for and a purpose to existence.'

"Bewildered, frightened, unnerved by the world as it
is, the potential cult member, in desperation, makes a
total surrender, a fanatical commitment to the cult in the
hope of overcoming the uncertainties of life," the Rubins
wrote.

"This surrender to absolute authority which relieves
the cult member of agonizing large decisions and even
sometimes small, day-to-day decisions is an abdication of
freedom and personal liberty in favor of security. A significant and growing number have turned their backs on
our society and have opted instead for a closed system of
belief, work, and friendship, but the price paid for such
security is high."

The Rubins contended that in a world of moral ambi-
guity and affluence, many were attracted by the self-
denial and sacrifice cults seemed to demand.

"A cult leader who demands personal sacrifices of
money, time, talent, energy, and as we saw in Jonestown,

even life itself, will find thousands of receptive converts only waiting to be told what to give up or surrender for a promised greater good. If the general society and established religious groups either neglect or spurn this urge to give, that powerful drive will be satisfied elsewhere. That is why many cult members joyously transfer their savings account to a cult, why they deliberately lead a rigid, Spartan life of self-denial while they are in a group, and why so many are willing to work long hours in often humiliating jobs, all enthusiastically done in the name of sacrifice."

But Utopia does not come cheaply.

"No matter how democratically advertised, visions of the New Jerusalem, Utopia or Edenic Jonestown are bathed in a totalitarian light," *Time* magazine essayist Lance Morrow wrote after Jonestown. "And they are shadowed by glimpses of their enemies: Antichrist, Gog and Magog; paranoia is often a cult's principle instrument of discipline. Even in 1978, one catches whiffs of an old dementia and witchfire."

Implicit in the new cult members' abdication, implicit in their sacrifice, is their idealistic faith in the leader's benevolence. But cult leaders who might initially have kept their followers' well-being foremost in mind didn't for long. Power intoxicated, and ultimately, no amount of worship was ever enough.

"Cult leaders become extremely impressed at how much power they get," said Cal-Berkeley's Singer, who has counseled more than 3,000 former cult members, more than any other therapist in the country. "It's as if they feed off the power they get from other people. It's a heady role to be in. That treatment makes them feel more and more sure of themselves, and other people more and more unsure of themselves. Jim Jones fed off the adulation he engendered."

So cult leaders demanded increasingly dramatic displays of loyalty from adherents who obediently followed along while weapons were stockpiled, wives were taken from husbands, mass suicides were ordered. At some point, the mind-control techniques—the sleep deprivation, food deprivation, isolation, constant bombardment of doctrine without an outside framework with which to compare—had taken hold.

"You don't have to be a behavioral scientist to know what works, said University of California at Los Angeles psychiatrist Louis J. West, a cult expert. "You have to fool them. You become a con artist all the time and you find out through trial and error how easy it is to deceive people. You see them as gullible hens to be plucked.

"It isn't that hard to get decent people to believe incredible things," West continued. "Sometimes you can get whole nations to go that route, as they did in Nazi Germany, which had been one of the most civilized societies in the world to that point."

Often only in retrospect, as bodies rotted in the Guyanan jungle, or federal agents lay dead in Texas, did the cult leader's ruse seem obvious. Then the backlash against cults began again. Immediately after the Mount Carmel shootout, people across the nation abandoned cult-like groups in droves.

"What I was in sounds too much like that cult in Waco, Texas," they told counselors.

But if history was a guide, this new awareness would not last long.

Bill picked up Rick Ross at his hotel, driving to a house in Santa Barbara that had been set aside for their meetings. It was the first of four days of discussions, eight hours a day with breaks for meals. At night, Bill dropped Ross back off at his hotel, and drove to spend the night at his brother's home.

Ross listened as eventually the truth of Mount Carmel came spilling out. On one level, Bill seemed to be happy in the communal life offered at the compound. Men roomed with other men, women with women, but everyone toiled together. One day, Koresh would set Bill to work on the new swimming pool. The next he would pound nails in some other Mount Carmel construction project. At night, he attended Bible studies with fellow Davidians Bill had come to love.

"I think there were happy times in the group," Ross said. "As a whole they were very idealistic and self-sacrificing. They had to deny self. They were a loving people, a caring people focused on the principles of the Bible. He really loved the people."

But increasingly, they were led down the road to insanity. To them, Koresh indeed was the Lamb of God who would unravel the mystery of the seven seals. Koresh was the last angel of the apocalypse upon whom the salvation of his followers depended. But beyond that, no one really understood what Koresh was saying. Puzzled friends and family members would ask just what it was that Koresh taught, and none of his followers could say. Perhaps that was by design. Koresh's message was unassailable that way.

"You have to talk to Dave," the disciples would say.

Koresh himself promoted the notion that his message could be fully understood only by visiting Mount Carmel.

"Come and spend a couple of weeks with us," he was fond of saying.

Then he descended on his visitors and sucked them in before they could get their bearings. Initially, all they saw was a charming young man who played rock music, knew the Bible like no one else, and promised to "open the book." To Koresh, the book was more than just the Bible. It was the "Lamb's Book" referred to in Revelation. Followers whose names were written in the Lamb's book were guaranteed eternal life.

Over time, his prophecies grew more bizarre and cruel. Koresh began to teach he was entitled to the cult's women—young girls and other men's wives included—for only the Lamb possessed the Holy Seed. To Koresh, "the oil of gladness" in the forty-fifth Psalm referred to the vaginal secretions of his female followers. Only his head was to be anointed.

Koresh had the final say on Mount Carmel diets. He prohibited his followers from eating during Bible studies, which consisted of fifteen-hour sessions on nights when he was really on a roll. Koresh kept his own strength up with ice cream, or by ordering out and eating in front of his famished followers. Such were the privileges of the Lamb. Bill once lost twenty-five pounds in two months.

Bill also told Ross of the Davidian arsenal. There were AK-47s, a .50-caliber machine gun, zip guns, night vision goggles. Koresh followers had begun to modify rifles into machine guns and talked of making their own hand grenades. Each male member was assigned a weapon, taught how to maintain it and break it down. Regular target practice was held at the Mount Carmel underground firing range. A cult-owned business called the Mag Bag, supposedly a gun shop, was in reality a front for the purchase of more arms. On one occasion, Koresh used Bill's credit card to purchase $4,000 in ammunition.

The guns would be oiled for the final confrontation, for fulfillment of the Koreshian prophesies. In one, Koresh promised to outdo Moses, whom he regarded as a second-rate prophet. He promised to part the Atlantic Ocean so his followers could walk to Israel. In the Promised Land, Koresh would slaughter all armies who met him. That was one version of his apocalypse. Later he spoke of another scenario involving an enemy closer to home, the federal government. The FBI would attack Mount Carmel, killing everyone, he said. Then Koresh would unlock the mystery of the seventh seal and the world would end, probably in June 1992, but no later than 1995.

As he listened, Ross saw the extent of Bill's programming, the genius of Koresh's technique. Slowly, gently, Ross began to attack, dissecting the Davidian leader's teachings, unmasking the methods of his manipulation.

Bill and Ross sat together at the dining room table, each with a Bible, studying the key scriptural passages of Koresh's teaching. The leader had roamed freely from Revelation to Psalms with no rational means of connecting them, Ross pointed out. It was all done on a whim.

How could Koresh be the Lamb of God when, according to the New Testament, the Lamb was Jesus Christ? When Jesus came again, according to the Bible, he would come in power and glory, and all men would know him. How did that fit David Koresh?

If Koresh owned spiritual discernment in sexual matters, why was it that God told him to have sex only with attractive white women?

"Why didn't God want him to have sex with the black or the ugly or the old?" Ross asked. "Is this part of God's plan for him or is this just Koresh's proclivities sexually?"

Ross reminded Bill that Victor Houteff split from the

Seventh-day Adventist church because it had become too worldly. Houteff strictly proscribed the use of alcohol. How did Koresh's beer drinking and rock and roll adhere to Davidian principles?

At Ross's suggestion, Bill studied literature on mind control. Together they watched a video on Jonestown and the techniques of Jim Jones. The framework of what Ross was saying began to emerge, the smoke began to clear away. Bill came to realize the teachings of David Koresh had nothing to do with the Bible and everything to do with advancing megalomania. A picture had emerged.

"It was an ugly, gruesome picture of a cult leader gone mad with a Bible," Ross said. "He saw a very evil man."

A huge breakthrough came on the third day. The terror seemed to lift and Bill actually began to joke about some of the nonsense of Koresh's teaching. By this time, Bill began to describe the Davidians as "those people" or "that group." On the fourth day, the tension started to disappear from his face. The burden of David Koresh was lifting. Bill smiled. He laughed.

"That's it," he said. "I don't want to go back. I don't want to go back to the group."

Koresh did not surrender his follower gracefully. A woman from Mount Carmel, one of Bill's closest friends, was the first to call.

"When are you coming back, Bill?" she said. "When can we see you? We miss you."

Steve Schneider called, also concerned. David Koresh spoke with Bill, too. He said Bill would burn in hell.

Ross considered Bill's deprogramming a victory over one of the most dangerous cult leaders in America. The dangerous cycle was obvious. The more power Koresh sucked from his followers, the more he demanded. The cycle had to end somewhere. Koresh was stockpiling weapons, breaking the law and eventually word would get out. Ross was certain Koresh's apocalyptic prophesies would be self-fulfilling.

"If there is a group that is going to go ballistic, it will be this group," Ross thought then.

He and Bill discussed approaching the authorities, but initially, Bill didn't want to be the one to precipitate trouble. But the outside world would soon find its way to David Koresh's doorstep. In November, Waco newspaper reporters called Ross as part of an extensive investigation into Koresh and his practices, and Bill agreed to be interviewed. Two months later, agents of the federal Bureau of Alcohol, Tobacco and Firearms were on the line.

On that Sunday morning, the last day of February, Rick Ross was brewing coffee at home in Phoenix when reports from Texas began flashing across his television screen. He hurried into the living room to watch. It happened sooner than Ross had expected. But the inevitable had indeed begun.

7

APOCALYPTIC SUPERMAN

It was a world of dark, smoky taverns where whining electric guitars rattled the shot glasses and Waco's heavy metal rockers dreamed of a shot at the big time, just one shot. Just like their idols in Los Angeles, they wore black leather and hair past their shoulders. They strutted around on stage with the appropriate amount of attitude. Yet for a rocker, Waco seemed about as far from the bright lights as you could get.

This was Baylor's town after all. The kids were well-scrubbed Baptists whose idea of an adventure was an evening excursion to Wendy's on the edge of campus. In Waco the rockers truly lived on the grungy fringe. They were the rebels, guys in their twenties, who played music instead of going to college. They played in bands like Rif Raf, Flashback, Whirling Dervish or Bonz X, floating from one Central Texas beer joint to the next, wherever they could jam and strut, and get paid a little in the process. They were definitely not the main stream.

Someday maybe a demo tape would fall into the right hands and they would land that big record deal, play to full stadiums, have their own roadies, their own legions of screaming teenage girls. That was the dream.

The reality was working a day job to make ends meet and at night playing grimy dumps such as the club Cuestick, where bikers and brassy women with tattoos made up a good part of the audience. Waco rockers played tough places. Not at all the kind of place where you'd expect to find a prophet.

But David Koresh wasn't your typical prophet. How many prophets watched MTV, fantasized about Madonna or decorated the walls of their homes with posters of Ted Nugent, the heavy-metal legend from Detroit? Revelation and rock and roll, that was Koresh's life. Indeed, the unlimited opportunity to indulge his musical fantasies seemed one of the major prerequisites to Branch Davidian leadership.

And Koresh would rock, no matter what. In the mid-1980s, while George Roden squatted at Mount Carmel and the Davidian people lived in squalor near Palestine, their leader found the means to take over a Waco tavern, converting it into his own music studio replete with thousands of dollars of sophisticated equipment. Later, at Mount Carmel, pews in the chapel were stacked aside, again ostensibly to make room for the speakers and the instruments. When Vernon Howell became David Koresh in 1990, the name change was explained in California court records as a marketing ploy, apparently part of a strategy to jump start his own rock-and-roll dream. Once established as a star, he would use his music as a pulpit, travel to Israel and deliver the biblical truth to the rabbis.

That fantasy led Koresh to seek like-minded souls at places like the Cuestick, or Chelsea's Pub in the Waco mall, where Jimbo Ward met Koresh one night in 1990.

Ward, the short, curly-haired lead singer of the band named Rif Raf, knew plenty about Koresh. Ward had moved to Waco in 1987 when the cult leader's one-sided shootout with George Roden hit the local news. A short time later, Ward crossed paths with the bass player in the Branch Davidian band that Koresh named Messiah. The attack on George Roden was just the beginning, the bass player said. The ultimate goal of Koresh—Messiah's lead vocalist and lead guitarist—was the conquest of the Holy Land. Koresh wanted to take on the Israelis, the Messiah bass player told Ward.

"He's building this military Christian group, getting ready for World War III," the bass player said. At the time, Ward thought he was joking.

Three years later, Rif Raf was playing Chelsea's when Ward and Koresh met through a mutual friend. Their introduction came during a break in the music, and the two joined several others around a table in the club. The notorious gun battle three years before quickly came up and Koresh calmly explained he was just trying to take back land that belonged to him. The discussion eventually turned to the book of Revelation. Koresh said he had been banned from Australia because of his teachings on that subject.

"I know things about Revelation and the seven seals that other people need to know," Koresh said.

Unlike most of the guys, Ward knew something about what Koresh was talking about, remembering the seven seals from his Methodist upbringing. Revelation was kind of neat, a lot of wild symbolic stuff in there, Ward thought. But Koresh dropped the topic as quickly as he had raised it. It was as if he was teasing Ward or didn't want to scare him off by saying too much too soon. The strange conversation turned to music and ended when Rif Raf's break was over a few minutes later.

Ward saw plenty more of Koresh in the coming months of 1990. He seemed to be anywhere rock music was played in Waco. Koresh would roar up on the huge Harley he was so proud of, wearing a black leather jacket and sunglasses, shoulder-length blond hair trailing behind him in the breeze. Or, he would show up in the souped-up Camaro, another in his seemingly endless supply of toys.

Wherever Koresh went, his entourage was sure to follow. They were guys in his band, mostly, neat-looking dudes in leather and long hair who looked straight out of the L.A. metal scene. But Ward thought it was curious how they always checked with Koresh before saying or doing anything, like leaving a club or going off someplace to pick up equipment. And Koresh was the only one in his group allowed to drink beer. Sometimes it seemed to Ward that Koresh was more guru than lead singer.

Those were the rumors, of course. Everyone heard them. Word on the street was that Koresh was the leader of a creepy cult that lived in the country east of town. People said he was some sort of apocalyptic prophet leading his people to the end of the world, which seemed to fit what the bass player had told Ward three years before. People around Waco also heard that lawyers and business people from all over the country had given up all their worldly belongings to follow Koresh to the place called Mount Carmel on the outskirts of town. Children and old people lived out there, too. Why they would follow a metal head like Koresh, no one could figure. There were other rumors, but they were too weird to be believed, like the one that Koresh claimed to be the Lamb of God and knew when the world was going to end. Or the one about Koresh keeping all the women in the cult for himself.

"He was the only one at the compound who could rap with the chicks," is the way Ward heard it.

No question that Koresh was a Bible-banger of some kind. He could be cranking out heavy metal one minute, spouting verses from the Bible the next. His habit of preaching, one that started in childhood, continued. One night in a Waco club, members of the rock band Hour Glass had finished their show and were breaking down their equipment on stage when Koresh rose from the audience to continue the evening's entertainment. He stood in front of the drunken crowd preaching the Bible until bouncers forced him to leave.

Koresh could be weird, no question. But he seemed tolerable for the most part, and despite all the strange stories, there were times when he seemed like a normal family man. He and wife Rachel and the kids could be seen out shopping in music shops or auto parts stores. And the way the Waco rockers figured it, anybody with all those toys, all that equipment, couldn't be all bad.

Cuesticks was the place he frequented most often. It was located on Old Dallas Highway in Bellmead, a little town adjacent to Waco. The building had been a pool hall before being converted. Koresh became friendly with the owner, a guy named Randall, and the next thing you knew, Koresh was turning the place into a concert hall. He and the guys from Mount Carmel built a stage, which was decorated by an artist from Koresh's cult. At the front of the stage on one end, the artist painted Koresh's head with a snake trailing out of it. He did the same with Randall's head at the other end. The two heads faced each other across the stage, smiling. Near Koresh's head were the words "Rock on Randall!"

Koresh installed a sound system at Cuesticks, monster speakers that were too powerful for the club. When bands were jamming, it seemed the roof would blow off.

But faulty sound or not, almost every local group came to play at one time or another. Band members enjoyed not having to haul and set up their own sound equipment. The only rule: Koresh ran the control board and mixed the sound. You would see him there at Cuesticks almost every night, sitting at the control board, drinking a Budweiser.Then, between sets, Koresh often went to the microphone, recited Scripture and gave out his Mount Carmel phone number for anyone interested in hearing more. At a place like Cuesticks, there weren't many takers.

You had to hand it to the guy. He had all that equipment at Cuesticks and plenty more at Mount Carmel. He had a Harley and those cars, a fleet of golf carts, an arsenal of guns and a huge customized bus that he took on trips to California every so often, disappearing for a couple of weeks at a time. All that, and the guy didn't seem to have a job. Nobody could figure out how he did it.

"Man, how can you afford all this equipment?" Ward asked him once.

Koresh said he restored and sold classic cars in California. Another time, a rocker asked Koresh the same question, and was told he owned a company on the West Coast that installed underground sprinkler systems. It all seemed pretty far-fetched.

If you stopped to think about it, a lot was strange about the guy. He seemed to have that spell over the band members he hung around with. Sometimes they seemed like his recruiters, like Koresh had asked them to find out who might be interested in coming out and spending time at Mount Carmel. Jimbo Ward remembered the time Dave Thibodeau called.

"Dave wanted me to call you to see if you wanted to go fishing," said Thibodeau, who had become a good friend.

Ward declined. If Koresh wanted him to come fishing, he could call and ask himself. Besides, Ward thought, the call wasn't about fishing. It seemed to him a thinly veiled attempt to get him to Mount Carmel so Koresh could preach. Ward wasn't in the market.

Another time, one of Ward's female friends was attracted to the bass player in Koresh's band, a handsome guy with long curly hair called Jaime. One night the two met in a club and the woman gave Jaime her telephone number. But Jaime wasn't the one who eventually called her. It was Koresh on the line, which the woman thought very weird. Their conversation didn't last long.

That's the way Koresh was. Everything rotated around him. And the Bible wasn't the only topic on which he was quite sure of himself. Nobody knew more about cars. Nobody knew more about music, either, an assumption which Waco rockers thought amusing after hearing his band play. Two or three times during the year, Cuesticks hosted huge barbecues and five or six local bands would set up to play, including Messiah. The band had no form. It just wandered around wherever its lead guitarist felt like going.

"They sucked bad," Rif Raf rhythm guitarist Trent Duffer said once. "It was like, 'You play some, then I'll play some. You play some, then I'll play some.'"

But Koresh insisted he had connections in Los Angeles who could give the Waco bands their break, and what Waco rocker wouldn't sell his soul for a chance. Koresh even offered to fly some groups to the West Coast. There was one condition: Everything needed to be done his way. The bands had to look and sound the way Koresh wanted them to. Rif Raf, for one, needed a complete overhaul, Koresh figured. One Rif Raf player looked like an auto mechanic, another like a Baylor student, yet another a flashback from the 1960s. That kind of look would never work. They needed to take his advice if they ever wanted to get out of Waco. Rif Raf was as ambitious as the next group, but after hearing the conditions, they decided maybe they'd stay in Waco. Maybe they didn't need Koresh's help so bad after all.

Jimbo Ward was real drunk that night and whatever reservations he might have entertained about David Koresh dissolved after several beers. A Waco club hosted a battle of the bands that night in 1990. Rif Raf was not among the winners, and Ward was thoroughly drowning his sorrows. By closing time he wasn't quite ready to call it a night. Ward wanted to drink more beer and play more music, and Koresh had the 2:00 a.m. solution.

"Hey man, you want to come out to my place and jam?" Koresh asked. "We can crank it up out there as loud as we want."

Ward and a few members of his band quickly accepted. Ward and his girlfriend piled into Koresh's Camaro. On the way, the group stopped at a local fast food restaurant. Ward was broke, so Koresh bought him a cheeseburger and french fries before they headed into the country, turning down desolate farm roads and finally onto a gravel path that led to Mount Carmel. It was dark and very quiet in a part of the world Ward had never visited. He thought about the rumors about Koresh and felt uneasy for a few minutes.

"It felt creepy," Ward later remembered. "But hey, we were there to jam and party."

Mount Carmel was being converted from a collection of ragged bungalows to the fortress the world would come to know on television three years later. But darkness obscured the construction. Koresh led Ward and his friends into a building that resembled a rundown chapel. Most of the pews were stacked to the side. A few sat in front of the guitars, drums and microphones. Ward found a meat locker stocked with Budweiser and Coors Light in one corner. A Mount Carmel resident disappeared into an adjoining kitchen and made popcorn, which was brought out to the guests in big bowls as the jamming began.

Dave Thibodeau's drums were set up and waiting, and Rif Raf drummer Gary Summers took a turn as Koresh sang and played lead guitar. They ripped through a version of "Cat Scratch Fever," Ted Nugent's heavy metal tune that was popular in the 1970s. Ward sang. It was a good night, nothing really weird about it. Everyone was amazed at Koresh's equipment, of course.

Ward noticed what must have been ten guitars. Koresh said that he had made most of them. There was a picture of an angel on the face of one guitar, a skeleton with wings on another. The talk that night never strayed from guitars and music. The only time religion came up was when Summers went outside for air and saw a man he didn't know standing there.

"May God be with you," the man said.

Dave Thibodeau was one of the nicest guys around: laid back, friendly, a hell of a drummer. It was hard to understand what he was doing hanging out with a guy like David Koresh. Thibodeau often hinted that he had given up a lot to live at Mount Carmel, but what he had sacrificed was unclear. There was no doubt Thibodeau was a true believer in Koresh. That was the thing about him that seemed strange.

"This guy knows stuff," Thibodeau told Ward once. "Just listen to him. You won't believe it. You've got to read about the seals. You've got to read about the seals."

Thibodeau was born and attended high school in Bangor, Maine. In 1990, his passion for rock music led him to travel cross-country. It was in Los Angeles, where Thibodeau studied drumming, that he ran into David Koresh in a music supply store, accepting his offer to join the cult leader's rock band in Waco.

The way his friends figured it, Koresh had lured Thibodeau with the promise to play music. Koresh had told him he would feed him and clothe him, take care of all his needs. Messiah's members didn't need day jobs like guys in the other bands. Dave Thibodeau's job was playing music. Who could resist a life like that? That's the way Koresh operated; it seemed he always had something to offer in addition to the Bible.

"I think he thought it was cool figuring out the religious stuff that went along with it," a friend later said of Thibodeau.

For some, apparently, the Bible and rock and roll were too potent a combination to resist. Others thought Koresh was just a nut.

"He said he had the power to open the seals," said Waco guitarist Shawn O'Bryant. "A lot of people seemed to believe it. Either he believed what he was saying or he was a terrific con artist."

O'Bryant remembered the time Koresh badgered him with biblical rhetoric.

"Hey, I'm not grasping what you're saying," O'Bryant told him. "You might want to talk to someone who grasps you."

Koresh never bothered O'Bryant again.

But one Rif Raf member, Richard, the lead guitarist at the time, was taken in. The guys said Richard was gullible, a born follower, just the kind of person Koresh seemed to prey on. Richard seemed spellbound when the two met.

"He went out there a couple of times and got interested in something he had seen," Trent Duffer, the Rif Raf rhythm guitar player, said later. "This guy had major equipment, a sound system out the teeth. Richard would say, 'Like wow, look at those stacks.' Koresh had guns out there. Richard was the kind of guy who liked to go out into the country and shoot guns."

"That's outstanding shit, Trent," Richard told Duffer once. "You ought to see what he has out there."

Richard began to spend more time out at Mount Carmel. After the band finished playing, he drove out for Bible studies in the middle of the night. He spent afternoons fishing in the Mount Carmel pond or riding golf carts in the country. Before he met Koresh, Richard had been carefree and outgoing, a real bullshitter. He loved to work on cars; cars and guitars were his life. But after a while, neither seemed important. He started acting spacey and introverted, like he was deep in thought most of the time. He seemed nervous, like he wasn't supposed to talk about what he was doing.

"My dad would kill me if he found out I was out there studying the Bible with this guy," Richard told Duffer.

The band grew worried when Richard started showing up late, then missing practice altogether. When they asked him what was going on, Richard defended Koresh.

"The man has a lot to say," Richard would insist.

Koresh then tried to bar Richard from traveling with the band, telling him it was more important for him to stay at Mount Carmel. The orders caused Richard to snap back to his senses. He abruptly ended his visits to Mount Carmel. Soon after, Richard bought a gun. Although he didn't like to talk about it, friends said they thought he was afraid of Koresh.

"That guy freaks me out," Richard said.

He was beginning to scare the other rockers, too.

"I thought it was freaky," Ward said. "I felt like he was a cult leader like Jim Jones."

Then a scenario involving another band's lead singer really got people thinking. Koresh had tried to preach to the guy, one of the only rockers who completely blew him off.

"You're full of shit," the singer told Koresh.

Several months later, the singer died from a brain hemorrhage. Some rockers whispered about a curse.

About that time, Koresh seemed to disappear—just up and vanished. The Cuestick shut down. Some guys said it was because of all the customers Koresh had driven away with his preaching.

Three years passed, but Jimbo Ward never forgot the rock-and-roll prophet. Then came that day in February "that tripped me out." The band had been up late the night before cutting a demo tape and it was after noon on Sunday by the time Ward woke up and turned on the television. News of the Mount Carmel shootout dominated every channel. Ward remembered what he had been told by Messiah's bass player back in 1987. Later he learned that his friend Dave Thibodeau was one of the people holed up inside Mount Carmel with Koresh.

"Oh, man," Ward said to himself. "It's come down."

Only a few months before, David Koresh had been Ward's inspiration. He thought it would be cool to write a song about an apocalyptic prophet. Ward called the tune "Apocalyptic Superman," the title cut from Rif Raf's first recording. The lyrics he had written gave Ward goose bumps:

"I can give you guidance,
I can be your friend,
I can save you from your decadence and sin
If you call me master
And give me all your praise
I will give you comfort
In your final days."

8

A GLIMPSE INTO HELL

David Jewell was shaking with outrage as he sat in lawyer Vic McFadden's office. McFadden had a trial lawyer's thick skin and was skeptical at first. But if half of what Jewell was saying was true, it was enough to make McFadden's stomach turn.

"We've got to do something for her," said Jewell, a thin, dark-haired disc jockey. "This is my daughter. No matter what the mother wants, I want that child out of there."

McFadden said he needed proof before he could take legal action. Jewell assured him the documentation would be forthcoming, and that witnesses would travel from Australia to testify if necessary.

It was a story that began in 1984, when his ex-wife, Sherri Jewell, told David about her new church friends. They were young and "on fire for God," she said. David Jewell met some of them that year during a visit to see his daughter, Kiri. He found nothing about them particularly unusual. But over the years, he noticed some strange things about his daughter. By the age of five or six, Kiri had been instructed that whenever she wore pants, a long shirt needed to come down to cover her bottom.

"She, at that early age, had a vast knowledge of Bible Scripture, which in itself I don't mean to condemn, but it became very clear that there was a very strong and unusual focus here being put on her spiritual development," Jewell said later on a morning talk show.

Then, in October 1991, a telephone call from an Australian computer programmer named Marc Breault sent David Jewell rushing into McFadden's office. Breault had been a member of the religious group Sherri Jewell had joined, a Bible-based cult known as the Branch Davidians that was headquartered near the Texas town of Waco. Since breaking away from the group in 1989, Breault had been waging a campaign to wrest its members away from Davidian leader David Koresh, a man the Australian had come to know as a sex-crazed megalomaniac. In the late 1980s, Koresh began to teach that all the Davidian women were meant for himself, building a harem known as the House of David. The harem included wives of Davidian members and girls as young as twelve. In the October phone call, Breault warned David Jewell that his eleven-year-old daughter was in danger of becoming the House of David's newest member.

Breault's sworn affidavit arrived in the mail a few days later, ten pages and single-spaced. It provided a chilling account of cult life, both in cult homes in California and at the country compound known as Mount Carmel in Texas. From illegal bakeries to military maneuvers, from sex with children to AK-47 assault rifles, Breault's statement provided the first public window into David Koresh's hidden hell.

The Marc Breault Affidavit

"I, Marc Breault... was a member of the cult known as the Branch Davidian Seventh-Day Adventists from January 1986 to August 1989. At first Vernon Howell appeared to be a conservative person whose only wish was to reform the Seventh-Day Adventist Church. As time progressed, however, Howell became power hungry and abusive, bent on obtaining and exercising absolute power and authority over the group. I lived separate from the group from January 1986 to January 1988. From January 1988, I lived with the other group members in either Mount Carmel, Texas, or Pomona, California. During my involvement with the group, I witnessed the following.

"In April of 1986, Vernon admitted in front of the entire group membership that he had sexual relations with one Karen Doyle, a girl who was only 13 or 14 years old at the time. Howell taught that this act was according to Bible prophecy. Howell related that God had said to him 'Give seed to Karen.' Upon hearing this, Vernon approached Karen Doyle and informed her what God had told him. Karen responded by saying that she would do whatever God told her to do. This is how Howell related the story. The girl's father, Clive Doyle, was in Australia at the time, and he did not know this had happened. In April of 1986, I assumed that Clive Doyle had been informed. I have since discovered my error in this regard. Clive's ex-wife, Karen's mother, was not a member of this group and she also had no idea of what had taken place.

"Once, during the Summer of 1987 (I think it was late May or early June), I was visiting the group's California residence in San Bernardino, California. At approximately

5:30 a.m., Howell's father-in-law, Perry Jones, called from Texas. I took the call and Perry informed me that it was urgent he speak to Howell. I put the phone down and proceeded to Howell's room. I knocked but learned he was not there. I went outside to look for him. Since Perry had informed me the matter was urgent, I called out for Vernon. There were three little shacks positioned at the side of the San Bernardino house. Karen Doyle was staying in one and Michelle Jones (then aged 12) was staying in another. When I called out, Michelle Jones called out from her shack asking if I was looking for Vernon. I said that I was and that Perry (Michelle's father) said it was urgent he speak to Vernon. Michelle said for me to hold on and she would get him. A moment later, I saw Vernon exit Michelle Jones' shack (where she was supposedly staying alone.) Vernon was not wearing a shirt, but pants only. He went inside and took the call.

"In October of 1987, Sherri Jewell, mother of Kiri Jewell, took me aside (we were good friends) and told me she was in love with Howell, and that she had become one of his 'wives.' She said she wanted me to know because she felt she could trust me with that knowledge. At the same time, Sherri Jewell and Dana Okimoto were sharing the same shack. Sherri said that she and Dana had become very good friends now that they were both in the 'House of David,' i.e. one of Vernon's wives. Some time before this incident, Howell had given Bible studies from the Song of Solomon saying that he was entitled to 140 wives. Howell further broke the number 140 down into 60 proper wives and 80 concubines. A concubine is a slave who acts as a mistress to her master.

"At about the same time as the incident with Sherri mentioned above, Dana confided to me that Vernon and her were having sexual relations as well. Dana even told me that her first night with him was 31 August 1987. Both Sherri and Dana felt I was going to be one of the group's evangelists and that I should know what was happening. Howell did not mind my knowing.

"Two of the cult members, Neil and Margarida Vaega, owned a bakery in Honolulu. When they joined the group they gave it to Vernon. This was done via a verbal agreement. While the bakery was operational, under Howell's control, Howell sent a number of group members to Hawaii to work. These were Bonnie Haldeman, (Vernon's mother,) Jimmy Riddle, Peter Hipsman, and Clive Doyle. These were the core workers. Howell also started up a bakery in San Bernardino, California. This bakery was operated without a license. Several group members worked for that bakery. At no time were any W4 forms filled out or filed. To my knowledge, little and, in some cases, no wages were given for the work done. At no time were the profits registered with the proper government agencies. Both Douglas Wayne Martin and myself strenuously urged Howell to discontinue this practice. Eventually, both bakeries were closed down. The one in Honolulu was sold (and I do not think it was legally recorded,) while the one in San Bernardino was just shut down.

"From January to May 1988, I lived on 19th Street in Waco, Texas. This is where we had the musical equipment. During this time, I personally witnessed Dana Okimoto, Robyn Bunds, Sherri Jewell and Rachel Howell (his legal wife) spend the night in Howell's room on various occasions.

"Later, in 1988/1989, we would occasionally stay at the Pomona House in California. Vernon would have his own room, and he would usually sleep in that room with a number of his 'wives.' Kiri Jewell would also sleep in the same room as Vernon and his women. I know this because I used to sleep in the living room and I often saw Sherri and Kiri enter Vernon's room to go to sleep for the night.

"Eventually, Howell moved into the garage of the Pomona house. He would pick his 'wife' for the night and she would come out to him in the garage. The wives all slept in Howell's former room in the house and Kiri continued to sleep in that room as well. On one occasion, Howell related the following story to me.

"Howell told me that one of his 'wives,' Nicole Gent, (now known as Nicole Little) was very depressed. Howell was sleeping on the floor in his room (before he moved out to the garage.) He was positioned near Sherri Jewell and Lisa Farris, and Kiri Jewell. Both Sherri Jewell and Lisa Farris knew that Nicole was depressed and they encouraged Howell to move from the floor to the bed where Nicole was sleeping so he could be with her. So Howell complied. Howell related this story to me saying that he was amazed that women (wives) would be willing to encourage him to go and 'make love' to another woman in their presence. Howell told me this story in an effort to convince me that the Holy Spirit was with his 'wives.'

"I can say for certain that Kiri Jewell knew about Sherri's sexual involvement with Howell. Sherri would often employ Kiri in covering for her when outsiders were involved. Sherri told me that she was drilling Kiri in case she was questioned by outsiders about her (Sherri's) involvement.

"During the Fall of 1988, I saw Howell put Kiri Jewell on his lap. Sherri Jewell also was present. Howell told Kiri that she (Kiri) was his (Howell's) daughter and he asked her if she (Kiri) would behave herself. From then on, Sherri Jewell emphasized to Kiri that she was Howell's daughter. By early to mid 1989, Sherri was beginning to prepare her daughter, Kiri, to become one of Vernon's 'wives.' By this time, I had become quite disenchanted with Howell, but I had no place to go. When I saw Sherri was doing this to Kiri I often took Kiri aside and explained to her that she was very young and that she should wait before she decided whom she should marry. I saw that Kiri and her girl friends Rachel, Sylvia and Audrie (about her age) were intensely interested in marriage and were primed to look forward to it. Sherri would often teach Kiri Howell's doctrine and even take pride in the fact that Kiri knew and memorized Scriptures Howell used to teach his 'wives' doctrines.

"In about April of 1988, I was breaking up with a girlfriend of mine. Howell took me aside and confided in me that he was having girl troubles of his own. He said it wasn't easy having all these women. He asked me to guess who his favorite 'wife' was. I guessed Rachel Howell or Sherri Jewell. Howell said I was wrong. He said that his favorite 'wife' was Michelle Jones and that he had been with her since she was 12 years old. 'Can you believe it, Marc, she's (Michelle) been with me since she was 12 years old.' Those were his exact words. That was the first time I actually knew for certain that Howell had slept with Michelle Jones. Previous to this incident, I had been suspicious, but I did not wish to believe Howell would do such a thing.

"In April of 1988 I saw Michelle Jones's baby, Serenity Sea. The baby was being looked after by its grandmother Mary Bell Jones. I went into the house to use their phone (as I did not have one myself) and Mary Bell was telling me how quiet the baby was, etc. The baby was only a month or two old. Mary Bell told me specifically that Howell had instructed her to hide the baby in case any outsider or fringe member happened to see it. This was because Howell did not want anyone to know he (Howell) had been sleeping with Michelle Jones. In June of1991, I discussed the matter with Michelle Jones's brother Joel, a very good friend of mine. He informed me that Michelle Jones (his younger sister) was born on July 4, 1974. I saw the baby Serenity Sea in April of 1989. Thus, Michelle Jones would have only been 14 years of age when she gave birth to the baby.

"On one occasion, Howell's right hand man, Steve Schneider, told me that Howell told him that he (Howell) would have to undergo a test greater than that which Abraham had to endure when God told Abraham to slay his son Isaac. Steve went on to say that Howell told him people would think he was crazy for doing what he was required to do.

"On one occasion, Howell's son, Cyrus, had misbehaved. As punishment, Howell forced his son, Cyrus, to sleep on the hard kitchen floor with only a thin blanket for covering. Howell had asked Cyrus to call Nicole Gent (now known as Nicole Little) mommy. The child's real mother is Rachel Howell. Cyrus would not call Nicole mommy. Thus, Howell instituted that punishment. On the following day, Howell ordered James Tom to prepare a place in the garage (Pomona house) for his son Cyrus to sleep in that night. Howell emphasized to the little child (about three years old) that there were large rats in the garage and that they would eat him because he had been naughty. The child was absolutely terrified and began begging to be allowed to stay in the house. Howell then tried once again to force Cyrus to call Nicole mommy but the child would not. James Tom also objected strenuously, but his objections were silenced by Howell.

"On one occasion, shortly after this incident, Howell asked his son, Cyrus, whether he liked him (Howell.) The child replied that he did not like his father, Vernon. Vernon was enraged and beat his son severely. He then asked the child again if he liked him (Vernon.) Once again the child replied that he did not. Vernon continued to beat the child until Cyrus finally said he loved his daddy. These and other incidents prompted me to begin planning my escape. I took Cyrus in hand, so to speak, and used to sneak out with him and some of the other guys, and we would play ball in the park. Cyrus enjoyed these times very much.

"In March of 1989, Howell told me that the Gyarfas family was scheduled to visit the group in the U.S. Howell asked me if I thought he should pay for Aisha Gyarfas's way over. Aisha was only 13 years old at the time. Howell said that since he wanted Aisha as one of his wives, he should be responsible for her upkeep. He also said that the Gyarfas family were not well off financially. I objected strenuously to Howell's intention.

"I was seriously considering leaving the cult in the summer of 1989 because of what Howell was doing to the young girls. But I wanted to make sure. I saw Aisha Gyarfas (now Summers) enter Vernon's room on a number of evenings. She entered alone. The next morning, she would emerge.

"To make sure of this, I stayed in the office downstairs the entire night, under the pretext that I had some work to do. My PC was in the office and I did write a few unimportant letters. In reality, I was playing a Star Trek simulation game. The point is, however, for Aisha to exit, she would have to come through that office and she did not. The next morning, Aisha emerged from Koresh's room and was somewhat surprised to find me in the office so 'early' in the morning. But by that time, it was feasible for me to be there so I did not have to give her any story.

"On another occasion, Howell gave me permission to practice in his room. While I was practicing, Aisha came up to retrieve some clothes which she had forgotten the night before. There might have been a couple of other belongings that she forgot, but I do not remember. When she saw me in the room, I explained that Koresh (then Vernon Howell) had allowed me to practice in the room. Indeed, I practiced in that room regularly, almost on a daily basis.

"On another occasion, around this time, Howell told me that a lot of people thought that 12 and 13 year old girls were not ready for sex. Howell assured me that this was incorrect. He said that girls that age were extremely ready for sex and that they were very good in bed. He said they were fast and eager at that age. He used Aisha Gyarfas as an example.

"During the summer of 1989, I was staying at Mount Carmel. Kiri and I were walking together to our respective houses. Sherri Jewell and Kiri were staying next door to where I was staying. Howell walked up and said hello. He asked Kiri whether she had been behaving. Kiri responded that she had been behaving. Howell said this was good because if she wanted to be in the 'House of David' (one of his wives) she would have to be good.

"In general, I have seen Howell order the deprivation of basic human rights. I have seen this primarily with food. On many occasions, he has commanded that no food be eaten during an interval of from one to two days. He has assigned various juice fasts to a number of people. He would often declare starch free diets. During April of 1989, Howell forbade all fruit except for bananas. Howell also forbade anyone buying food for themselves for any reason whatsoever. All meals had to be eaten in the dining area and only the association could purchase food, and only by Howell's direction. Howell maintained strict and meaningless dietary rules. For instance, Howell forbade anyone to eat oranges and grapes at the same meal, but they could eat oranges and raisins at the same meal.

"During 1988, many children were not allowed to go to school. And even when Vernon allowed children to go to school during the 1988/89 school year, he would often call studies during the afternoons and evenings, preventing the children from completing homework assignments.

"On 5 August 1989, Vernon gave a Bible study in which he stated that he was the Lamb of God. As the Lamb of God he was entitled to have all the women and girls sexually. Only he had the right to procreate. Howell stated that he would give married couples time to adjust to this new 'revelation' as he called it. At one point during this study, Howell saw that the married couples were very upset. Howell commanded everyone to look at Sherri Jewell. Sherri was actually quite taken with the study and Howell pointed this out and said Sherri liked this doctrine because she had been sacrificing for years and now it was the married couples' turn to sacrifice. In fact, Sherri Jewell was quite enjoying this study. Howell commanded that no one tell anyone of this 'new light' as he called it.

"Shortly after this study, Sherri Jewell wrote a letter to the group members in Texas. She stated that people were having difficulty coping with some 'new light' Vernon had given. The letter was quite condemning of those who would not go along with Howell's doctrines. A copy of the letter was read to me.

"When Howell discovered I had left the group and joined my wife, Elizabeth in Australia, he forbade anyone to communicate with Elizabeth and I without his permission. When Howell arrived in Australia he had Steve Schneider call me up. Howell was prompting Steve what to say. At one point, I heard Howell tell Schneider to tell me that he would kill my wife Elizabeth because she was his enemy.

"Later on I was told three things by former Australian members. One was that Vernon had created a hit list and that I was on top of that list. This was because I had been instrumental in causing Australian members to break away from Howell. I was also told that during that time the Australians were following Howell, Howell told them that if I came to visit them at their home, they were to open the door, kick me in the balls, and slam the door in my face. Finally, we were told that Howell had sent some of his followers to spy on us, driving by our home at about 2:00 in the morning to see if any Australians who were considering breaking away were, in fact, visiting us.

"In June of 1991, I confronted Sherri Jewell regarding Howell's sexual activities with young girls. I verbally backed Sherri Jewell into a corner and she admitted, in front of her mother, Ruth Mosher, that Michelle Jones had been pregnant and had given birth to a child by Howell when she was only 14 years of age. I forwarded the details of this confrontation to Barbara Wiggins of the La Verne police department.

"Ruth Mosher also told Elizabeth and I that Kiri had gone to Mount Carmel Texas around April of 1991 to see a baby being born, that is, to physically witness a baby being born. We have since received confirmation of this story from an ex-member, one Doreen Saipaia. Doreen related that Kiri was with the women delivering the baby of one Dana Okimoto. Doreen informed us that Kiri was sent to inform Howell that he (Howell) had a new son. Doreen also indicated that Kiri's participation was in preparation for her (Kiri) becoming one of Howell's 'wives.'

"During my involvement with the group, Sherri would often take on a maternal role with regard to the women in Howell's harem. To my knowledge, Sherri was the oldest member of that harem and girls would sometimes confide in her for advice. Rachel Howell, being Vernon Howell's legal wife, would also sometimes assume this role. Lisa Farris, another of Howell's women, would often seek Sherri out for advice. Because Sherri and I were good friends, I often saw this take place. During 1988, Sherri would also console Robyn Bunds, Dana Okimoto and Lisa Farris. Both Dana and Robyn were pregnant and were often upset at Howell's various actions towards them. Sherri also drove a number of Vernon's women from Texas to California, or visa versa. Once Sherri had 'repented' from her adultery (early 1988), Howell felt he could trust Sherri with many responsibilities regarding the harem.

"On one occasion, Sherri and a few other young women made what was to become the Branch Davidian flag. It depicted a white unicorn surrounded by both visual and textual references to scriptures Howell used to formulate his harem theology. Sherri led out this activity.

"During the months of May through July of 1989, Howell conceived of the idea of heavy physical training.

He had shown the entire group movies such as Platoon and Full Metal Jacket, movies about the Vietnam war. He required little children to attend these violent, R-rated movies. Kiri was also required to attend and watch. In some of the war movies, Hamburger Hill was another such movie, Marine training exercises were shown in great length. Among these scenes were marching songs, the type one sings during forced marches and runs during boot camp. Many such 'songs' were very sexual, as one might expect from Marines.

"When Howell decided everyone needed physical training, the women and girls did their own training. Jaydeen Wendel and Sherri Jewell were inspired by the Marine songs in the above mentioned movies, and they created songs about Branch Davidian doctrines. These songs, as I recall, included references to killing 'Babylonians,' i.e. Vernon Howell's enemies. Sherri and Jaydeen would lead both women and girls on marches and runs, acting as drill sergeants, even to the extent of 'left, left, left, right, left' chants, followed by the various songs which they had written. Sherri or Jaydeen would call out one line, and the rest would answer, just as a drill sergeant does in military boot camp. Even Kiri was obliged to participate in these 'exercises.' They usually began at 5:30 in the morning.

"Howell also had a theory that people should not hydrate themselves in hot weather. He felt that not drinking during exercises in hot weather was a sign of toughness. The women would exercise two or three times a day, each exercise period consisting of the above mentioned marches. During that summer, the weather would consistently exceed 100 degrees and no one was allowed to hydrate themselves during those exercises in the heat.

"The men only exercised once in the early morning and there were no Marine-style chants. The rest of the day was spent in building the new church which now stands on the Mount Carmel property.

"Howell was increasingly obsessed with guns and the need to use them. Howell mounted a 24-hour-a-day, seven-days-a-week, armed guard at the front gate of Mount Carmel. Some of the women stood guard duty, including Sherri Jewell and Jaydeen Wendel. Even Dana Okimoto stood guard duty, a loaded gun at the ready. Very few, if any had adequate fire arm training and little children would often come up to visit their parents despite the fact there were loaded guns in the vicinity.

"One summer night (I think it was in 1988) I had just arrived at Mount Carmel. It was very late and I was just preparing to go to sleep. I heard a noise and when I looked out, I saw Wally Kennett, who was standing guard duty at the front gate, fire his gun at an intruder. It was about 5:00 in the morning. The intruder was the newspaper delivery man. He had surprised Wally and Wally had panicked. Those in charge had forgotten to tell Wally about the newspaper delivery man, who delivered papers to the Chuns, an elderly couple. When Kennett panicked he cried halt, and then fired his gun. He said later it was in the ground but I have no way of verifying that. All I saw was the shadow of a figure, Wally cry out halt, and then the gun being fired. The poor newspaper man cried out something like 'Holy Shit. Don't shoot. Please don't shoot.' I saw him run away in panic. Wally was badly shaken up. That very morning, the newspaper called and refused to deliver any more papers to that property. My point is that the firearm situation within the group is a serious accident waiting to happen. In the above-mentioned case, someone was literally nearly killed or seriously hurt. In fact, I was so frightened for the poor newspaper man that without thinking, I ran out and yelled to Wally to take it easy. I explained who the man was.

"Howell is very paranoid and instills that paranoia to members. Howell would often walk around the property late at night and shoot his AK-47 rifle at various objects.

"During my time at Mount Carmel, the sanitation conditions were appalling. Howell had promised both his members and the media to put running water on the property. Because there was no real toilet facilities, raw sewage was simply buried in the ground where ever there was room. Some people in that area get their water from wells. Mount Carmel also has a well but it was never restored. Water would be brought in on a large yellow container, situated on a flat bed truck. Drinking, cooking and bathing water was obtained from this yellow container. It was rarely, if ever cleaned. Thus, this container was literally crusted with algae and Howell eventually forbade anyone from obtaining their own water. Compounding this sanitation problem was the fact that one of Howell's followers is a carrier of Hepatitis B, a highly contagious condition. When people carried their excrement to be buried, it would sometimes spill out of the bucket and fall unburied on the ground.

"When food was prepared in the dining hall, no hair nets or gloves were used. Someone on the property was always sick. During the winter, there was virtually no real heating and there was no way to get firewood. At one stage, Howell forbade any store-bought firewood. In fact, I cannot recall one instance in which firewood was brought in for anyone.

"I have been told by several persons that health and

sanitation conditions are far worse now than they were when I was at Mount Carmel. In my opinion, anyone, especially children, who lives on Mount Carmel for any length of time is in extreme danger of disease and infection. Compounding this is Howell's belief that he is sufficiently capable of handling most medical situations.

"On one occasion, the children brought lice back to Mount Carmel from school. Sherri and Kiri were both affected, Kiri severely so. The lack of running water made it virtually impossible to alleviate the lice plague. Poor Kiri had lice for months and I am not certain she was rid of them by the time I left the group in August of 1989.

"Finally, Howell is obsessed with sex. I have often witnessed Howell give Bible studies, if you can call them that, in which literally hours of time was spent describing sex, sexual acts, and sexual preferences in graphic detail. Little children were also forced to listen. During a number of studies, for example, Howell would describe what he felt to be the difference between male and female genitalia of different races. In Kiri's presence, Howell would describe Sherri's sexual habits with him, as well as her genitalia. These studies were especially sexual in nature in 1989, but sex was always part of Howell's studies. I could even say that when I first met Howell, he was mindful of children's sensitivities in that area, but by 1989, he had lost all restraint.

"I affirm under penalties of perjury that the foregoing is true to the best of my knowledge and belief."

McFadden and Breault later went over the affidavit line by line. By the end of the session in McFadden's South

Bend, Indiana office, the lawyer was convinced Breault's statement was true. On January 3, 1992, while Kiri was visiting her father's home in nearby Niles Michigan, McFadden filed a legal motion in the Michigan courts that alleged Sherri Jewell had abdicated her role as a parent to the cult. The motion, which quoted liberally from Breault's statement, begged the courts to intervene and keep Kiri from the cult until the case could be heard. To allow Kiri Jewell to continue living with David Koresh and the Branch Davidians, would condemn her "to a life of moral uncertainty and irreparable harm," the motion said.

Veteran Michigan Judge Ronald Taylor later described the subsequent hearing held a few weeks later as the most bizarre case he had ever heard. Breault and several other former members of the cult from Australia had flown in to testify. Sherri Jewell was present as well. She was a small, well-groomed woman who wore conservative suits and her hair pulled into a bun. The mother testified that Marc Breault's allegations were preposterous.

But after three days of testimony, Sherri Jewell agreed to a compromise custody arrangement. Kiri would now live with her father, but the mother would maintain visitation rights with the proviso that Kiri be kept away from David Koresh and the rest of the Branch Davidians. Sherri Jewell left Michigan when the agreement was signed, and returned to live with Koresh in Texas. She did not exercise her visitation rights in the year before the shootout at Mount Carmel.

9

THE ICONOCLASTS

Bob Lott had known about the Branch Davidians virtually from the time he set foot in Waco in 1979, arriving from Atlanta to take over as editor of the *Waco Tribune-Herald*. By then, the Davidians were an accepted, if fairly inconspicuous, part of the local landscape in the country. At least, that is, until November 1987, when Lott directed his paper's extensive coverage of Vernon Howell's shootout with George Roden at Mount Carmel. The bizarre trial of Howell and his followers the following spring also made interesting reading for Waco newspaper subscribers.

After the verdicts, Lott had read enough about Vernon Howell. There were many others stories competing for his staff's time and attention, such as an attempt by the conservative wing of the Baptist church to take over Baylor University. Vernon Howell and his cult again disappeared into the fabric of local life.

Not until the spring of 1992 did discussion of the Davidians resurface in the *Tribune-Herald* newsroom. Ex-cult members began calling to tell reporters that Howell and his followers were planning a mass suicide on Easter. It seemed like the kind of crazy tip reporters heard all the time, but they were on alert that weekend nonetheless.

Easter came and went without incident, but the phone calls from former Davidians didn't stop. *Tribune-Herald* reporter Mark England, who had covered the 1987 trial, began to do some checking on his own. What he heard seemed more than idle rumor, and by autumn, the story increasingly began to command Lott's attention and involvement. The information about the man now named David Koresh was bizarre and highly troubling, and Lott believed too many people were saying the same things for the rumors to be dismissed.

In October, Lott sent England to California to interview ex-cult members living there. England came back with stories about Vernon Howell's use of the Bible to create a concubine for himself, a harem that reportedly included other men's wives and young girls.

"It became more and more likely to me that there was something here that we had to let people know about," Lott said. "Freedom of religion comes before freedom of speech and the press in the Bill of Rights. I don't want to be questioning anybody's practice of their religion, but it became apparent to me that this man had taken liberties with religious freedoms to the point that it led to the abuse of people."

The *Tribune-Herald* investigation by England and fellow reporter Darlene McCormick stretched over eight months, an unusual commitment of resources at a paper the size of the *Tribune-Herald*, with a Sunday circulation of 61,000 readers. Typically it was the larger papers like those in Fort Worth and Dallas that could afford to undertake long projects and investigations. Most often, reporters were stretched thin at smaller publications, scrambling to keep up with the day's events.

Lott demanded his paper be different, often telling the reporters and editors he wanted to give the town of 100,000 residents big-city journalism and was willing to commit the resources that it required.

Lott was a courtly man, a life-long southerner, tall and reserved with a soft southern accent. He was raised in the 1940s in a tiny crossroads village in Alabama that consisted of four stores, a few churches and a cotton gin. As a young man he studied journalism at the University of Alabama, and took his first newspaper job in Columbus, Georgia, nine credits short of graduation. He moved to the *Atlanta Journal* in 1968, eventually rising to assistant managing editor.

While Lott enjoyed the resources the metropolitan paper brought to bear covering the news, he often envisioned himself as a country editor. Maybe it was the result of his rural upbringing, but he felt a nagging desire to move to a smaller place and a smaller paper where he actually got out to meet readers and could find out first-hand what was really important in their lives.

"At a larger paper...there wasn't that sense of connectedness," Lott said. "I had worked at a smaller paper and I had seen my colleagues in smaller towns and they seemed to have more of a sense of community than I did. I sensed they saw the impact of their work. I thought that if you could point to smaller papers that had sufficient resources and enough editorial integrity, that would be ideal."

The publisher from Waco called in 1979, and Lott liked what he heard.

"I felt I could do the kinds of things at the paper here that a smaller paper had to do," Lott said.

The new editor in Waco set out to make his point.

"It's a small paper in an out-of-the-way place, but he was really adamant about having big-city journalism in a small place," said Elizabeth Simpson, a former *Tribune-Herald* reporter. "He said that a lot. He expected a lot of the staff."

Under Lott, the *Tribune-Herald* would undertake to report the news more aggressively in all areas, religion among them. Traditionally, it had been a topic shunted by newspapers to the back pages, but not in Waco. Readers needed news about economics, public education, politics and crime, Lott knew. "But you figure in an average person's life, even a person who's agnostic or an atheist, spiritual matters, things you can't see, make up an important segment of life," Lott said.

Religious coverage must be nonpartisan and nonsectarian, Lott believed. One of his first actions as editor was to rename the *Tribune-Herald* church page. From then on it would be called the religion page because not all faithful people—Jews being a prominent example—worshiped in churches. The *Tribune-Herald* frequently editorialized against religious practices "that sought to exercise tyranny over the minds of men and women," Lott said, including the attempt by the fundamentalist wing of the Baptists to take control of Baylor.

In March 1987, the paper's reporting on religion landed the *Tribune-Herald* a major journalistic coup. Several months earlier, Lott called in Elizabeth Simpson to issue an ambitious assignment. Simpson was to take several months and travel across the country to examine the phenomena of televangelists. Pat Robertson was planning a run for the White House at the time, and others, like Jim Bakker, Jerry Falwell and Jimmy Swaggart, had fashioned massive followings and million dollar industries through their television pulpits.

"It was really Bob Lott's baby," Simpson said of her series years later. "It was something that he was really concerned about."

Simpson's series, a compelling chronicle of the televangelists' growing power and questionable morality, was scheduled to begin on Sunday, March 21. Three days before the series was to start, Jim Bakker resigned from his $172 million Praise the Lord ministry. This was after Bakker admitted to a sexual liaison with church secretary, Jessica Hahn, setting in motion a chain of events that eventually led to Bakker's imprisonment. The Waco series was quickly re-edited to include the latest development. With information about the topic available virtually no place else, Simpson's series was published in papers around the world.

Six years later, with reports coming in on Vernon Howell, the *Tribune-Herald* marshalled its resources again for a major story that had its roots in the Bible. It was the kind of unflinching journalism that Lott had come to Waco to achieve. Beneath his genteel exterior beat the heart of an iconoclast.

In that respect, he had one very prominent Waco ancestor. Waco's most famous historical figure was an editor, too, one who secured his legend a century before with unbridled vitriol and acidic wit that most often was directed toward the local Baptists. A "Mean Mark Twain" is what some would call William Cowper Brann, the yellow journalist on the Brazos.

It must have seemed a reasonable enough proposition at the time, even to the Baptists. Brann, a newcomer to town, would publish the first issue of Brann's *Iconoclast* in February 1895 for a dime apiece, or one dollar for a year's subscription.

"The *Iconoclast* makes war upon no religion of whatsoever name or origin that has fostered virtue or added aught to the happiness of the human race," Brann wrote in the first issue. "It is simply an independent American journal, exercising its constitutional prerogative to say what seemeth unto it best, without asking any man's permission."

But Brann would not remain diplomatic for even a few paragraphs. He quickly set out after the hypocrisy of late Victorianism that he found to be so abundant in Waco. To him, no group exemplified that more than the local Baptists and their cherished institution, Baylor University.

Waco of the late 19th century indeed seemed a schizophrenic place. On one hand it was deemed the Athens of Texas for a concentration of colleges unmatched anywhere in the state. Fifteen periodicals were published there. But on the other, the town was appropriately hailed as Six Shooter Depot, a sinful enclave that had its rowdy origins in the cattle and cowboys of the Chisholm Trail.

In 1894, in fact, Waco shared a unique distinction with Omaha, Nebraska. They were the only two communities in America with ordinances that set aside parts of town for prostitutes who were free to sell their wares unhindered by the law. The Waco red light district, three or four blocks north of Second Street which was known as the Reservation, survived well into the next century. On Sunday mornings, the prostitutes and their customers shared the streets with those en route to worship, for Waco had almost as many churches as saloons. It was a duality that Brann found delicious.

"Waco, we would have you know, is the religious storm-centre of the Universe, and one of the few places that licenses prostitutes—a fact for consideration of students of cause and effect," he once wrote.

"Of course, Waco, like other places, has its drawbacks; but, taken by and large, there is no better. While it is true that you can not secure a bath, shave or clean shirt here on Sunday, the saloons and churches are open, and the Reservation hath all seasons for its own...."

"All trains stop at Waco. You will recognize the place by a structure that resembles a Kansas section-house that has been held by the vandal Time while criminally assaulted by a cyclone."

Brann had arrived in the dusty Texas town in November 1894 at the age of thirty-nine after being hired as an editorial writer for the *Daily News*. He was a tall, thin, dark-haired family man with a wife and two children whose life to that point had been a compilation of hardship, tragedy and discord. Born in Coles County, Illinois, Brann would later brag in a column of stealing a locomotive engine as a boy. As an adult, he became a self-schooled intellectual widely conversant in the classics. He authored several plays and worked at several Texas newspapers as a writer, but never at one place long. The contentious and opinionated young man rarely left on good terms.

In 1890, while Brann worked at the *Houston Post*, he found his thirteen-year-old daughter, Inez, dead in a hammock behind their home, having taken an overdose of morphine. Brann later wrote that he believed it was his overbearing manner that led to his daughter's act of self-destruction. Several newspaper jobs later, Brann arrived in Waco, desperate for a means to feed and clothe his wife and two surviving children, but stubbornly continuing to nurse a long-held dream: ownership of a publication in which he could speak his mind and answer to no one.

Three months after his arrival, without financial backing, Brann published the first issue of the *Iconoclast*, rushing out to sell the first few copies, then bringing the money back to the publisher to buy some more. Despite his diplomatic mission statement in his first issue, Brann wasted no time in setting the editorial tone. He antagonized thousands in the fundamentalist community by proclaiming the Bible as only one of several sources of religious truth.

"I gather them together—the Old Testament and the New, the Koran and the sacred Vedas, the northern Sagas and the southern mythologies; I search them through, not to scoff, but to gather with reverent soul, every gleam of light that since the birth of Time has been vouchsafed to man," Brann wrote. "I go forth beneath the eternal stars—each silently pouring its stream of sidereal fire into the great realm of Darkness—and they seem like the eyes of pitying angels, watching man work out, little by little, through the long ages, the mystery of his life."

In the same issue, Brann also set out after the popular syndicated columnist DeWitt Talmadge, who had labeled Brann "the Apostle of the Devil," for expressing similarly heretic notions in the past.

"The *Iconoclast* will pay any man $10 who will demonstrate that T. DeWitt Talmadge ever originated an idea, good, bad or indifferent," Brann wrote. "He is simply a monstrous bag of fetid wind."

In a later edition, Brann generally skewered Christian missionaries.

"The religion of the Turks and the Chinese is just as dear to them as that of the Christian cult to its communicants; yet missionaries from Europe and America go among them uninvited and tell them that the time honored faith of their fathers is but a tissue of falsehoods...Is it any wonder—keeping Deuteronomy and the history of Medieval Christianity well in mind—that these self-expatriated apostles sometimes get it where the bottle got the cork?"

Brann's utter irreverence and wicked humor made his writing irresistible, even to many of his enemies, and built a worldwide following for the publication headquartered in such an unlikely place. The *Iconoclast's* circulation eventually swelled to 120,000.

"In a setting of general public interest in morals, in religion, in literature, and in affairs more reminiscent of Plato than of Post (Emily), Brann's mind and extraordinary writing ability burst upon the last decade of the 1800s like a rocket," Charles Carver wrote in 1957 . "The fact that the point of origin was a tiny, tin-roofed Texas town only made the event more impressive."

Brann also became a much sought-after public speaker, entertaining his listening audiences with more of the same. On one occasion, Brann said, "I confess to a sneaking respect for Satan, for he is preeminently a success in his chosen profession...He sat into the game with the cash capital of one snake: now he's got half the globe grabbed and an option on the other half...I have been called a defender of the devil; but I hope that won't prejudice the ladies against me, as it was a woman that discovered him."

He addressed the topic of piety this way:

"Too many people presume that they are full of the grace of God when they're only bilious...They put up long prayers on Sunday; that's piety. They bamboozle a green gosling out of his birthright on Monday; that's business...They even acquire two voices—a brisk business accent and a Sunday whine that would make a cub wolf climb a tree."

Yet over time, Brann would manifest as many contradictions as the community he ridiculed. He demanded religious tolerance on one hand, but was unabashedly racist on the other, stating his feelings in that area in appalling, if typically blunt terms.

"I once severely shocked the pseudo-philanthropists by suggesting that if the South is ever to rid herself of the Negro rape-fiend, she must take a day off and kill every member of the accursed race that declines to leave the country," Brann wrote. "We have tried restraining influences of religion and the elevating forces of education upon the Negro without avail...We must consider ourselves first, others afterwards. The rights of the white man are paramount, and if we do not maintain them at any cost we deserve only dishonor...."

Others contended his outspokenness was less the product of deeply held belief and courage than the manipulative attempt of a brilliant wordsmith to build circulation.

"Brann had arrived at a journalistic truth—that dissent, a sharp attack upon the status quo, was the surest way to acquire a following and to sell newspapers," Carver wrote. "In Waco the established targets were the Baptists, and from the first he joyfully ridiculed those of that faith whom he felt to be particularly narrow in their religious outlook."

Baylor became a frequent target of Brann, who often accused its Baptist hierarchy of hypocrisy. In 1895, Brazilian exchange student, Antonia Teixeira, who had been brought to Waco for missionary training, became pregnant. Her alleged seducer was the brother of the son-in-law of Baylor's president. Brann gleefully seized upon the greatest scandal of Waco's early history, fueling already inflamed passions that would result in bloodshed in the town's streets.

"The *Iconoclast* is not in the habit of commenting on particular social ulcers and special sectarian scandals. It prefers to deal with broad principles, not individual offenders," Brann wrote. "But once or twice in a decade a case arises so horrible in conception, so iniquitous in outline, so damnable in detail that it were [*sic*] impossible to altogether ignore it. Such a case has just come to light, involving Baylor University, that Bulwark of the Baptist church."

The scandal eventually subsided, but Brann's attacks on Baylor did not.

"I note with unfeigned pleasure that, according to claims of Baylor University, it opens the present season with a larger contingent of students, male and female, than ever before," Brann wrote. "This proves that Texas Baptists are determined to support it at any sacrifice— that they believe it better that their daughters should be exposed to its historic dangers and their sons condemned to grow up in ignorance than that this manufactory of ministers and Magdalenes should be permitted to perish..."

A few days after this appeared, Brann was abducted at gunpoint, driven to Baylor, rope thrown around him as a mob gathered, and severely beaten.

"These intellectual eunuches, who couldn't father an idea if cast bodily into the womb of the goddess wisdom, declared positively that I would be permitted to print nothing more about their beloved Baylor," Brann wrote.

He was unbowed. But not surprisingly, "threats were as thick as the bluebonnets in the meadows," Carver later wrote. Brann began carrying a pistol. Mobs of Baylor boys frequently gathered in front of Brann's house. On one occasion, the mob would not retreat until firehoses were turned on them by the authorities. Brann's wife, Carrie, became increasingly reclusive. Her husband planned to take her on a national speaking tour during which the couple hoped their frazzled nerves would heal.

On April 1, 1898, shortly before he and his wife were to depart, Brann and a friend were walking down Fourth Street in late afternoon when Tom Davis, the father of a girl who attended Baylor, emerged from a real estate office, and shot Brann in the back. Brann whirled and fired his own weapon. Both men suffered fatal wounds.

Brann's enemies predicted no ladies would attend his funeral and no flowers would be sent, but never had a Waco funeral been so well attended. Hundreds lined the streets for his funeral procession. Friends erected a monument over Brann's grave—a stone profile of the Iconoclast himself. Shortly after his death, a visitor to Oakwood Cemetery kicked over the flowers at his grave and planted a bullet hole in the temple of Brann's stone likeness, the final act in a brief but searing local drama.

What may have been the first chapter in Waco's history of Bibles and bloodshed would not be the last. David Koresh would add another ninety-five years later. Once again, a newspaper would play a prominent role.

10

A TIMELY TALE

On February 22, 1993, *Tribune-Herald* reporter Mark England interviewed David Koresh for the last time to allow him a final chance to respond to the newspaper's allegations. England's editors ordered him to conduct the conversation by telephone.

"We did not want to go to the compound," Lott said. "We specifically told him we thought it would be better if he interviewed him by phone. We knew the people had a lot of firearms and a commitment to protect what they saw as their mission."

All the pieces were then in place. Senior editors discussed beginning the series later that week. But as the paper added its finishing touches, another complication had arisen. Agents of the Bureau of Alcohol, Tobacco and Firearms contacted the paper, telling editors that the federal agency had been conducting an investigation of the Davidians.

The probe centered on allegations that Koresh was violating federal weapons laws, agents said. They asked the paper to delay its series until the probe could be completed. Lott believed the comments of the agents were vague, and the government offered no assurances that any action would be taken. *Tribune-Herald* editors refused to withhold publication.

"If someone asks you to hold up on publishing, you can't do it on blind faith," Lott would say later.

The meeting with federal authorities ended with editors promising to notify the ATF when their series would begin. On Friday, February 26, newspaper editors discussed the ATF's request one last time. After hours of discussion with his editors, Lott ordered the series to begin the next day. A newspaper representative told ATF agents that the presses would roll at 12:15 a.m. Saturday.

"We had had the information in shape to be published for close to a month for all intents and purposes, and we had been holding it up for other considerations," Lott said. "We needed to tell people in Waco what was going on in the shadows of their city. It was in the greater interest of the public to publish. It was my decision. I don't duck that responsibility."

The next morning, the fruits of the long investigation were waiting on the doorsteps of *Tribune-Herald* subscribers, the first installment of a seven-part series under the bylines of Mark England and Darlene McCormick. The series was entitled, "The Sinful Messiah."

"If you are a Branch Davidian, Christ lives on a threadbare piece of land 10 miles east of here called Mount Carmel," the series began.

"He has dimples, claims a ninth-grade education, married his legal wife when he was 14, enjoys a beer now and then, plays a mean guitar, reportedly packs a 9mm Glock and keeps an arsenal of military assault rifles, and willingly admits that he is a sinner without equal."

"David Koresh is now his legal name."

In the series, for the first time, a defiant Koresh publicly admitted his own claims to divinity.

"If the Bible is true, then I'm Christ," Koresh said. "But so what? Look at 2,000 years ago. What's so great about being Christ? A man nailed to the cross. A man of sorrow acquainted with grief...If the Bible is true, I'm Christ. If the Bible is true. But all I want out of this is for people to be honest this time."

Koresh dismissed his accusers, saying some, like Marc Breault, were false prophets who were motivated by jealousy.

"We're doing what we're doing, and no one is going to stop us," Koresh said.

Koresh's self-proclaimed divinity was hardly a burden to him, however. The *Tribune-Herald*, citing interviews with more than twenty former cult members, provided a riveting and often graphic chronicle of physical and sexual abuse of Koresh's followers, of the leader's boasts of sex with underage girls, and his biblically ordained right to the wives of the Davidians.

Only in passing did the series refer to the weapons, a decision made after deliberations at the newspaper.

"Most rational people are concerned about those kinds of weapons," Lott said. "But the greater evil to us was the manner in which he was taking little girls into a harem. For us, it was not primarily a story about stockpiling weapons. It was a story about the abuse of human beings in the name of religion, including sexual and other physical abuses of children in the name of religion. We were careful not to let the imagery of the weapons overshadow the images of the abuse."

The imagery included a tape made by Koresh and sent

to his followers in Australia. It referred to the leader's frequent claims that only the Lamb possessed the Holy Seed.

"You have only one seed that can deliver you from death," Koresh said on the tape. "There's only one hard-on in this whole universe that really loves you and wants to say good things about you. Remember Mary and God? Yeah? God couldn't make any advances because the world would misjudge."

Koresh used different reasoning with recruits.

"He said God was really lonesome, and he wanted grandchildren," one woman said. "It was like the Scriptures kind of said it, but they didn't really. It was like he was giving God grandchildren."

Another former cult member, Robyn Bunds, described a Bible study in which Koresh bragged about having sex with one of the cult's children, a thirteen-year-old girl. Koresh told his followers that the girl's heart pounded so hard he could hear it.

"You know when an animal is scared, how its heart just pounds?" Bunds quoted Koresh as saying. "That's how Vernon said her heart sounded. Like when you're hunting something is how he put it. That's how he said the heart of all girls sounded when he was with them for the first time."

Koresh was aware that the world would frown on his sexual conduct, even if he felt it was justified by Scripture. Several babies born to women at Mount Carmel and apparently fathered by Koresh were not legally registered, apparently at the cult leader's order. Too many babies born without named fathers might bring questions from authorities, Koresh reasoned. Beginning as early as 1987, Koresh taught that a jealous world would eventually cru-

David Koresh, then known by his birth name of Vernon Howell, holds son, Cyrus, while standing next to wife, Rachel.
(Elizabeth Baranyai, Sygma)

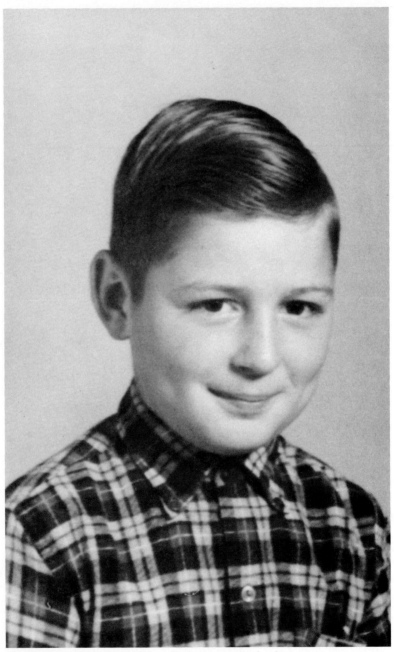

Vernon Howell as a young boy in elementary school.
(Erline Clark)

One of his family's favorite photos of him, showing Vernon Howell, at age eleven in the spring of 1971, holding a fish he had just caught. His pet dog's name was Jet Fuel. (Erline Clark)

A family portrait of stepfather Roy Haldeman, mother Bonnie Haldeman, brother Roger and Vernon Howell (who changed his name to David Koresh in 1990). This was taken in March, 1971.
(Erline Clark)

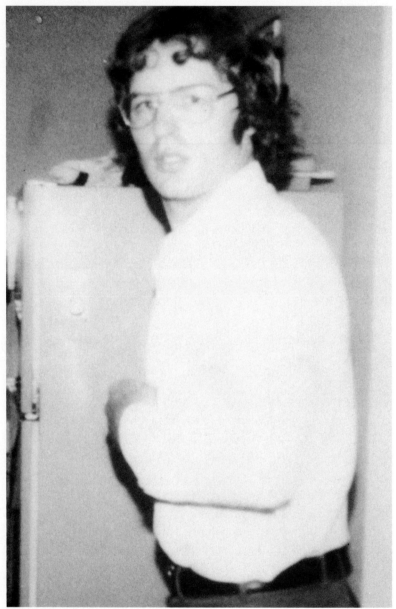

This 1981 photo of Howell shows him inside the Mount Carmel compound of the Branch Davidians. This was still several years before he wrested control of the Waco cult from George Roden.
(Associated Press/Wide World Photos)

Three weeks into the stand-off between the Branch Davidians and federal law enforcement officers, a Texas Department of Public Safety officer keeps watch at a checkpoint as two agents of the Bureau of Alcohol, Tobacco and Firearms (ATF) take a break in the background.
(Associated Press/Wide World Photos)

An ATF agent holds an M-16 rifle aloft as he watches traffic approaching a barricade north of the Branch Davidian compound. (Associated Press/Wide World Photos)

*An ATF agent takes a break from the tension of the stand-off to play with a
kitten in some tall grass outside the compound.
(Jim Winn, Fort Worth Star-Telegram)*

A woman who identified herself as "a Talmidad" carries a cross while walking with her two dogs outside Waco, not far from the compound under siege. She said she was walking across the country from Santa Cruz, California. The woman, not affiliated with the Branch Davidians, was quoted as saying, "A little Jesus doesn't use guns." (Associated Press/Wide World Photos)

The Mount Carmel compound with some cows grazing in the foreground. (Paul Moseley, Fort Worth Star-Telegram)

This is a document that was left unclaimed in a Fort Worth print shop for twenty years before being identified in March 1993 as scrolls somehow linked to the Branch Davidians.
(Mark Rogers, Fort Worth Star-Telegram)

Former Branch Davidian sect leader George Roden goes public from inside the Vernon State Hospital.
(Tony Record, Fort Worth Star-Telegram)

Bonnie Haldeman, David Koresh's mother, is stopped and queried by an ATF agent at a checkpoint outside the Mount Carmel compound. (Rodger Mallison, Fort Worth Star-Telegram)

Dick DeGuerin, attorney for David Koresh, and attorney Jack Zimmerman, who represented Davidian "lieutenant" Steve Schneider, meet with the media after meeting with their clients. (Carolyn Bauman, Fort Worth Star-Telegram)

Much of the accessible area outside the Mount Carmel compound became a makeshift media village as evidenced by this line of television reporters and cameras.
(Paul Moseley, Fort Worth Star-Telegram)

Five women released from the Davidian compound into police custody are led out of a Waco courthouse and walk, wearing leg chains, through a sea of reporters and photographers.
(Ron Jenkins, Fort Worth Star-Telegram)

Two more Branch Davidians leave the Waco federal courthouse following a hearing a little over three weeks into the stand-off.
(Associated Press/Wide World Photos)

Various entrepreneurs took advantage of the 51-day stand-off to cash in on souvenir sales. Here, vendor Bill Powers sells David Koresh T-shirts emblazoned with the message "We Ain't Comin' Out", as in W. A. C. O. (Jerry Hoefer, Fort Worth Star-Telegram)

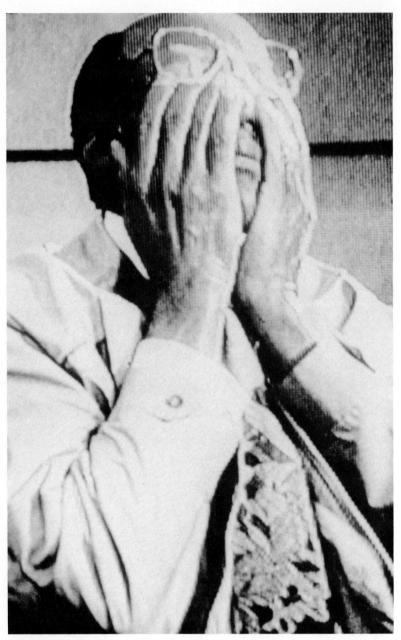

Samuel Henry of Manchester, England lost his wife and five children to David Koresh and, subsequently, the fatal compound fire of April 19, 1993. (Sygma)

Within minutes, just after noon on April 19, 1993, a fire allegedly set in several places inside the compound turned Mount Carmel into a blazing inferno. Dozens of Davidians perished in the fire.
(Jerry Hoefer, Fort Worth Star-Telegram)

After the devastating fire, experts spent weeks sifting through the charred debris for bodies, weapons and other pieces of evidence. It took two weeks for searchers to locate and identify the body of cult leader David Koresh, who reportedly had a bullet wound to the forehead.
(Rodger Mallison, Fort Worth Star-Telegram)

cify him because of his many wives. He used paranoia about the imminent attack of the outside world as a means to keep his flock united. Koresh frequently cited a passage from Psalm 38.

"Mine enemies are lively, and they are strong;

And they that hate me wrongfully are multiplied."

The Branch Davidians followed reverently along, fearful of the man who possessed the God-like grasp of Scripture. Koresh's power, however, likely had more to do with brainwashing than biblical inspiration. Mount Carmel life described by the newspaper could have been taken directly from the best mind-control manuals. Koresh kept his followers exhausted, underfed, isolated and confused. Husbands and wives lived separately.

"It gave him more control," said Robyn Bunds's mother, Jeannine Bunds, another former cult member. "He's big on control. If you're married, you talk. You discuss things. But if you're not with your mate at night, you can't talk, you can't put Vernon down. You don't have anybody. You're isolated."

The typical day at Mount Carmel began at 5:30 a.m. Men exercised, then ran an obstacle course Howell had designed before spending most days repairing Mount Carmel. Modestly dressed women cooked and cleaned and educated the children, who had been removed from neighboring public schools several years before and later were rarely seen outside the compound. Children's birthdays were never celebrated. Television was forbidden.

Koresh would be all the entertainment they would need. The leader typically slept until early afternoon, and was fresh for marathon Bible studies that began in the evening when everyone else was exhausted. Koresh also frequently practiced rock music until the wee hours, then roused his followers for more study.

"You don't have time to think," a former cult member said. "He doesn't give you time to think about what you're doing. It's just bang, bang, bang, bang, bang."

Over time, Koresh's methods proved highly effective. Followers surrendered to their leader, body and soul. "You begin to live for a pat on the head," as one former cult member described it.

His biblical teaching, however, would have been difficult for a rested person to decipher. Koresh spoke rapidly, peppering his lectures with rhetorical questions that his followers could not answer.

"He roamed back and forth across the chapters of the Bible, arcane biblical references rolling off his tongue," England and McCormick wrote. "Before the listener could grasp what was just said, he was on to something else. It was like a roller coaster ride: thrilling, but it was almost impossible afterward to say what you had seen or heard."

"But Howell's followers got hooked on the feeling— that sense of glimpsing truth, even if it was awful and apocalyptic. Some compared it to a drug. You felt like you were in the know. Others might consider you average. Let them. They were unbelievers. But you knew something they didn't—something that put you in the ultimate In Crowd, the ones who wouldn't be taking a dip into the Lake of Fire."

Koresh promised that the world was about to end, but his followers need not fear Armageddon if they listened to him, but only to him.

"This planet is just like a cemetery," Koresh follower, Paul Fatta, told the *New York Times*. "We're all just waiting to die."

Fear was perhaps the most important component of

Koresh's brainwashing. It was the common dread of being incapable of finding their way alone. Branch Davidians came to believe Koresh and not the Bible.

"I don't think anyone ever knew what his understanding was, honestly," said Karl Hennig, a teacher from Vancouver, British Columbia, who studied the cult for two months in 1987. "If you had given them pencil and paper, I don't think they could have written down his message. They might have a piece here and there."

Hennig later would include his experience at Mount Carmel in a psychology paper submitted at the University of British Columbia.

"Generally, in the quiet evenings, an introspective, self-absorbed malaise seemed to overshadow the place as individuals perhaps contemplated their grim future. The only consolation was that the world would get even worse."

Robyn Bunds grew up with the Branch Davidians and remembered a time when the cult was a benign part of her family's middle-class California existence. Her father, Don Bunds, was a design engineer; her mother, Jeannine, a nurse. The couple frequently sent money off to Ben and Lois Roden, and the family occasionally visited Mount Carmel, where cult members cultivated crops and the children rode horses.

"Before, it was harmless," Robyn Bunds told Waco reporters. "You sent tithes, had services."

Then Vernon Howell began making periodic visits to the Bundses' home in Southern California. Robyn Bunds thought the young man arrogant. It soon became apparent he was in control of her family's life. Robyn's parents spent $10,000 for a van for the cult and purchased a $100,000 home in Pomona at Howell's request.

"When Vernon came along, he totally changed it," Robyn Bunds said. "He said you had to give him all your money. You had to live on the property. You had to give up everything else. You had to give him your mind...your body."

Robyn was seventeen when she attempted to escape the growing influence Howell seemed to possess over her family, moving to live with relatives in Massachusetts. When she asked to return home a few months later, her parents told her that Howell had other ideas. She was ordered to join other members of the cult, who were then living in exile in the pine woods near Palestine. From middle-class comfort, Robyn was forced to share a plywood hut with another young woman.

Despite the hardship, Robyn had a change of heart. Howell, who had once seemed so full of himself, now seemed inspired, charming and humble. The woman fell in love. At seventeen, she became one of the leader's wives. Only later did Robyn realize how thin Howell's affections would be spread. His harem soon would come to include at least fifteen other so-called wives.

"It was like a beauty contest," she said. "All of us battling against each other to be this woman that God thinks is the greatest. It was like a fairy tale."

The romance would not last long. Wisdom Bunds was born November 14, 1988, a boy that Robyn Bunds maintained was fathered by Howell. She later accused him of beating her son—whose name she later changed to Shaun—until his bottom bled.

"Vernon said even if a child died from a spanking, they would go to heaven," Robyn Bunds said.

Howell's New Light doctrine, delivered in 1989, was the last straw. Recent inspiration had directed him to take all wives of the cult for himself, Howell told his startled followers. Robyn's mother, Jeannine Bunds, was among the first Howell would claim. Jeannine Bunds later told Waco reporters that Howell's interest made her feel young again, gave her the chance to contribute to building the House of David. Howell prophesied that she would become pregnant if they had sex and that she would bear a child for the Lord. Jeannine's daughter was disgusted.

"I've had his child. He's slept with my mother," Robyn Bunds said. "I can't think of anything weirder. He doesn't even try and justify it."

In 1990, while they were together in a California cult house, Robyn Bunds told Koresh she was leaving. The Davidian leader was visibly upset. While Robyn was away working, Koresh ordered another follower to take Shaun to Texas, prompting Robyn to file a kidnapping complaint with police in LaVerne, a suburb of Los Angeles.

Detectives arrived at the Davidian house in LaVerne in the summer of 1990, finding a place set up like a dormitory. Upstairs, they found Koresh and twenty women, including Jeannine Bunds.

"He was there by himself with all the women," said LaVerne detective Ron Ingels. "And all the women indicated that they were dedicated and loyal to Howell[4] and would do anything he said. It was a strange situation. All the men stayed in Pomona. All the women stayed with Howell."

Police told Koresh he had forty-eight hours to return the boy. Two days later, Shaun was back from Texas with

---

[4]Vernon Howell changed his name to David Koresh in 1990.

his mother. Jeannine Bunds also left the cult within months. Of family members, only Don Bunds would stay behind, choosing David Koresh over his wife and children.

Three years later, Robyn and Jeannine Bunds would become celebrities, their faces and stories familiar to people around the world. David Koresh had been transformed from an obscure cult leader to an international villain by the shootout at Mount Carmel. The mother and daughter were the only wives known to have shunned him, the only women who could describe the insanity inside his harem.

Cameras from the CBS news magazine show "48 Hours" visited their California home.

"I was one of the first ones, one of the first ones that anyone knew about anyway," Robyn Bunds told a national television audience. "I want to talk to you later. That was his way of telling you, 'Come up and see me.'"

Oprah Winfrey was perplexed a few weeks later. How could seemingly normal people end up under the spell of a man like David Koresh?

Jeannine Bunds: "Well, you've got to understand when (Howell) took Robyn for his wife, I did not know."

Winfrey, gesturing to Robyn: "Uh-huh. He took her back to Texas and you were fourteen years old."

Robyn Bunds: "But I came home several times because I just couldn't take it. The time that I..."

Winfrey: "What couldn't you take? What was going on?"

Robyn Bunds: "It was just very hard. You don't— when I went there the first time, I was fifteen. And we didn't have any heat, and we didn't have hot water and it was winter."

Winfrey: "Mm-hmm."

Robyn Bunds: "And I was freezing my butt off. So I called my parents and said 'I want to come home.' And they came and got me."

Winfrey: "Was he having sex with you at fifteen?"

Robyn Bunds: "Uh-huh."

Winfrey: "Had you been taken his wife at fifteen?"

Robyn Bunds: "No. Not until I was seventeen."

Winfrey: "Not until you were seventeen."

Robyn Bunds: "That's when I really started getting into it, when he started sleeping with me. Because by then, you feel kind of stuck. You know, you're having sex with this man and he's really got you by your mind, your body. You know, it's really..."

Winfrey: "So one of the questions, I—I think, we all want to know, is—we all see this as a cult. We all see this as somebody who's taken over your mind."

Jeannine Bunds: "We didn't."

Winfrey: "Did you, at the time, recognize that—that it was indeed a cult and that you were being brainwashed?"

Jeannine Bunds: "No. I didn't feel that way."

Winfrey: "You just believed him?"

Jeannine Bunds: "I didn't feel that way at all."

Winfrey: "Do you believe he's evil?"

Robyn Bunds: "I believe he's lost his mind."

Winfrey: "Mm-hmm."

Robyn Bunds: "I don't believe that he's evil."

11

HOLY WAR

The prophecy was fulfilled about 9:30 on a cold, rainy morning in the country when many of the faithful in nearby Waco were in church. It was the moment David Koresh had preached about for years, the arrival of the infidels, the Babylonians at the gate. "Mine enemies are lively, and they are strong, and they that hate me wrongfully are multiplied," he warned his followers. The Davidians listened, dutifully marching off with their weapons to target practice each day. When the Babylonians came, Koresh's soldiers were ready.

They arrived in cattle trailers meant to disguise their approach, speeding down the empty country roads, then onto the dirt driveway leading to Mount Carmel. The infidels came by the dozens, hefting weapons, dressed for war in blue jumpsuits, helmets and body armor. It wasn't the FBI, as Koresh had predicted. The full authority and force of the United States government would be borne that day instead by agents of the Bureau of Alcohol, Tobacco and Firearms. That day in Texas, they would be no match for an even greater force, a Davidian juggernaut.

For years, Koresh gathered firepower for just such a moment. But the arsenal of guns more typically carried by soldiers, the AK-47s, the AR-15s, the massive .50-caliber airplane killer, were not his most destructive tools. The leader's deadliest weapons were his Branch Davidian followers, fanatical acolytes who conformed to his every whim, who would follow him to the death as they would prove so dramatically that Sunday morning.

Later, it was easy to forget that they once had been lawyers, engineers, nurses, students, mailmen, mothers and fathers. They were not killers before that day. But when the moment of reckoning came, when the infidels approached the place dubbed by Davidians as Ranch Apocalypse, they were stirred into a blood-thirsty froth by their leader. In those minutes they were transformed by the force of their beliefs into ruthless warriors who fired on wounded adversaries even after they fell. Their hearts were cold in defense of their leader and his muddled biblical vision. The prophet had trained them well.

Hindsight dictated that the ATF raid that left four agents and several cult members dead, was an ill-advised debacle plagued by faulty planning, loose lips and bad judgment. While it was widely agreed that law enforcement intervention was necessary at Mount Carmel, ATF methods spawned needless bloodshed, critics maintained. News reports indicated the agents were ordered to press on with the raid despite evidence that the element of surprise, a crucial component of the ATF plan, had been lost. Unknowing officers thus stumbled into an ambush that should have been anticipated and avoided, some of the agents themselves later maintained.

Yet in one respect, the debate and acrimony engendered by the assault was academic. No matter what the government's timing, no matter what its tactics, the ultimate confrontation with the Branch Davidians was inevitable. David Koresh had fashioned his followers into instruments of destruction. Now or later, he would have his Holy War, and it seemed assured that when he did, many would die.

The march to the inevitable confrontation began innocuously with routine parcel deliveries to the country compound. Only when one of the packages fell open was a deadly chain of events set in motion. For years, Mount Carmel had been part of United Parcel Service employee Larry Gilbreath's route. But in early 1992, the frequency of the deliveries increased, deliveries that included firearm parts and accessories and chemicals, according to invoices. The Mount Carmel purchases were always made in cash. Then, in May 1992, another package headed for Mount Carmel reportedly broke open while it was being loaded onto the delivery truck, exposing fifty hand grenade hulls.

Gilbreath reported his discovery to superiors, who in turn notified local authorities. By June 1992, a long ATF investigation had begun, one that ultimately would snatch the agency from its traditional obscurity.

ATF agents point out they are the successors to Eliot Ness, whose photograph still hangs in agency headquarters in Washington, D.C. Ness, the famous nemesis of Al Capone in Chicago during the 1920s, was incorruptible, the original Untouchable. His agency, the Federal Prohibition Bureau, evolved into the ATF. Sixty years later its agents still were expected to adhere to Ness's example.

In the beginning, the focus of the ATF and its various federal ancestors was crimes spawned by the nation's whiskey trade. In 1791, Congress imposed the first tax on distilled spirits in an attempt to pay off debts remaining from the Revolutionary War, a tax so unpopular that President Washington was forced to summon 15,000 militia—in effect the first ATF agents—to quell what became known as the Whiskey Rebellion.

The onset of Prohibition in 1918 forced distillers to pour out sixty million gallons of alcohol, heaving open a black market soon to be filled by Mafia mobs, moonshiners and bootleggers. The U.S. government responded with the Prohibition Bureau and puritanical agents like Ness.

The bureau was ultimately absorbed into the Department of the Treasury, and assigned to regulate the cigarette and firearms industries, in addition to alcohol. As decades passed, its focus shifted from whiskey to more glamorous crimes involving bullets, bombs and arson. ATF agents took only twenty minutes to trace the revolver John Hinkley, Jr. used to shoot President Ronald Reagan in 1981. Its commando-style units known as Special Response Teams undertook over 230 high-risk raids across the nation in 1992. But until that last weekend in February, the agency had existed in the shadows of its more prestigious federal law enforcement brethren, the FBI (Federal Bureau of Investigation) and the DEA (Drug Enforcement Administration). Indeed, no one had ever made a television series about the ATF.

Then, around lunchtime on February 26, 1993, the terrifying specter of international terrorism visited the United States: A massive explosion rocked an underground garage at the World Trade Center in Manhattan and ATF agents found themselves on the front lines. In the television coverage that followed, men and women dressed in blue uniforms with agency initials emblazoned in large white letters across their back were depicted in their attempts to piece together evidence of the crime. That publicity paled in comparison to the coverage the bureau would receive in Texas only two days later.

The case against the Branch Davidians and their leader, David Koresh, involved allegations of the possession and manufacture of automatic weapons, and the manufacture of bombs in violation of federal statutes. The purpose of the ultimate raid would be to arrest Koresh and execute a search warrant for his compound.

It was no great secret that Koresh was stockpiling weapons designed for combat. He had become a fixture at Texas gun shows, later described by one Texas gun dealer as someone who seemed like a "rich and eccentric guy."

Henry McMahon, a shadowy but apparently legitimate Texas gun dealer in the little town of Hewitt near Mount Carmel, considered Koresh a business partner of sorts. It was McMahon, the owner of a business called Hewitt Handguns, who helped Koresh accumulate a large part of his arsenal, including the Davidian leader's legal purchase of dozens of AR-15 assault rifles and a .50-caliber sniper rifle capable of blasting targets a mile away, according to a story by reporter Lee Hancock of the *Dallas Morning News*.

On one occasion in Dallas, Koresh displayed McMahon's federal firearms license while trying to make a wholesale purchase of twelve Colt AR-15 assault rifles. The sale was denied when the Dallas gun dealer couldn't contact McMahon by telephone. Koresh quickly whipped out $7,000 in cash and bought the weapons retail instead.

The same Dallas wholesaler shipped another dozen AR-15 assault rifles to Hewitt Handguns to fill a $7,000 order reportedly placed by Koresh, and sold several pistols to the same business, guns that the dealer understood were meant for Mount Carmel.

In 1992, Koresh purchased the .50-caliber Barrett Firearms sniper rifle, a thirty-two-pound weapon mounted on a bipod, and about 100 rounds of .50-caliber ammunition, Hancock reported. The deadly acquisition came after Koresh admired the weapon at a Houston-area gun show. The rifle, used by United States forces during the Persian Gulf War to disable light Iraqi armored vehicles, apparently later greeted arriving ATF agents from the Mount Carmel watch tower.

Each of Koresh's purchases apparently was made legally. Even the grenade hulls did not violate federal weapons laws. But in addition to the legally obtained weapons, federal agents said they monitored the Davidian leader's purchase of material normally used to convert rifles into illegal machine guns and to manufacture bombs. They believed both activities were taking place inside the compound.

A federal affidavit later used to support the search-and-arrest warrants portrayed Koresh and his followers as an army in training, one bracing for a confrontation with the government.

Young males were designated by Koresh as the Mighty Men, a term from the Old Testament that described the warriors of King David. But combat training was not limited by gender. All adult residents and some children were schooled in the use of military assault rifles. Only the very young, the elderly or infirm were excluded. All able-bodied adults were issued weapons that were routinely kept in the Davidians' bedrooms. In the personal notebook of seventy-year-old cult member Catherine Matteson, authorities later found detailed handwritten instructions on how to use a gun, including notes on how to shoot a person wearing a bulletproof vest.

There were roughly three guns to a person at Mount Carmel in Koresh's staggering stockpile of weapons that, according to federal agents, included:

123 AR-15 assault rifles similar to the M-16 carried by U.S. soldiers
44 AK-47 assault rifles
26 M-1 assault rifles
11 long guns
60 hand guns
two assault shotguns (known as street sweepers)
two Barrett .50-caliber rifles
one M-76 grenade launcher
40 to 50 pounds of black gun powder
50 hand grenade casings

Boxes of ammunition were stacked two deep in one room, reaching to the ceiling of a ten-foot wall. Between October 1991 and February 1993, the cult spent at least $199,715 on the acquisition of weapons and related equipment, federal agents said.

In February 1992, neighbors reported hearing automatic gunfire coming from the compound. Koresh followers began to rearm hand grenades. Women in the compound began to sew tactical vests used to carry ammunition during military-type exercises.

Joyce Sparks saw hints of the buildup in February 1992, when the caseworker for the Texas Department of

Human Services visited the compound to investigate child abuse complaints. A boy about eight years old told Sparks he couldn't wait to grow up so he would be issued "a long gun" like the other men in the cult.

During a second visit two months later, Sparks said she was assured by Koresh that weapons were kept away from the children. Koresh's guided tour seemed to indicate otherwise. At one point, Sparks noticed a trapdoor at one end of the building. She wasn't expecting what she saw when Koresh allowed her to look beneath it. A ladder led to a buried school bus from which all the seats had been removed. A large refrigerator riddled with bullet holes sat at one end and three rifles were lying on the floor. Koresh told the curious case worker that he used the bus for target practice so as not to disturb his neighbors.

Koresh refused to allow her to see any of the children and her visit turned increasingly ominous. The cult leader told Sparks he was the "Messenger from God, that the world was coming to an end, and that when he reveals himself, the riots in Los Angeles would pale in comparison to what was going to happen in Waco, Texas. Koresh said that it would be a 'military type operation' and that all non-believers would have to suffer," a federal affidavit said.

Child welfare officials insisted they found no evidence of child abuse during their visits to the compound. But Sparks later told authorities about the case of a ten-year-old cult member who said she had been sexually abused by Koresh. The girl told Sparks she was taken to a motel room in Waco by her mother, where Koresh was waiting for her in bed with no pants on.

"She stated that, while in the hotel room, Howell sexually molested her," Sparks told agents. "When asked how she was feeling when this happened, she responded 'scared' but 'privileged.' It was understood in the group that this is what happens. They did not need to talk about it. That was just the way it was and everyone knew it."

In the waning months of the Bush Administration, periodic reports about the investigation began to circulate at the highest levels of the Treasury Department. Probes into activities of professed religious groups were as a rule viewed as sensitive, ATF officials said. But it had also become apparent that thwarting Koresh and searching his compound presented unusual dangers.

ATF agents came to consider the Davidians among the most volatile groups they had encountered in recent years. Their firepower was not the only reason for concern. Other theocratic groups were well-armed, too. But other groups, such as white supremacist organizations, were engaged by an earthly agenda, such as purging the world of people they considered undesirable. Koresh, on the other hand, built his arsenal and drilled his followers in preparation for the final battle, the Apocalypse. Former cult members spoke of the possibility of mass suicides. To ATF investigators, the Branch Davidian leader clearly was spoiling for a fight.

"There was no doubt the guy was a dangerous, heavily armed leader of a group of people who clearly had shown they would follow him to extraordinary lengths," ATF official Jack Killorin said later. "He was going to be a tough nut no matter which way we went at it."

By late 1992, the decision was no longer whether to move against Koresh, but when. In an attempt to gather current information, undercover officers—including an agent named Robert Rodriquez—posed as college students and were put in place in a house 260 yards down the road from the Branch Davidian compound.

Koresh was immediately suspicious. His new neighbors claimed they were students, but seemed too old. They drove expensive cars, didn't burn their lights at night and never used the front door. Nonetheless, after the agents made contact with Koresh's followers and expressed an interest in their philosophy, they were invited to take part in Mount Carmel activities. They joined numerous Bible studies, were given tours and even were assigned weapons by cult members for target practice.

Court documents described one meeting between Koresh and the undercover agent.

"(Koresh) played music on a guitar for thirty minutes and then began to read the Bible to Special Agent Rodriquez," the document said. "During this session, Special Agent Rodriquez was asked numerous questions about his life. After answering all questions, Special Agent Rodriquez was asked to attend a two-week Bible session with David Koresh. This was for Special Agent Rodriquez to learn the seven seals and become a member of the group. Special Agent Rodriquez was told that by becoming a member he was going to be watched and disliked...David Koresh stated the Bible gave him the right to bear arms."

In the process, the undercover agents confirmed the extent of Koresh's arsenal. Based on their description of Mount Carmel, a government plan to raid the compound began to take shape.

"We were getting close when we put our undercover agents in place," Killorin said. "There had been months of discussions about how to go forward, how to attack the cult and seize evidence. Plans were drafted and amended."

After weeks of deliberation, senior ATF agents decided on a morning raid to take place after a regular Bible study when the men were likely to be at work, the women and children off by themselves, and the guns locked away in a second-floor room adjoining Koresh's bedroom. They hoped to catch the leader in a morning nap.

Special Response Teams in New Orleans, Dallas and Houston began to rehearse for the raid, which was tentatively set for March 1. Agents studied photographs of the beige-colored compound that included a four-story watch tower, underground tunnels and storage areas, living quarters, chapel and gymnasium built into one interconnected building.

Several days before the raid, strike team members from the three cities said goodbye to their families and gathered at Fort Hood's army installation near Waco. In a mock village normally used by army soldiers to train for urban warfare, ATF agents simulated the coming operation, winnowing the time necessary to accomplish their assignments and subdue Koresh. One team was assigned to climb to the Mount Carmel roof by ladder, crash through a second floor window and secure the gun room. A second team was to isolate the women and children, the third team to secure the men.

In thirteen seconds, according to the plan, more than 100 agents were to scramble from the two cattle trailers. Seven seconds later they were to have crashed through the front door. In twenty-two seconds they were to have gained the roof. In less than a minute, the gun room was to be secured. By the end of rehearsals, the agents could reach their objectives with seconds to spare.

The surprise attack was designed to subdue Koresh and his followers without gunfire or bloodshed. But if the Davidians opened fire, the agents were told, they were to fall back as soon as possible, establish a perimeter and begin telephone negotiations with the cult. With women and children inside, prolonged gun battles were to be avoided. Agents could not return fire without an identifiable hostile target.

For most, it would be the most dangerous assignment of their careers. But the agents were confident as final preparations for the assault were completed. Some in the strike force called relatives, telling them to keep tuned to the Cable News Network over the weekend because something big was about to come down. Shortly before nine o'clock that rainy Sunday morning, the agents, armed with 9mm handguns and clad in full battle armor, squeezed beneath tarps into the cattle trailers and set off for the ten-minute ride into the rolling country.

The tip to the *Waco Tribune-Herald* came the day before, and by 8:30 a.m. that Sunday, seven reporters, two photographers and an editor from the paper had fanned out into the country around Mount Carmel. A Waco television crew was on hand. David Koresh would be waiting for the agents as well.

Later speculation centered on a deliberate tip by someone at the paper to the cult leader, an allegation *Tribune-Herald* editor Bob Lott vigorously denied. And as time wore on, a different scenario emerged, one pieced together from federal records and published reports. It involved a seemingly innocuous conversation between a mailman and a visitor to the country.

The mailman was cult member David Jones, the brother of Koresh's legal wife, Rachel. On the morning of the raid, Jones was driving near Mount Carmel in his mail truck when he noticed a white vehicle parked along the normally deserted road. Jones stopped to ask if the driver was lost, but soon suspected that the person wasn't lost at all, but a journalist in the country for a very specific purpose. Jones continued on to the compound, telling others about his suspicious visit a few minutes before. Meanwhile, as Jones arrived, agent Rodriquez visited with Koresh inside Mount Carmel, the final act of his undercover assignment.

The Davidian compound already was on edge that weekend because of the newspaper series, and the situation was about to grow even more tense. Jones and other cult members devised a plan to alert Koresh without tipping off the government agent. One Davidian telephoned a relative and asked the relative to call Koresh back at Mount Carmel, according to a magazine account. When Koresh left Rodriquez to take the call, he was told about Jones's suspicions. When Koresh returned to the agent, he was screaming that the ATF and the National Guard were on their way.

"Neither the ATF or the National Guard will ever get me," Koresh said. "They got me once and they will never get me again. They are coming. The time has come."

Rodriquez quickly left the compound, telling cult members he was going home to breakfast. Davidians watched Rodriquez hurry down the road to his residence, which he left a few minutes later, further fueling suspicions inside the compound. The Davidians took up battle stations. Boxes of hand grenades were placed on a table in the dining room. Cult member Douglas Wayne Martin, a Harvard-educated lawyer who practiced in Waco, wore a string of hand grenades around his neck. Twenty men and fifteen women were seen taking up weapons.

"Assyrians are coming," cult member Neil Vaega cried.

Within minutes, the cattle trucks were speeding toward them down the country road, racing past the mailboxes and small frame shack at the entrance to the Mount Carmel driveway.

ATF official Jack Killorin said the undercover agent saw nothing to indicate Koresh had been tipped off. But as federal affidavits conceded later, Rodriquez obviously was made aware of Koresh's alarm about an imminent attack. News reports also indicated that senior ATF officials were warned of Koresh's suspicions, but decided to move ahead with the raid before he and his followers could fully prepare. Shortly before the cattle trailers approached the target, the readiness of the Davidians became dramatically apparent. Three government helicopters carrying senior federal agents were struck by gunfire, two eventually being forced to land. Agents on the ground later told reporters they were not warned that the helicopters had come under fire from the compound.

"That was inexcusable," one career agent told the *New York Times*. "As soon as those shots were taken, the raid should have been aborted. Instead, we were ordered to walk right into it."

Koresh, dressed in black, wearing a bulletproof vest and carrying an assault rifle, stood smiling in the front door as agents approached. The strike team scrambled out before the vehicles had fully stopped, announcing themselves as government officers carrying warrants. Koresh slammed the front door shut.

Within seconds the agents were met with withering gunfire. Agents smashed through the front door and moved toward their objectives, but were met by bullets at every turn. Agents on the second story crashed through the window and advanced toward the gun room, but were pelted by gunfire through walls, the floor and down through the ceiling. An officer on the roof was blasted through the wall and tumbled down a ladder.

Agent Bill Buford was hit twice in the leg, but was lucky compared to the fate of colleague Robert J. Williams.

"I saw Robb huddled behind what appeared to be an abandoned safe," Buford said of Williams, one of the four officers killed. "I saw him fall back once, as if he had been pushed by a bullet, and then I saw him look up and over it. And I saw him get hit. I sort of knew that he wouldn't get up."

Buford was pinned down for two hours. While he lay there, fellow agent Ken Chisholm covered Buford's wounded body with his own.

"I remember telling Ken, 'Hey, they don't give the congressional medal of honor out here,'" Buford said later from his hospital bed. "But Ken wouldn't leave me."

"It was a nightmare, just a nightmare," said Buford, a Vietnam combat veteran. "I've been in some well-planned ambushes in my time, but never anything as deadly as this one. We were taking fire from everywhere, even through the wall. At first, I didn't realize I'd been shot. I felt no pain, just a hard impact in my leg. It took a few moments to realize what had happened."

The bullets kicked up dirt and splintered wood all around Jerry Petrilli from the moment the agent rushed from the trailer toward the front door. Petrilli was felled by fragments from what was either a grenade or a bomb that struck him in the left arm, right forearm, wrist and hand. Another was deflected by his bulletproof vest.

Agents reported seeing Davidians dressed in black pajamas, wearing black ski masks. Gunfire showered them from forty to fifty locations inside the compound. A sniper blasted away with the .50-caliber rifle from the watch tower. Agents exposed themselves to gunfire to retrieve wounded comrades who continued to be targets after being felled. After forty-five minutes of frantic telephone negotiations with Koresh, agents finally secured a cease-fire so both sides could tend to their wounded and count their dead.

Adrenalin flowed as the reporters shivered in the mist that morning near Mount Carmel. Reporters and editors of the *Waco Tribune-Herald* had wondered how David Koresh and the Branch Davidians would react to the series that began the day before. And now, the paper had learned, ATF agents were en route to stir the pot even more.

"We went out expecting the worst," *Tribune-Herald* reporter Tommy Witherspoon said later. "But we didn't expect what was going to happen."

Witherspoon was paired with reporter Marc Masferrer. The two loitered a good distance from Mount Carmel until another reporter notified them by radio that the federal strike force had left its staging area in Waco. The reporters moved closer, pulling their car into the driveway of the house that had been used by the undercover agents.

The federal agents were sitting ducks as they scrambled from the trailers, showered immediately by a horrifying barrage of gunfire. Hundreds, maybe even thousands of volleys made high-pitched, whining noises as they pierced the air. Dozens of agents fell or were pinned down behind the trailers and other vehicles. The stunned reporters realized they also were targets. Bullets rippled the water of the pond in front of them, shattered the windshield and flattened a tire of the Chevrolet station wagon that had been their shield. Witherspoon and Masferrer dove into a small ditch for cover.

"We became one with the ground," Witherspoon said. "It became very cold and very wet, but we weren't going to move. We were kind of resolved to be there for a long time. I thought a lot about my wife and two kids. I knew Marc was a good Catholic, so I told him to start sending up the 'Hail Marys.'"

Television reporter John McLemore was even closer to the fray, so close he said he could hear people inside being struck by bullets. McLemore and cameraman Dan Mulloney also had been tipped about the raid and were sure to be in place in plenty of time to cover the action. They found themselves in the middle of the story that would reverberate around the world.

"The ATF agents came right in, parked right by the front door and made a frontal assault on the building," McLemore recounted later. "They went inside. There's thousands of holes in the building right now. A couple of them were shot when they were inside. They jumped out of windows and were dragged off to the side...It was like a war zone. People were being hit. You could hear people screaming with agony, the pain of it."

Bullets whistled about Mulloney's head and riddled the ground as his camera rolled, gathering footage of the surreal scene—helmeted agents busting through a second floor window, then tumbling off the roof after being blasted through a splintering wall—pictures that would be broadcast to an international audience within hours.

"I didn't know if I was going to die, but I figured I was going to get shot," Mulloney said later. "I started thinking of my kids, my two daughters."

Agents apparently without their own medical backup began pleading for the journalists' help.

"Hey, TV man, call for an ambulance," one yelled.

McLemore dashed to his truck, exposing himself to the bullets and radioed for assistance as a shot struck his vehicle. The 45-minute battle seemed to continue for a lifetime. When it finally stopped, McLemore and Mulloney helped load wounded ATF agents into their truck. An agent hit in the leg took the back seat. One with a shoulder wound sat in front. A third, hit in the chest, was draped across the hood, held in place by colleagues as the truck drove slowly from the rural battlefield.

The heaviest gunfire ended after forty-five minutes, but it was two hours before Witherspoon and Masferrer noticed agents retreating from the compound. They plodded slowly down the country road. One had been hit in the leg, blood splattered across the back of his pants. A female agent held a wounded hand. Stunned officers embraced each other. Some wept.

"We did a good job," one agent said.

"It was like a war," said another.

A Holy War.

12

THE WORLD MEETS KORESH

Erline Clark had warned her grandson six years before. Vernon Howell was charged with attempting to kill George Roden, but when a Waco jury couldn't reach a verdict, the charges against him were dismissed. Vernon, his followers, his mother and grandmother, were relieved he wasn't going to prison. But Erline was angry, too.

"Vernon, don't you ever do anything like that again," she told him at the courthouse. Vernon did not reply.

Now, late on February 28, 1993, Erline was heartbroken and frightened. She didn't want Vernon or anyone else to die. But she was angry now, too. She never spanked her children, never swatted Vernon during those years she raised him as one of her own. But now, if she could get her hands on him, she would give him a good wallop.

It was 11:30 p.m. when the phone rang in her wood-frame house in the East Texas countryside where Erline lived alone. The late-night caller was no longer her grandson, Vernon. Now he was an international celebrity named David Koresh, the cult leader in the middle of that awful shootout in Waco earlier that day. She and Vernon's mother, Bonnie Haldeman, watched that day's news reports and wept for hours. When he called, his high-pitched voice sounded weak and raspy.

"Well grandma, I've been shot," Vernon said. "I wanted to tell you I love you and I want to tell you goodbye."

"Where were you shot?" Erline asked in a shaking voice.

"In the stomach and the hand," he said.

"Vernon, I heard a child has been shot," Erline said. "Is that true?"

"Yeah," Vernon said.

"Whose was it?" she asked.

"It was one of mine," Vernon said.

"Was it a boy or a girl?"

"It was a girl. It was a twin."

Until then, Erline didn't know Vernon had twins. She knew Vernon had two children, not twins, with his wife Rachel.

Erline learned many things that day, things that contributed to her pain. Vernon—or David, or whoever he was now—told her that night he really had eight wives and thirteen children. He spoke of a biblical message he said he was trying to spread throughout the world.

From the time he was a little boy, Erline knew Vernon was religious. That didn't change when he grew up. Once she told Vernon that he lived his life looking backward because of his preoccupation with the Old Testament. But Erline never knew about a special message.

"I tried to tell you, Grandma, but you would never listen," Vernon said that night. "Well Grandma, it's not so bad to die. I'll be resurrected when Jesus comes back. Don't worry Grandma. It will be all right."

Then he hung up, leaving his weeping grandmother alone with her thoughts. Erline reached back through years of memories for some clue, some warning it would turn out this way. It all seemed too odd. Before that day, she never heard anyone refer to Vernon as a prophet. Now people called him a false prophet and Vernon had admitted to doing those things Erline knew were wrong.

Vernon always had big plans. From the time he was twenty he would travel back and forth to California with his guitar, trying to make a name for himself. Later, when Erline went to Mount Carmel for a lunch and a Bible study, Vernon seemed the one in charge.

But he still seemed the nice, easygoing boy she had helped to raise. And he seemed a good leader at Mount Carmel. George Roden had just left Mount Carmel when Erline first visited, and the place was a mess. The cluster of homes looked more like a garbage dump. But Erline heard Vernon was restoring Mount Carmel. He was adding on to the buildings and clearing out the junk. One time, Vernon, Rachel and the kids came to visit, offering to take Erline to dinner. Erline declined, saying it was too late, but it was so nice to see them. They seemed a happy family.

Several years before, Bonnie had even gone to live with her son. When she and Roy were having marital troubles, Bonnie stayed with Vernon and his people in Palestine. She sometimes accompanied him on his frequent travels to California and Hawaii. But she spent most of her time with Vernon at Mount Carmel. She was happy there. The women did things together and took turns cooking. Some had jobs outside the compound. Others cared for the children. Bonnie enjoyed Vernon's Bible studies and long walks in the country.

When Bonnie and Roy reconciled, the couple lived at Mount Carmel for a time. Vernon's stepfather hauled the group's water and mowed the grass with a tractor. But Roy was a strong-willed, independent person who didn't take orders easily. That quickly put him at odds with Vernon. At Mount Carmel, only one person gave the orders.

So Roy and Bonnie moved to Waco, where Bonnie went to nursing school. Later, the couple moved back to East Texas and their home just down the road from Erline's. Bonnie worked fulltime caring for an invalid, but she visited Mount Carmel regularly to see Vernon and her grandchildren. She never mentioned any problems with Vernon or Mount Carmel to Erline. She never said anything about guns.

It was about 2:00 in the afternoon when Bonnie called, frantic and crying.

"Mom, will you come down here? They're having a shooting at Mount Carmel! There's a shooting out there!" she cried.

"What? People are shooting at them?" Erline said.

"Yes," Bonnie said, weeping. "It's happening on TV!"

Erline rushed in her car to her daughter's place. The television was on when she arrived. Erline saw bullets hitting the side of the houses, splintering the brown walls. The scene stunned her. Erline had no idea this might happen. Bonnie wept. She was unable to work that day.

Then Bonnie's anguish was compounded. Erline needed to return home for a few minutes. While she was gone, Bonnie's dogs escaped and needed to be penned back up. The phone rang while Bonnie was outside. The caller left a brief message on her telephone answering machine.

"Hello Mama," the voice on the answering machine said. "It's your boy. They shot me and I'm dying, all right? But I'll be back real soon. See y'all in the skies. Bye."

When the smoke at Mount Carmel cleared, David Koresh's call list included more than just relatives. Armored vehicles and hundreds of law enforcement officers rushed to the scene as news of the shootout spread. Satellite trucks and reporters from around the world camped out in the chilling drizzle, creating a small city on the prairie previously shrouded in silence. Black cows grazed in the distance. As the world closed in around him, Koresh began talking. He kept talking. He seized the chance for a worldwide pulpit.

He was interviewed live by CNN in the early evening, telling the network he had been wounded and a two-year-old daughter had been killed.

"They fired on us first," Koresh said. "There are a lot of children here. I've had a lot of babies these past two years. It's true that I do have a lot of children and I do have a lot of wives."

Earlier, a Dallas radio station agreed to broadcast his statement in return for the release of children from the compound. Koresh also granted a lengthy telephone interview to a newspaper reporter in Dallas.

In the morning, he had introduced himself with a barrage of bullets. The sordid images of the battle still flickered across television screens when he began to make himself known with words. It was the gospel according to David. People around the world pulled out their Bibles in an effort to decipher his strange message.

That message was old news to some—people like Bill, the former cult member in California, Rick Ross, Robyn Bunds and Marc Breault. In Manchester, England, Samuel Henry knew the message, too. Now millions of others were treated to his bizarre rantings. Koresh declared himself the Lamb of God described in Revelation, chapter eight.

"And the twenty-four elders fell down before the Lamb, each having a harp, and golden bowls full of incense, which are the prayers of the saints. And they sang a new song, saying:

"You are worthy to take the scroll,
And to open its seals;
For You were slain
And have redeemed us to God
by your blood."

Millions learned for the first time of the seven seals, biblical symbols of the catastrophes to befall the earth at the Apocalypse. Opening the first seal, for instance, would reveal a white horse that symbolized evil. A red horse appeared as the second seal opened, symbolizing war and political strife. The black horse of the third seal represented famine. A pale horse appeared with the fourth seal, symbolizing death. The fifth seal prophesied suffering. Earthquakes would come when the sixth seal was opened. The sun would darken and the moon would be like blood. Strong winds would blow. Mountains would move. The opening of the seventh seal was the moment of Armageddon, the second coming of Christ. Koresh held the key to them all, he said. Only the Lamb could open the seals.

"I am the Lamb," Koresh told a Dallas newspaper reporter.

He was many other things, too. He was above the law.

"I am the law," he said. He was a polygamist with many children. "It's true," he said. He was Jesus Christ incarnate.

"They've gone and done it again, not knowing what they do," Koresh said after the shooting, echoing Christ's words during his crucifixion 2,000 years before. "All I've ever done is to try to teach the world the seven seals...The next thing, the world will be darkened. That is the sixth seal. We're pretty close...All I do is open the book and make it plain...The only way I let people worship me is by learning these seals."

"...My father is the one who wrote the book," Koresh continued. "It says about me that He loves me more than any of you. But I love you. I came to reveal the love that can set you free."

They wouldn't listen to him in Tyler or at the job site when he was a young man. They wouldn't listen at Cuesticks in Waco. But now, David Koresh had the world's attention.

"Your world is not going to be the same," Koresh said. "When this boy is gone, my mother in heaven will be angry...I'm sorry that this had to happen. The world has got to do what it's got to do, and now I've got to do what I've got to do...I tried to keep the world from having to deal with my father. Now you're going to have to learn the hard way."

As Koresh talked and darkness came to the bloody day in Texas, three disciples attempting to return to Mount Carmel encountered ATF agents. Again, there was an exchange of gunfire. Two Davidians was arrested. Another was killed. The dead man was still clutching a pistol when authorities drove into a field with an armored vehicle to retrieve his body a few days later.

Charlie Seraphin planned a quiet day with his family. It was Sunday and the world seemed relatively calm. KRLD-AM 1080, the only Dallas radio station with an all-news format, that afternoon planned a live broadcast of a Ross Perot appearance. Otherwise it looked like an uneventful news day. Seraphin, a personable forty-three-year-old, KRLD's vice president and station manager, was free to relax.

Seraphin was tired. He and his wife, Diane, had attended a charity ball the night before and had stayed out late. He was up early that Sunday morning, rousing five children for church. Later in the day, the family attended a lawn and garden show in Arlington. His relaxation was soon cut short.

It turned out David Koresh was a KRLD listener. Soon the station, like the Waco newspaper and television crew, would be sucked into the whirlpool surrounding the cult leader. By midafternoon, Koresh offered this deal: If KRLD would broadcast his written statements, he would release some of the children still inside.

Seraphin conferred by telephone with KRLD news director Rick Ericson in Waco. Koresh's request went against the station manager's journalistic instincts. In the past, he had encountered similar kooks who threatened to blow up buildings if they weren't granted air time. Seraphin didn't flinch then. But this was different.

The station finally agreed to broadcast Koresh's rambling statement and the cult leader kept his word. In early evening, shortly after the first statement hit the air, two small figures stepped from the compound into the night. They were whisked away by officers, and driven past the throng of cameras and lights at the media compound that had sprouted a few miles away. Two more children came out when the statement was rebroadcast a few hours later. Seraphin had made the right decision, it appeared. But another dilemma soon presented itself.

Seraphin arrived at the station about 6:00 p.m. and was still there after midnight when the call came in on the KRLD 800 number. Earlier, someone claiming to be from the compound called to complain the station was mispronouncing Koresh's name. Seraphin was dubious. This latest call, he was sure, was some kind of fraternity prank.

"Who's this?" Seraphin asked.

The caller, a man, spoke in a Midwestern accent.

"Steve Schneider," he said. "I'm inside what you all call the compound."

Schneider spoke calmly and casually, like he and Seraphin were old buddies just catching up with each other.

"Pretty exciting day, huh," the station manager said, playing along.

The two chatted briefly. Then the conversation took a dramatic turn.

"I'm going to turn you over to David Koresh," Schneider said.

Another man got on the line. Within seconds, Seraphin recognized the voice from the CNN interview earlier in the day. The exhausted radio executive's adrenalin began pumping again.

"Are we on the air?" Koresh asked.

"No, we're just going to talk," Seraphin said.

"I want to go on the air," Koresh insisted.

He kept referring to himself as the Lamb of God. Seraphin couldn't get a word in as Koresh launched into a four-minute biblical monologue. He spoke too fast for Seraphin to keep up, spoke without breaking for air, it seemed, making a mockery of Seraphin's attempt to conduct an interview.

"I would ask him a question, and he would quote me Psalms," Seraphin said later. "I would ask another question and he would quote me Revelation. I would ask another question and he would quote me Job."

Seraphin said the cult leader's attitude toward federal authorities also became quickly apparent:

"We're here. You're there. We've got guns. You've got guns. I'm the Lamb of God. It's your move," Seraphin said, quoting Koresh. "I knew early on that this guy was going to be tough."

In his business, crazy callers were part of the job. But no one in a quarter-century of radio compared to the one he had on the line now. Seraphin and Koresh talked off the air for nearly forty minutes, the station manager worrying the line he tied up might be put to better use by federal negotiators. He feared his long conversation might ultimately cost lives.

"I felt it was really a dangerous situation," he said later. "I sort of knew that one slip-up and it could get bad. He had to be scared. He had a lot of adrenalin going. I really felt out on the edge. There were no branches to grab onto, nothing to keep from going down the river and over the falls."

With Koresh on the line, Seraphin managed to contact ATF agent Jim Cavanaugh, the prime negotiator to that point. Instead of being rebuked, Seraphin felt that Cavanaugh was asking for his help, almost as if the agent was saying, "I can't reach this guy. See what you can do."

"You can put him on the air," Cavanaugh said. "Just let him say his thing on the air and tell him I'm trying to get in touch with him. See if you can steer him back toward me."

By then, Seraphin knew a thoughtful, on-air exchange was out of the question. Koresh's incessant, incoherent rambling pretty much precluded that. But with Koresh on the air, millions of KRLD listeners could get a sense of his twisted mental state, a firsthand glimpse at the man holding the world's attention. Seraphin also felt compassion for Koresh, who increasingly moaned with pain as their long conversation wore on. It was one of the oddest conversations in the history of the medium: radio newsman counseling a cult leader.

At one point, Koresh's biblical ranting stopped. His voice weakened.

"I've been shot. I'm bleeding bad," Koresh told Seraphin as a baby cried in the background. "I'm going home. I'm going back to my father."

Seraphin's hair stood on end. He gently urged Koresh to come out and receive medical attention for his wounds.

"I could see him putting a gun in his mouth and pulling the trigger on the air," Seraphin said later. "I said to myself, 'Not on my air time you're not.' I knew I was in real deep. I just wanted to extract myself in a gentle sort of way. I kept telling him that he should come out, that he shouldn't allow himself to die, that a lot of people wanted to hear his message."

Koresh regained his strength. He rambled on for another few minutes, then hung up, leaving Seraphin emotionally drained. The next day, FBI agents took over negotiations from the ATF and pulled the publicity plug on the Branch Davidian leader. If Koresh was going to be talking to anybody, it would be to them.

Even though he remained under guard at an East Texas mental institution, George Roden didn't seem so crazy anymore. Guards brought Roden out to meet reporters that Monday. He was a huge, middle-aged man with dark-rimmed glasses and a bushy gray beard. Roden was sent there four years earlier after a jury found him not guilty by reason of insanity in the killing of another man. That man, now dead, had been sent by the cult to kill him, Roden insisted. Now maybe people would listen.

"Nobody believed what I told them about this man, not even the doctors here," Roden said a day after Mount Carmel exploded. "But I guess everybody is beginning to see I was right about him."

He tried to warn authorities long before Koresh, then known as Howell, attacked him at Mount Carmel in 1987, Roden said. Koresh didn't even belong to the sect once led by his father and mother.

"He's a rock guitarist," Roden said. "He's a meat eater and drinks beer. All true believers are strict vegetarians...He's a chameleon. He's got one side one time and one side another. He changes colors. He recognizes he has to be gentle to people to get their attention, but once he gets his hooks into them, then he puts the screws to them."

By then, there were many other people not confined to mental institutions saying the same thing.

Attorney Wayne Martin didn't show for a scheduled appearance in a Waco court that Monday morning, March 1, but no one asked why. The forty-two-year-old lawyer was scheduled to represent a teenager in a juvenile delinquency case. Instead, Martin was under siege with David Koresh and the rest of the Branch Davidians at Mount Carmel.

To Waco judges and lawyers who knew him, Martin's predicament made the bloody event even more inexplicable. Martin was a 1977 graduate of Harvard Law School, a quiet, idealistic man who always handled his cases with the utmost skill and professionalism. His reputation among his peers was in stark contrast to the more sinister portrayals of the Davidians in the media.

"He's always been an aboveboard, moral kind of guy," State Judge Bill Logue said. "I feel badly about this. Things are a little inconsistent, aren't they? Some people get involved in matters...Bless his heart."

Martin and Logue, a Waco judge for thirty years who had presided over litigation involving the Davidians decades earlier, often discussed the group's local history, but never its theology.

"First I'm worried about the loss of life," Judge Logue said that Monday. "But beyond that, there are some people we know out there. I'm concerned because I know Mr. Martin."

Waco lawyer Gary Coker knew Martin, too. In fact, he was well acquainted with many of the Davidians, having represented Vernon Howell in 1987 when Howell and his followers were accused of attempting to kill George Roden.

"I bet they get this worked out, because of that lawyer. He's just not a radical," Coker said that Monday afternoon. "They're not violent people. They're vegetarians."

Coker had just spoken with Martin by telephone. Earlier in the day, the Hollywood production company of a well-known actor had called Coker in Waco, expressing an interest in making a television movie about the real-life drama.

"They asked me, if I had a chance to talk to Vernon, would I pass that along," Coker said. "Before the corpse was even cold, they wanted to get the movie rights."

But Coker figured television stardom might induce Koresh and the others to surrender. He dialed a Mount Carmel telephone number that he knew Martin used for business. Martin was at the other end of the line.

"Is Vernon there?" Coker asked.

"Yeah, he's right over there," Martin replied.

"Tell him, 'Hi,' from me and pass this word along," Coker said.

Martin assured his colleague that he was in good health. Then he hung up.

The woman told Erline Clark her name was Gloria. Gloria was calling from Hollywood, but said a man was waiting in Tyler to take Erline to dinner. It was a day or two after the shootout.

"That won't be necessary," Erline said. "I'm not much for eating out."

"You could eat in then," Gloria said.

Gloria was after a movie deal. Her company had called Bonnie's house and talked to Roy, but Bonnie was at work. So Gloria called Erline, offering dinner and a lot more. Gloria's company would pay Erline and Bonnie $75,000 each for the rights to their story.

"There was so much competition, they started calling right away," Erline said later. "They were afraid they were going to miss out."

Bonnie discussed it with her mother the next day. She didn't think accepting money for what happened at Mount

Carmel was a good idea, especially since it wasn't even over yet.

"I told her she might as well do it," Erline said. "Somebody is going to be making money off of it. The FBI is going to make their money. She might as well, too. She could use the money for the children there, or maybe to hire lawyers for some of them."

Bonnie eventually agreed. True, people at Mount Carmel would need money. Koresh's mother ended up signing for $75,000 with another production company that said Erline's contributions weren't needed.

"That was okay," the grandmother said a few days later. "I don't need the money. I don't want it for anything."

By Tuesday, March 2, scriptwriters prepared for a peaceful resolution. David Koresh said he had just one more request. Koresh had prepared a taped message and wanted it broadcast nationally on a Christian radio network and on KRLD. As soon as the broadcast was completed, Koresh and his followers would lay down their weapons and come marching out.

Contacted by federal authorities, Seraphin agreed to go along one more time.

"Boy, I hope this works," he thought at the time. But he had his doubts.

Koresh sent the tape out with one of the eighteen children released. Later that morning, an FBI agent in Waco told KRLD news director Rick Ericson to be ready. Shortly after noon, the agent handed over the tape to Ericson who prepared it for the air. Koresh's sermon was fifty-eight minutes long, Ericson was told. At 1:30 p.m., the cult leader took to the airwaves for what authorities hoped would be the last time.

"I, David Koresh, agree upon the broadcast of this tape to come out peacefully with all the people immediately," Koresh began. "My name is David Koresh. I'm speaking to you from the Mount Carmel center. The first thing I would like to introduce in our subject is the reason for the revelation of Jesus Christ. The Book of Revelation doesn't clearly state what John has written in Scripture, nothing other than the revelation of Jesus Christ, which God gave to him, to show that his servant David must shortly come to pass...In the first chapter it says, 'Blessed is the man, blessed is he that readeth and who hear the words of the prophecy, and those that keep the things that are written therein, for the time is at hand.'"[5]

It would later be described as a typical Koresh sermon, a rambling missive laced with arcane biblical references about Revelation and Armageddon. But the message of the raspy-voiced cult leader had moderated since his introduction to the world two days before. There was no mention of his many wives or children, no mention of himself as the son of God. Instead, Koresh spoke as one concerned about his followers and the rest of the world.

"I'm sure you're all aware of how I'm involved in a very serious thing right now, and I'm sure that a lot of you realize that I should possibly be scared, and hurt," Koresh said. "There's women, children and men involved in our situation here at Mount Carmel. But I am really concerned about the lives of my brethren here, and also would

---

[5]The text of Koresh's fifty-eight minute sermon is reprinted in Appendix A.

be even greater concerned about the lives of all those in this world."

Koresh even injected mild humor at times. He referred to the ancient practice of sacrificing lambs, turtle doves and red heifers.

"It was a very sophisticated and very holistic type of worship," he said. "Of course, God had to give these people their own country and had to give them...things to be able to perform the rituals and...It would definitely keep a man on guard not to sin too much, because otherwise he could lose his livestock pretty quick in the end."

Yet his implication was clear. Authorities had violated the anointed one, the one true holder of the sacred mysteries. He had long taught his followers that those who knew him but turned their back would burn in the Lake of Fire. The language of his radio sermon was far less dramatic, but his message seemed the same.

"We see in Psalm 45 the Lamb only has to destroy his enemies. And who are his enemies? Those who do not believe the word of God. Now if a person never had the chance to know, you gotta forgive 'em because they know not what they do. But should anybody dare try to go against the word of God and try to hurt Christ because they know not and refuse to know, well then we're talking something serious," Koresh said.

Citing a passage from Revelation, Koresh said mortals who tamper with apocalyptic prophecy would be punished by God.

"Now that's spiritual," Koresh said. "That means the book is not to be messed with or pranked with by anybody who would dare think that they can make speculation or private opinions or unlock the mystery of the seven seals and what they contain."

Those biblical proscriptions against false prophets clearly did not apply to him.

"We have made an agreement with ATF agents that they would allow me to have national coverage of this tape that I might give to the world all of the information that I have tried so hard to share with people—that if I would do this that all the people here at the facility, compound here, which y'all call it, will give ourselves over to the world, give ourselves out to you. This is what I promised. This is what we're going to keep....We're all brethren. But let's get into unity with one God, one truth, one Lamb, one spirit, and let's receive the reward of righteousness. Thank you very much. God Bless."

Texas clergy members promptly panned the message. Some said they pitied Koresh.

"I felt a poignancy in listening to him," said Reverend Eugene Price, a Protestant minister in Forth Worth. "He talked sincerely, earnestly. But he is a poor, poor misdirected man."

Barry Bailey, a United Methodist pastor, said the leader "believes that some big God out there is going to destroy the world. True believers are going to be saved, while others are going to be destroyed by fire."

If that was true, "that makes God a vicious God who is not acting any worse than poor Vernon Howell," Bailey said.

To Protestant minister J. Don George, Koresh's theology was blatantly self-serving.

"Jesus Christ laid down his life for his followers," George said. "This man has laid down others' lives for propagation of his own propaganda. This is just another tragic example of a false Christ."

Federal authorities weren't concerned about the quality of Koresh's preaching. They kept their part of the deal. Now it was time for the cult leader to make good on his. Buses roared through the country toward the compound, ready to whisk Koresh's followers away from Mount Carmel after they surrendered.

"We're coming out the door momentarily," Koresh told federal negotiators after his statement was finished.

An hour passed. At KRLD, Charlie Seraphin's eyes were red and swollen from lack of sleep.

"I feel like the father of a baby that's halfway in and halfway out," he said. "I just want to grab these people and pull them out and get this thing over with."

Two hours passed. Then three. Koresh and the Davidians were not moving any time soon. Late in the day, a dejected Seraphin was interviewed by one of his own reporters. What should people do now? the station manager was asked.

Seraphin struggled with his emotions, coming close to breaking down on the air.

"Close your eyes and say a prayer," Seraphin replied.

The next day, federal agents explained the delay. God had told David Koresh to wait.

13

WAITING FOR THE PROPHET

By the Saturday afternoon of March 20, 1993, the twenty-first day of the stand-off at Mount Carmel, Woodie Lambert had his instructions down pat. Dozens of carloads, truckloads, busloads of people arrived each day, parking at the crest of the hill on the country road outside Waco. They borrowed Woodie's old field glasses and squinted off into the rolling farmland. Woodie handed the glasses from one visitor to the next, then stood by to assist.

"Look straight ahead at the tall tree," Woodie instructed the visitors, one after another. "Look to your left and you'll see a tank. If you've gone too far, you'll see a satellite dish. That's a man's house. Go back to the right until you see the flag. That's their flag, the Mount Carmel flag."

Woodie, a seventy-four-year-old decked out in wire-rimmed glasses and an old denim jacket, quit counting the day before. By then, he tallied 5,000 people who had looked through his glasses at the most famous site in Texas. The visitors came from New York and California, Japan and Germany. On a clear day, using Woodie's binoculars, they were granted a distant glimpse of the beige buildings sitting two miles away. They saw the Davidian flag with its Star of David flapping in the breeze, even the government's Bradley armored vehicles as they rumbled about the compound. They saw a bit of history through Woodie's glasses.

Woodie, a retired Air Force man, lived across the road for years. He remembered when Mount Carmel was just a bunch of shacks, and he was as stunned as anyone when shooting broke out that Sunday morning. The next day he hiked to the top of the hill, curious, and stayed there all day. Everyone wanted a peek through Woodie's glasses and he was glad to oblige, free of charge, all day long.

"Everything is free," Woodie said, still there that Saturday nearly three weeks later. "I haven't made a dime. Why would I want to charge a kid for looking through these field glasses so these parents can explain to them what this means?"

Yet as the stand-off continued, on Woodie's hill and elsewhere, plenty of others were cashing in.

Days wore on. The seasons changed. Easter came and went and David Koresh remained in Mount Carmel, surrounded by hundreds of federal officers. Koresh continued to feed Leno and Letterman with a steady supply of new material. Crews from network news magazines showed up one after another, scrounging for fresh angles. One film crew began shooting a television movie, using buildings in Oklahoma as substitutes for the real Mount Carmel.

In Waco, hope ebbed and flowed from day to day that Koresh would surrender, if not soon, then at least peacefully. The surreal drama became darkly comic. Frustrated FBI negotiators tried to crack the capricious cult leader with psychological warfare—nightly blasts of Andy Williams ballads, a Nancy Sinatra tune, military marching music, Christmas carols, chants from the Dalai Lama. If things really got tough, it was suggested they try "Achy Breaky Heart" by Billy Ray Cyrus. The negotiators endured his arcane babble, and publicly labeled Koresh a coward who hid behind the Mount Carmel children. Or sometimes they tried kindness, delivering milk to the compound, and copies of national magazines that featured Koresh on the cover.

The effect was the same. Koresh and his top lieutenant, Steve Schneider, dangled hope from Mount Carmel. On some days, they let a trickle of children and adult Koresh followers depart. But then, in a fit of righteous pique, Koresh would again slam the door on negotiations. And the days of the stand-off droned on.

Telephones were installed at what became known as Satellite City, the media compound. Porta-potties were brought out, too. Reporters ate about twelve dozen Salvation Army donuts a day, several dozen sandwiches, bowls of chili, stew, cups of coffee and hot chocolate. The first two Salvation Army canteen trucks broke down so a third was brought out. Reporters practiced golf swings and had their hair cut on the roadside while the vigil continued. They held an Easter egg hunt and a dance. The crew from CNN made itself at home in style, installing green Astroturf over the mud, erecting a picket fence, flowers, a mailbox, setting up lawnchairs next to statuettes of a fat farm couple bending over in their garden. Not long into the stalemate, it became apparent to everyone that they would be there for awhile.

Two miles down the country road, where Loop 340 and Farm Road 2491 intersected, Woodie's hill became a center of commerce, one of the state's hottest tourist destinations. Dallas college student Rowdy Poteet and two buddies rolled up on Day Twenty-One in a red pickup. They were headed back to Dallas after spring break on the Gulf Coast beaches of South Padre Island. Their trip would end with a Mount Carmel memory.

"We came so we could tell our grandchildren we saw it," said Rowdy, a short, stocky nineteen-year-old. "I'm buying a T-shirt. I'm still on vacation."

He had quite a selection to choose from. Several tents sprouted on Woodie's Hill, a place ankle deep in quagmire after the rain and tourist traffic. One T-shirt, for instance, billed Waco as headquarters of the "World Association of Cult Observers." Another maintained Waco was an acronym for "We Ain't Coming Out."

"My parents went to Mount Carmel and All I Got Was a Lousy AK-47," another $15 shirt said.

"Mount Carmel Erupts, The Sinful Episode," said another.

"David Koresh's 'Let's Get It On World Tour,' Australia, Great Britain, Jerusalem, New Zealand, Palestine Tx, Waco," the front of one shirt said.

"Hey Vern, Spank Me!" said yet another.

Bill Powers, a guy in a Mount Carmel baseball hat, stood beneath a green and white canvas canopy, blasting Rif Raf's "Apocalyptic Superman" at full volume on a tape player to lure customers.

"This is the original song about Koresh," Bill announced on a public address system. Powers had been there from the time the stand-off started, selling the T-shirts as fast as he could get them to the top of the hill.

Later, Powers had an announcement for the several dozen visitors who had gathered in late afternoon. He was slashing his shirt prices by $2. "Attention Kmart shoppers, a Blue-Light Special for the next ten minutes only."

A middle-aged man wanted the "Mount Carmel Erupts" model

"Do you have it in extra large?" he asked.

Woodie Lambert's business boomed, too, though the clouds limited visibility that day. The only thing to be seen through the mist was the Davidian flag. But people continued to drive up. They looked through his glasses and pointed, looked and pointed.

"I've been on Dan Rather. I've been on '48 Hours,'" Woodie said proudly. "A lady came by and patted me on the shoulder, and said she had seen me last week on TV in Germany."

A family with small children approached.

"Here, young man," Woodie said, offering the binoculars. "Do you want to look?"

The boy eagerly grabbed the field glasses and pointed them in the direction of Mount Carmel. Woodie rattled off his instructions one more time.

A routine settled in after a while. Reporters made themselves comfortable at Satellite City, monitoring Mount Carmel through high-powered television lenses. FBI negotiators wrangled with Koresh and his lieutenant Steve Schneider by telephone each day, then gathered reporters in Waco to discuss the latest developments in a story where the bizarre became commonplace. Everyone cringed when the FBI mentioned Christmas in Waco.

The Stand-off, March 8, Day Nine

In an apparent attempt to annoy his federal adversaries, Koresh blasts rock music from the compound. Negotiators report the Davidian leader is growing irritable, profane and confrontational.

"Let's get it on," he tells negotiators on one occasion.

"We are ready for war," Koresh says on another.

"Your talk is becoming in vain."

"I'm going to give you an opportunity to save yourself before you get blown away."

Koresh also brags he possesses the firepower to destroy the government's armored vehicles circling the compound.

"We can cause those (Bradley) vehicles to go forty or fifty feet in the air," Koresh says.

Federal authorities take him seriously and summon Abrams tanks. There is no word from Koresh on whether he can kill the tanks, too.

Koresh conducts a burial service for one of his followers killed in the raid. Reporters watch as three cult members remove a red bag from a van, place it in a hole fifty yards from the complex and cover it with dirt.

March 9, Day Ten

Koresh breaks off negotiations, suffering from a splitting headache. Federal agents say they have no plans to attack.

"We have sufficient firepower, if we chose, to completely neutralize this situation at any moment," said FBI agent Bob Ricks. "We do not choose to do that."

The media-savvy Davidians find a sympathizer. While on the air, conservative radio commentator Ron Engelman asks the besieged cult if they need food or medicine, instructing them to move their satellite dish or hang a sign outside to reply. The Mount Carmel satellite dish moves. Soon after Engelman's broadcast, a white banner is slung out a compound window. "God help us. We want the press."

March 11, Day Twelve

Steve Schneider promises negotiators that three Davidians will soon surrender, the first hopeful sign in days. Nothing happens. A pattern of raised hopes and broken promises begins to emerge. By now, twenty-one children and two elderly women have been released. Schneider does most of the talking with negotiators, but Koresh remains firmly in control.

Koresh's mother, Bonnie Haldeman, and high-powered Houston defense attorney Dick DeGuerin attempt to drive to Mount Carmel to speak with the cult leader, but are stopped at a checkpoint and turned back.

March 12, Day Thirteen

Two Davidians leave the compound and the FBI is again hopeful that the 105 others still inside will soon follow. One who emerges is Kathryn Schroeder, the thirty-four-year-old mother of four children released earlier. Schroeder's husband, Michael, was shot to death the first day.

Federal affidavits later describe Schroeder as the only woman allowed to live on the compound's first floor with the men. Gunfire came from her room during the February 28 shootout, the affidavit alleges. Schroeder carried an AR-15 assault rifle the morning of the shootout, and gave other women orders concerning their responsibilities and guard positions. The affidavit states that on the morning of the shooting, she was dressed in commando-type clothing.

Oliver Gyarfas from Australia is the second Davidian who leaves Mount Carmel. Both the nineteen-year-old Gyarfas and Schroeder are immediately jailed.

In a hearing in federal court a few days later, Gyarfas's lawyers claim he was asleep when the shooting started. A Texas Ranger tells a different story during the hearing, quoting Gyarfas from his conversation with an FBI negotiator a few days earlier.

"I couldn't shoot the guy because he was behind the cement. So he's lucky," Gyarfas told the FBI. "I'm ready for any action you guys give out."

Later, the handcuffed Gyarfas, a tall, thin man clad in orange jail clothes, has a message for reporters as he is transferred to jail. "I love David Koresh," he says, smiling.

March 14, Day Fifteen

Bible studies at Mount Carmel now are conducted in smaller groups because Koresh's wounds have worsened and he has more trouble addressing the larger group. The leader spends more time in his room and off his feet, FBI agents report.

The Davidians use a flashlight to send out an SOS distress signal in Morse code. A new banner hangs from the Mount Carmel watch tower. "FBI broke negotiations," the banner says. "We want Press." In a new tactic, the FBI bathes the compound with bright lights at night.

In her house in East Texas, Erline Clark studies her Bible, trying to understand what her grandson is trying to say, why he did what he did. She sits on a sofa in her living room, a woman with short gray hair and glasses.

"I'm pretty depressed," she said quietly. "I've been reading most of the day, watching the news, reading the Bible and other books trying to put things together, trying to find some reason for it. Mostly I'm studying the Old Testament. That seems to be where my grandson is coming from right now. King David and Solomon and all, that's the way they lived."

There is a picture of David Koresh as a child, wire-rimmed glasses, wavy blond hair, a blue shirt, sitting on the mantel in her living room with the photographs of several other grandchildren.

"I just keep praying that Vernon will repent," Erline says. "The Lord is always willing to forgive. I hope if he gets out of there, he will repent. I don't feel what Vernon did is right."

March 15, Day Sixteen

Frustrated FBI agents cut electricity to the compound.

"They've released two people in the course of a week, and at that rate we'll be here more than a year," FBI agent Richard Swenson says.

Swenson says agents are weary of Koresh's preaching.

"Frankly, we're not here to get converted," he says.

March 16, Day Seventeen

Authorities meet with the Davidians for the first time since the shootout. A federal negotiator and McClennan

County Sheriff Jack Harwell meet Wayne Martin and Steve Schneider sixty yards from the compound and talk for an hour, but little progress is reported. Koresh's wounds apparently prevent him from attending the meeting.

"I think his condition, as he and others have relayed it to us, is a progressive downhill condition," Swenson says. "Initially, he was in some pain, but ambulatory. Now he's basically lying down or sitting down most of the time. He said himself he can't go from room to room very easily."

March 17, Day Eighteen

The FBI says as many as thirty Davidians have expressed a desire in coming out. None do.

March 21, Day Twenty-Two

Eight cult members emerge over the two days and are taken into federal custody. The Davidians, women and elderly men for the most part, smile as they are driven past reporters. Before leaving, each reportedly receives Koresh's approval and a final Bible lesson. By Koresh's count, seventeen children, forty women and thirty-nine men remain inside, but FBI negotiators now are more publicly optimistic about a resolution than at any other time since the shootout.

In Manchester, England, Samuel Henry monitors the developments as best he can on the British Broadcasting Corporation. For days, the story of Henry's wife and five children at Mount Carmel was blasted across the front pages of the British press. Now, reporters in England have moved on to other things. Henry busies himself with his construction business. And he prays they will come home safely.

"I forgive my wife and I still love my children 100 percent," Henry says. "I trust that they will come to their senses. I have my arms open like the prodigal."

March 22, Day Twenty-Three

Federal authorities, expecting a quick end to the standoff, are disappointed again. They retaliate by blasting meditational chants of the Dalai Lama through refrigerator-size speakers in the middle of the night.

"We are not going to be jerked around," FBI Agent Bob Ricks says. "If they back away from what they promise, we will continue to exert the pressure we feel necessary...We were pretty much led to believe we had a substantial number coming out as a prelude to an end to this situation. We saw nothing."

Ricks says that the Davidians who came out wouldn't have helped Koresh in a gun battle, anyway.

"He says that the government prepared for their situation for nine months. He's been preparing for this situation since 1985," Ricks says. "He's been stockpiling weapons, food, water, whatever to enable him to withstand a lengthy situation."

Among the released Davidians are three cult members reportedly punished by Koresh for getting drunk after the shootout. For their transgression they were selected to bury the body of the Davidian casualty several days before....Koresh, however, is said to have a private liquor supply.

March 23, Day Twenty-Four

Federal authorities offer Koresh a two-hour stint on "America Talks," a show on the Christian Broadcast Network, in return for his surrender.

"This is an extraordinary opportunity for you," the FBI tells Koresh.

Koresh disagrees.

"It's not worth the paper it's written on," the cult leader says.

Negotiators respond by blasting Mount Carmel with "These Boots are Made For Walking," by Nancy Sinatra.

March 24, Day Twenty-Five

Koresh ends his discussions with negotiators, letting his released followers carry his message. The Davidians grant telephone interviews from jail and collect reporters' business cards at court hearings.

As Brad Branch leaves the federal courthouse after a detention hearing, he turns to reporters shouting questions at him. "Don't sweat it; I have your cards," Branch says. He and others claim the ATF fired first in the February raid.

In the morning, Branch chats live from the McClennan County Jail with Bryant Gumbel on NBC's "Today" show.

"We can come and go as we want," Branch says. "I don't know why they're saying all that. I don't know why they're calling it a cult...why they're calling it a compound. We read the Bible."

The reason Koresh didn't come out, Branch tells Gumbel, was that "God told him to wait."

Gumbel then asks what it would take for Koresh to surrender.

"He wants to put on a challenge to all the churches and all the heads," Branch replies referring to competition to interpret the seven seals. "The Pope, Billy Graham, Pat Robertson. If they want a peaceful resolution, that's a good way. That's my idea."

Livingston Fagan, another of the released Davidians, is asked when he thought the stand-off would end. "It's right on schedule," Fagan says. "God's schedule."

March 25, Day Twenty-Six

The Mount Carmel population grows when a religous fanatic slips past hundreds of federal agents. Louis Anthony Alaniz, twenty-four, an outcast member of the Assembly of God church, manages to reach the compound, peer through its windows and knock on the front door about 7:00 p.m. Agents spot him walking toward the compound, but decide to let him continue without a confrontation.

The Davidians are shocked by the new arrival, at first suspecting he is another undercover agent, but eventually they take him in.

"Obviously, it's easier to control people coming out of the compound than going in," an embarrassed Ricks says. Alaniz apparently believed that the compound "was the center of action that involved perhaps biblical prophecies and he wanted to be a participant in that."

March 26, Day Twenty-Seven

Another man, this one named Jesse Amen, sneaks into Mount Carmel. No one comes out.

March 27, Day Twenty-Eight

The tone of FBI agents turns more hostile and ominous.

"We believe that for him, it would be a marvelous achievement if he can get a substantial number of his people killed," Ricks says. "We believe though, that in the end, he is going to protect himself. He looks for the lonely, the lost, the unloved, the innocent. These are the people he's brought into his fold who will do anything that he orders them to do."

Negotiators say they will not be able to accomplish one task.

"We are not required to prove that David is not the Christ," Ricks said. "I don't believe that there's anybody out there in the world who can prove to his satisfaction that he's not the Christ."

March 29, Day Thirty

Television cameras capture Koresh's attorney, Dick DeGuerin, arriving at Mount Carmel on a motorcycle. DeGuerin walks to the front door about 4:00 p.m. and is met by someone inside, who brings out a chair for the visitor. DeGuerin sits and talks with someone through a cracked door. The two-hour conversation ends with DeGuerin shaking hands with someone inside. A white dog accompanies him as he walks away.

In response to negotiator's concerns for the children inside, the cult sends out a videotape showing two adults and sixteen of the youngsters. The children all profess their love for David Koresh. Some say they believe that God will destroy his enemies.

"They feel okay and everything is all right. They love David. And they don't want to come out," Ricks says.

Zachary Gordon, of Waco, is arrested as he heads through the bushes and woods toward Mount Carmel, a lighted cigarette in one hand and a longneck bottle of beer in the other.

March 30, Day Thirty-One

DeGuerin and Koresh continue their meetings, which now take place inside Mount Carmel. An end to the stand-off seems imminent.

"I'm very hopeful that it's going to end peacefully," the handsome, sandy-haired attorney tells reporters later. "I think it went very well. We made a lot of progress. I hope it doesn't take too long. As far as feeling fear, no. I am not afraid of my client or any of the people in there."

March 31, Day Thirty-Two

DeGuerin says it might be tougher to coax Koresh out than it appeared at first.

"I have a more realistic idea of the time and effort this is going to take," the lawyer says.

Federal negotiators temporarily halt their own discussion with Koresh to give DeGuerin's efforts a chance.

"It would appear that perhaps he's going through some of the same things we're going through," Ricks says.

April 4, Day Thirty-Six

Jesse Amen is embraced by a Davidian, then leaves the compound. DeGuerin and Steve Schneider's attorney, Jack Zimmerman, leave Waco, saying nothing at Mount

Carmel will change until after the cult celebrates Passover, which is expected to last seven or eight days.

"It's pretty clear that were we not on the eve of Passover, they would be out by now," Zimmerman says.

FBI negotiators agree that significant developments might be imminent.

"Many of his followers who have come out and those around the world have said that David has said this is the last Passover they will celebrate together," Ricks says.

April 7, Day Thirty-Nine

The *New York Times* reports that DeGuerin has finalized plans to auction Koresh's book and movie rights. New York lawyers faxed letters to publishers soliciting bids for the right to Koresh's story.

The letter says "because of the timeliness and importance of the story," the rights would be auctioned quickly for no less than $2 million. The Koresh story would include "events which led him and his followers to the situation they now find themselves in."

FBI negotiators say the book deal is a good sign.

"It's a hopeful situation in that he (Koresh) is looking to the future," Ricks says.

April 9, Day Forty-One

The Davidians deliver a four-page letter to federal agents that they say is from God. The letter warns of imminent disaster for those who oppose Him and His flock.

Steve Schneider sets the letter on the ground south of the compound, where it is retrieved by agents in a Bradley armored vehicle. The letter addressed to "friends," is written in the first person and refers to Koresh as "my servant."

FBI agents are skeptical.

"Now we have not had confirmation from those inside that this is a letter from God...But if it is a mesage from God, then we have to know what the heck the message is," Ricks says. Agents and religious experts attempt to decipher the letter's meaning.

"Do you want me to pull back the heavens and show you my anger?" the letter from God says. "Do not fear the fear of man—fear Me for I have you in my snare....

"I am your God and you will bow under my feet...Look and see you fools you will not proceed much further," it continues. "I offer you my wisdom. I offer to you my sealed secrets. How dare you turn away my invitations of mercy."

The letter, signed Jahweh Koresh, also threatens to destroy the dam at nearby Lake Waco. The FBI wonders whether the letter is the sign from God Koresh is waiting for.

"When you have a letter from God, to me that's a pretty big event," Ricks says. "However, according to Mr. Schneider, they apparently are waiting for a more direct message from God...(Koresh) is looking for certain natural disasters...certain cataclysmic events to take place—either fire or earthquake or an event of that nature."

Reporters hold an Easter egg hunt and an outdoor social called A Dance in a Ditch.

April 10, Day Forty-Two

The FBI receives another letter from God. "This is a warning," God writes. "Please don't harm my Lamb."

April 14, Day Forty-Six

Koresh authors his own letter to Dick DeGuerin, saying he will surrender "and stand before man and answer any and all questions regarding my activities," but only when he finishes his written explanation of the seven seals.

"As far as our progress is concerned, here's where we stand," Koresh wrote. "I've related two messages from God to the FBI, one of which concerns the present danger to the people here in Waco.

"I was shown a fault line running throughout the Lake Waco area. Many people here in Waco know we are a good people and yet they have shown the same resentful spirit of indifference to our warnings of love.

"I'm presently being permitted to document in structured form the decoded messages of the seven seals. Upon completion of this task, I will be freed of my waiting period. I hope to finish this as soon as possible and stand before man and answer any and all questions regarding my activities.

"This written revelation of the seven seals will not be sold, but it is to be available to all who know the truth.

"The four angels of Revelation, chapter seven, are here now, ready to punish foolish mankind, but the writing of these seals will cause the winds of God's wrath to be held back a little longer. I've been praying so long for this opportunity to put the seals in written form.

"Speaking the truth seems to have very little effect on man.

"I was shown that as soon as I am given over to the hands of man, I will be made a spectacle of and people will not be concerned about the truth of God, but just the bizzarity [sic] of me in the flesh.

"I want the people of this generation to be saved. I'm working night and day to complete my final work of writing out these seals. I thank my Father. He has finally granted me this chance to do this.

"It will bring new light and hope to many and they won't have to deal with me, the person.

"The earthquake in Waco is something not to be taken lightly. It will probably be the thing needed to shake some sense into people.

"Remember, the warning came first and I fear that the FBI is going to suppress this information. It may be left up to you (DeGuerin). I will demand that the first manuscript of the seals be given to you.

"Many scholars and religious leaders will wish to have copies for review. I will keep a copy with me.

"As soon as I can see that people like (biblical scholars) Jim Tabor and Phil Arnold have a copy, I will come out and then you can do your thing with this beast.

"I hope to keep in touch with you through letters. We are standing on the threshold of great events. The seven seals in written form are the most sacred information ever."

14

APOCALYPSE

The weekend in Waco was among the quietest of the stand-off. David Koresh, it was assumed, was busy writing inside Mount Carmel. When FBI agents canceled the Sunday news briefing, few reporters complained. By all appearances, frustrated federal negotiators planned to wait it out like everyone else, settling in for the several weeks it would take for the cult leader to finish his interpretation of the seven seals of Revelation.

He would surrender then, Koresh promised. That Sunday, agents even sent in a typewriter ribbon to facilitate the production of Koresh's much-anticipated manuscript. News of the stand-off, meanwhile, had moved from the front to the inside pages of newspapers across the nation. The ongoing saga had vanished from the morning talk shows and most nights from the evening news. The population of Satellite City shrunk noticeably.

But placid appearances in Waco deceived. In Washington, D.C., the siege at Mount Carmel dominated discussions at the highest levels of American government.

The siege had begun before Attorney General Janet Reno took office in March, and now the decision about how to end it would be among the toughest she would ever be called on to make. The plan the FBI placed on her desk on Monday, April 12, was a dramatic escalation in the agency's attempts to force Koresh's hand. Agents proposed flushing him and his followers out with a skin-stinging tear gas, with nonlethal agony almost impossible to bear for long. Koresh would have no choice. He and the Davidians would have to surrender.

Reno agonized over the decision for days. Wait it out or move now? How would Koresh respond to the provocation? How would the gas affect the children? Would the assault prompt mass suicide?

No doubt the escalation would pose heightened risk. But by then it had become apparent the more conservative course, further negotiation, was pointless. Negotiators claimed they had heard firsthand the futility of their efforts. Concealed amid the magazines, batteries, milk, and videotapes the FBI sent in to Koresh and his followers were fingernail-sized electronic bugs that allowed them to eavesdrop on the cult leader, at least for brief periods, they said. Agents claimed they heard a belligerent sociopath spoiling for a fight. Koresh was growing more irritable, they said. Interpreting the seven seals was just another sham, and his discussions with attorneys that had seemed so hopeful were just another stalling tactic. Agents said Koresh and his followers railed against the negotiators, and complained about how they were unfairly maligned at the daily FBI briefings.

To his lawyer, Dick DeGuerin, Koresh was a misunderstood prophet who had promised to surrender. But to the agents, Koresh was, in the words of one FBI statement, "a determined, hardened adversary who has no intention of delivering himself or his followers into the hands of his adversaries."

Negotiators increasingly became concerned about the lengths to which he might go to initiate a battle with the Babylonians. FBI agent Bob Ricks said he feared Koresh would order the women to run from the compound with babies in their arms, firing at the agents in an attempt to provoke an attack.

"He was making statements to the effect that either he could die in jail or he could die 'in here,'" Ricks told Dallas newspaper reporter Lee Hancock. "He preferred to die 'in here.'"

Other factors dictated a more aggressive approach. The FBI's hostage rescue team, poised since the stand-off began, would soon begin to tire, Reno was told. Alternatives, such as building a wall around Mount Carmel, were rejected because of the risk from Koresh's arsenal to construction workers. Conditions inside the compound, rotting bodies and accumulating human waste, were increasingly inhumane.

And the most chilling scenario, mass suicide, didn't seem a significant threat with this leader. After weeks of study, the FBI's Behavioral Science Unit drafted a profile of Koresh that virtually precluded self-destruction. Agents in Waco grilled each adult who left the compound. They were told Koresh had no suicide plan. For one thing, agents felt Koresh didn't have the guts. After his March 2 radio speech, Koresh had planned to walk outside the compound and kill himself with hand grenades on national television, authorities were told. He "chickened out," in the words of the FBI.

Koresh's favorite prophecy was a roaring gun battle

with the infidels, not suicide, Reno was told.

Risks were inescapable, but new tactics obviously were required, the agents argued. Tear gas was the next logical step, they argued. On Saturday, April 17, after a long meeting with her aides, Reno agreed. One more person needed to be convinced.

"Why now?" President Bill Clinton asked the attorney general the next day. "We have waited seven weeks. Why now?"

Reno relayed what she had been told. There was a limited amount of time that federal resources could be maintained in Waco. Negotiations weren't working. The chances of disaster were likely to increase, not decrease, as the stand-off stretched on. Finally, Reno told Clinton, there was evidence that children were being abused.

"Now, I want you to tell me once more why you believe—not why they believe—why you believe we should move now rather than wait some more," Clinton said.

"It's because of the children," Reno said.

The president said to do what she thought was right.

Agents in Waco were amazed by the Davidians' unwavering devotion to their leader. The agents planned to inject an irritant known as CS Gas into the compound, permeating every corner of Mount Carmel for days, if that's what it took. The gas burned on contact, and caused coughing and dizziness. Agents hoped the women would grab their children and rush out to spare them the pain.

"There was a friendly dispute amongst ourselves," Ricks told Hancock, the Dallas reporter. "In effect, we were kind of wagering among ourselves on when they would come out. Some people thought they'd get a taste of the gas and run out immediately...My bet in the pool was probably that zero would come out on the first day...People just didn't realize how hardened those people were in there."

The wakeup call to Steve Schneider came at 5:55 a.m. There would be no more negotiations, FBI agents told him, no more time for the seven seals. If the Davidians did not surrender, the compound would be filled with tear gas. Schneider responded by ripping the phone from the wall and tossing it out the door.

Within minutes, authorities made good on their promise. At 6:04 a.m., an armored vehicle idling in the darkness outside Mount Carmel moved in, smashing through a wall of the compound with a battering ram, leaving a gaping hole eight feet high and ten feet wide. The vehicle's special rigging injected the tear gas as an agent blared instructions over a loud speaker.

"This is not an assault," the voice in the darkness said. "Do not fire. If you fire, your fire will be returned. We are introducing non-lethal tear gas. Exit the compound now and follow instructions. You are responsible for your own actions. Come out now and you will not be harmed. You will be provided medical attention. Come out and you will be treated professionally. No one will be injured. Submit to proper authority. Do not subject yourself to any more discomfort."

The Davidians responded with a barrage of seventy to eighty gunshots. The FBI guns remained silent. But as the sun came up on the warm, windy morning, the relentless probing with 60-ton vehicles continued. Mount Carmel's brown walls crumbled like cardboard beneath the weight of armored vehicles. Powder-like tear gas wafted to every corner of the building. At one point, a white flag was seen waving through a door, but Koresh and his followers held fast through the morning, greeting each new probe with a volley of shots.

"I think you have a totally fanatical, committed group to David Koresh," Ricks told reporters at the 10:30 a.m. news conference. "It is going to have to require extreme discomfort, we believe, and a signal from Koresh, that now is the time to get out."

Each adult was equipped with a gas mask, Ricks said, but even the best models wouldn't remain effective beyond eight hours, and the federal onslaught would last much longer than that. The siege was about to end.

"We will continue to gas them and make their environment as uncomfortable as possible until they do exit the compound," Ricks said. "Is suicide a possibility? We thought that this was probably the best way to prevent that type of suicide pact from taking place...Also we thought that their instincts, the motherly instincts, would take place and that they would walk their children out of that environment. It appears that they don't care that much about their children, which is unfortunate," the agent said in response to a reporter's question.

By sunrise, news of the assault had filtered back over the airwaves, focusing renewed international attention at the place in the Texas prairie. The government's confrontation with David Koresh, speculated about for weeks, was now unfolding through high-powered television lenses that broadcast the scene live. The cult leader's world was literally crumbling around him. His air was soured by gas. The men, women and children who followed him had to be suffering. Millions waited for David Koresh's next move.

It was a few minutes after noon in Texas. Stiff winds whipped across the grasslands in gusts up to thirty miles per hour as reporters squinted in the bright sunlight toward the compound where an armored vehicle was crumbling another corner of Mount Carmel. The first wisp of smoke came from a window near where the vehicle last struck. A finger of flame appeared in the same window seconds later, and in a horrifying instant, it was obvious the siege indeed was about to end. Without a firefighting unit nearby and fanned by gusting winds, the compound's wooden walls would burn like matchsticks. Mount Carmel would be gone in minutes.

Then flames appeared at the opposite side of Mount Carmel. Jonestown was unfolding again, this time on live television. They were images forever seared into the memories of those who saw them, like the bloated bodies of Jonestown in the jungles of Guyana, or the spindly streams of smoke that traced the sky after the explosion of the space shuttle Challenger. Minutes after the first smoke, Mount Carmel was an inferno. The cameras captured one man stumbling onto the roof, finally leaping down and scrambling to safety. An FBI agent dashed from cover behind an armored vehicle to pull another disoriented Branch Davidian from the blaze. But passing minutes brought the awful certainty of mass incineration for David Koresh and eighty-five of his followers. Among them were seventeen children younger than ten years old.

"Oh my God, they are killing themselves," Rick thought as he watched the blaze from the FBI command post.

In Manchester, England, Samuel Henry held his head in horror as he watched his family obliterated on television. His wife, Zilla, and each of his five children, Diana and Paulina, Vanessa and Stephen and his favorite, Phillip, all would perish in the flames he saw devouring Mount Carmel.[6] Their Manchester friend, Sandra Hardial, was also caught in the fire and later presumed dead.

"There is no way they will escape," Henry said. "I can't understand. I can't understand how my family can be so involved in this thing. I can't understand."

After thirty minutes, fire trucks roared down the country road, but were delayed by authorities as they reached the law enforcement checkpoint near the compound. Massive explosions from the stockpiles of ammunition inside were rocking what was left of Mount Carmel.

In the end, nine cult members escaped. Three women and a man were rushed to hospitals with massive burns. Five others, pale, emaciated and dazed, were driven from the grisly scene. Among them was David Thibodeau, Koresh's drummer in the band Messiah. Thibodeau's wife and three children perished.

"He was not very religious," Thibodeau's uncle, Robert Ganem, later told the *New York Times*. "David Thibodeau would not die for David Koresh. He told his mother: 'I didn't do anything wrong. I didn't do anything illegal and I haven't done anything I'm ashamed of.'"

Some survivors insisted the FBI vehicles started the fire by knocking over gas-filled lanterns and smashing a propane tank. There was no mass suicide, they said.

"No one inside started the fire," said twenty-nine-year-old Renos Avraam, one of the survivors.

FBI agents insisted they saw fire break out almost simultaneously in three different places. They said one survivor told investigators he overheard cult members

---

[6] A list of those presumed dead is found in the Afterword

making plans to splash lantern fuel throughout the complex. Another survivor reported hearing someone say, "The fire's been lit. The fire's been lit." A cult member clad in black was spotted kneeling with his hands cupped near a second-story window, government officials reported. Flames erupted nearby.

Agents insisted Koresh ordered the inferno. Minutes earlier, they said, Koresh had assured his followers that the children would be spared, tucked safely away in the buried bus that served as their bunker. But the children apparently perished in the second-floor living quarters, in the worst of the inferno.

"It was his final lie," Ricks said.

Three miles away, on the hill overlooking Mount Carmel, a crush of people bought up commemorative mugs and T-shirts, even as the huge plume of black smoke billowed on the horizon.

"If Koresh would have stayed in there for a year, we could have retired rich," souvenir salesman Bill Powers said as the children burned.

To DeGuerin, David Koresh was a loving man of God who had promised in writing to surrender when he finished his work with the seven seals. The FBI assault was a "terrible thing to do," DeGuerin said later that night. Janet Reno has "seventeen burned babies at her feet," the Houston lawyer said.

Reverend Jesse Jackson also weighed in during the spasm of fingerpointing that followed the tragedy.

"The Branch Davidians were not a threat to society, only an embarrassment to the government and its tacticians," Jackson said. "The government lost its patience and the people lost their lives."

Janet Reno offered her resignation, a suggestion President Clinton immediately rejected. The President ordered cabinet-level inquiries by both the Treasury and Justice Departments, promising that enforcement actions would be scrutinized. But the president believed only one person was to blame for what happened at Mount Carmel.

"Koresh was dangerous, irrational, probably insane," Clinton said. "He killed those he controlled and he bears ultimate responsibility for the carnage that ensued.

"We did everything we could to avoid the loss of life," Clinton said. "They made the decision to immolate themselves, and I regret it terribly, and I feel awful about the children."

To Rick Ross, the fire was the act of a man who saw his empire crumbling. With the FBI closing in, Koresh had known he soon would no longer be the Lamb. He would just be another prisoner. Koresh feared his treatment at the hands of other prisoners because of his reputation as a child molester, reports said.

"This was the act of a sick bastard," said Ross, the Phoenix deprogrammer who had been working with the families of seven Branch Davidians when Mount Carmel burned. "This man was a monster."

Investigators began poking about the rubble. They said they found charred bodies still clutching weapons. In an interview the day after the fire, FBI agent Bob Ricks's voice broke when he talked about the children he had seen on the videotape sent out by the cult during the stand-off.

"We felt deeply for those children," said Ricks, whose face became familiar in households around the world as the siege wore on. "I looked at those tapes. I looked them in the eyes. They're etched in my memory. And there are voices that will always be there. They will never go away. David Koresh, his voice is in my head."

Andy Leamon followed his cousin's exploits from his home in San Diego, taping any television news program that even mentioned the man he knew as Vernon Howell. Each day, as the siege at Mount Carmel continued, Leamon added to the stack of newspapers growing in a corner of his apartment. He rose each morning, poured a cup of coffee and turned on the morning news to keep up with the latest developments in the odd drama surrounding Vernon and his followers in Texas.

Like many, Leamon figured the stand-off would drag on indefinitely. Relatives back home in Texas told him Vernon and his cult had stored enough food to last a year, and Leamon knew his cousin well enough to know there was no way he would surrender on his own. From the time he was a boy, Vernon was determined to have things his way, determined to get people to listen to his biblical rantings. He wasn't about to relinquish his world stage now. One way or another, Leamon thought, the man known to the world as David Koresh would put off the FBI.

Early on, Vernon broke his promise to surrender after the fifty-eight-minute radio sermon. Then, Leamon heard about Vernon's promise to come out after Passover. Now came the news from Texas that the siege would end when Vernon finished writing his interpretation of the seven seals. Fat chance, Leamon thought. Vernon would still be holed up at Christmas. He was wrong.

His wife woke him at about six that Monday morning.

"Andy, something big's happening in Waco," Debbie Leamon said. "They're poking holes in the compound. They're ramming the compound."

Leamon, a self-employed cement contractor, rose and turned on the Cable News Network, watching in amazement as armored vehicles crumbled the walls of Mount Carmel, reportedly pouring in tear gas.

Debbie and the kids left for the day, but Leamon skipped work and stayed glued to the television set. He sat alone on the sofa, transfixed by the images of the story unfolding before him. It was just after 10:00 a.m. on the West Coast when Leamon watched an armored vehicle punch another hole in a Mount Carmel wall. It would be the government's final probe.

In seconds, a puff of smoke spilled from a window.

"I wonder what that is?" Leamon thought.

Then a finger of flame appeared. Minutes later, fire broke out in another part of the compound, and Leamon knew in a sickening instant that this was the beginning of the end for Vernon Howell and his sheep.

"That looney ass Vernon has done set the place on fire," Leamon thought as he watched, stunned, a helpless feeling spreading through him. With the rest of a horrified world watching the tragedy on television, he waited for human figures to emerge from the flames. But the television screen revealed only fire and a few people stumbling from the inferno. No children were seen. As the dreadful minutes passed, Leamon's rage at his cousin grew.

In days to come, friends in California would ask Leamon why the children weren't spared.

"How in the hell am I supposed to answer that?" Leamon said. "He's a sick individual. He's a sick bastard. I don't care if any of my family members hear me say that. If any of them would tell the truth, they'd say the same damn thing."

Two days later, Leamon's anger still smoldered.

"I don't put the blame on the FBI or the ATF," he said. "Everything that's happened is totally Vernon's fault. He's to blame. He's the bastard that started it. I can't get over the kids that he killed.

"That's exactly what he wanted, to make a name for himself," Leamon said, his voice shaking with anger. "Now he'll be right with that asshole Manson and that asshole Jim Jones. I hope that's how they treat him in hell, too, as an asshole, because he sure as shit isn't going to heaven."

Steve Schneider was forty-three years old when he died. Perhaps more than any of his followers, it was Schneider who embodied the dark mystery of David Koresh and his entrancing powers.

He was born in Wisconsin to deeply devout Seventh-day Adventist parents, a kind and loving son and brother, idealistic to a flaw. He was highly intelligent. He remained deeply in love with his wife, Judy, and was heartbroken when Koresh took Judy for his harem, fathering their two-year-old child. Once, while visiting relatives alone, Steve Schneider began to weep when he saw his wedding picture.

"Isn't she beautiful?" Schneider said. "Isn't she beautiful?"

In recent years, loved ones noticed doubts. There were

times he wasn't sure about David Koresh, but then Schneider's mask of worship would snap back. Once again he ceased thinking for himself. Once again, in Schneider's mind, David Koresh had become fused with God. No one would ever be able to explain why.

Schneider's family contacted Rick Ross in Phoenix in early January, inquiring about a deprogramming. Something needed to be done to get him back from the cult leader they had come to consider evil. The problem was that while Schneider visited them alone, Judy always remained at the compound. Even after a successful deprogramming, Schneider was certain to return in an effort to take his wife from Mount Carmel, re-exposing himself to Koresh and his powers, Ross believed. Before Ross and family members could develop a plan, time ran out.

Even after the ATF assault, it was Schneider who provided FBI negotiators with a window of humanity into the mad realm of David Koresh. Schneider cared about the people there, agents were convinced. Koresh was concerned only about himself.

"If Schneider would have had the decision-making power, those people all would have come out alive," Ross said later.

As the stand-off continued, doubts began to emerge among the Davidians and Schneider listened sympathetically. Koresh prophesied that Armageddon would come and they all would die in a hail of bullets from the FBI. But day after day passed and it wasn't happening. The agents just sat outside, surrounding them, while Koresh and his followers rotted away in the dank rooms of the compound. Thirty followers hinted they wanted to leave, and Schneider tried to secure their freedom. But Koresh spoke to each individually. He was the Lamb. Those who reject the Lamb would burn in the Lake of Fire, they were told. So they stayed.

Even Schneider had doubts. Once, he and Koresh managed to call Schneider's sister in Wisconsin, Sue Johnson, using a cellular phone after agents cut off the compound phone lines.

"You know, you can walk out," Schneider's sister told him. "You can be safe."

"Do you think we can?" Schneider asked, sounding confused. "Do you really think we can walk out?"

Schneider turned to Koresh.

"Sue says we can walk out," Johnson heard her brother tell Koresh. "We can be safe."

Johnson couldn't hear Koresh's reply.

"We can't right now," Schneider told her when he returned to the line.

"Why not?" Johnson said.

"You just don't understand," Schneider answered. "It's deeper than that."

Ultimately, Steve Schneider clung to the vision of David Koresh as the Lamb. At 5:55 a.m. on April 19, he ripped the phone from the wall of Mount Carmel and hurled it out the door. A few hours later, he died with the rest, led into fiery destruction by the man who said he was the Messiah.

APPENDIX A

In what turned out to be his last verbal message to the world and with the blessings of federal law enforcement officials, Branch Davidian cult leader David Koresh rambled on for fifty-eight minutes in a statement that was broadcast over radio stations on Tuesday, March 2, 1993. This was just two days after the Bureau of Alcohol, Tobacco and Firearms had launched an unsuccessful and fatal raid against the Davidian compound at Mount Carmel near Waco, Texas. Following is a transcription of Koresh's confusing sermon as transcribed by the *Associated Press* and reprinted in the March 3, 1993 edition of the *Fort Worth Star-Telegram*. Minor edits, including deletions, have been made to the text to enhance its readability. Readers can draw their own conclusions. As it is clear from Koresh's very first statement and subsequent refusal to come out of the compound, he obviously didn't keep all of his promises.

David Koresh's Final Message

"I, David Koresh, agree upon the broadcast of this tape to come out peacefully with all the people immediately.

My name is David Koresh. I'm speaking to you from Mount Carmel center. The first thing I would like to introduce in our subject is the reason for the revelation of Jesus Christ. The Book of Revelation doesn't clearly state what John has written in Scripture, nothing other than the revelation of Jesus Christ which God gave to him, to show that his servant David must shortly come to pass. And he signified it by his angel to his servant John.

Now, John bears the record of God as the word of Christ of all things to come. In the first chapter of Revelation it says, 'Blessed is the man, blessed is he that readeth and who hear the words of the prophecy, and those keep the things that are written therein, for the time is in at hand.'

The Scripture says that John writes this of the seven churches that are in Asia: Ephesus, Smyrna, Thyatira, Philadelphia, Laodicea, so forth. Naturally we must understand that we're not in Asia. These churches once existed long ago, being beneficiaries powered in the gifts of the gospel which was originally introduced by the man himself, people who knew him as J. Christ; others knew him by Shua.

What we're trying to present today may in someway shed a better light in regards to my situation, my predicament here at Mount Carmel. One point I'd like to bring out before we continue: that if we take a look at Matthew, Mark, Luke, and John, we see the burden of these ancient writers to learn to part the burden of mind and spirit, to put in a scriptural record, their crucial experience with Christ, a record that is to be received by all men that will receive it.

The point is true that not all have seen Christ, but invented the wisdom of God in certain men who were witnesses of his life, death and resurrection that they would bear witness...to come of the terrible happenings that took place...he was challenged now that he was the son of God.

It's sad to say that if we take a look of the record of John..., say chapter seven, we see a Scripture John writes that after certain events, after these things, Jesus walked in Galilee; he would not walk in Jewry, he would not walk amongst the Jews because the Jews sought to kill him. You might wonder why? Wasn't Christ a good man? Now the Jews seized the Tabernacle that was at hand...and go into Judea...so there is no man that knows anything...to get to be known openly if thou do anything, show thyself to the world for neither...brethren believed in him.

Strange statement, isn't it? It's funny how the man lived with...the realities of life, that even a man like Christ would have to meet with unbelief even from his own brethren. When Jesus said unto them, "My time is not yet come, but your time is always ready." And I'm sure most of my students will agree the time referred to is the time of his crucifixion.

They wanted to kill him, and he didn't want to show himself openly. Then Jesus said unto them, "The world cannot hate you...It is me that is hated, and I have testified that the works of every evil...My time is not yet full come."

And he said these words while still in Galilee. When his brethren had gone up, then went he also up into the fields, not openly, but in secret.

You would wonder why a man like Christ had something to hide. I mean surely, the angels would protect him, obviously. A person would think a lot of things about this strange character and disposition of character.

But we're sure that Christ knew what he was doing. That if you had thought he was a thief and said, "Where is he?" there was much...among the people concerning him, but some said, "He is a good man," only today. But he didn't see what the people, how be it no man say hopefully again for fear of the Jews.

Now we understand that Jews at that time had their own religious political network, didn't they? They were pretty strong in the religious sector, although they had no actual political power and were subject to the Roman government. And that was traditionally the law.

Now about the...of the scene. Jesus went up to the temple and talked. The Jews...having never learned. Now the days of Israel, most scholars, teachers, will agree that the schools of Israel ordained by the king of Egypt and also the Pharisees were still subject to the...theological...of today.

I wish they could fulfill the Scripture that nowhere is it written in the gospel that Christ ever attended these schools. But at the age of twelve he did enter into the temple...the most unique and interesting discussions with the religious leaders and they were amazed at the young man's knowledge of the Scriptures.

Now this man was teaching...Christ that is, that as far as the teachings go, you know, how low is man that he never learned. They marveled. Jesus went to them and said, "My doctrine is not mine, but his that sent me." What does that mean? My doctrine is not mine, but his that sent me. If any man will do his will, he shall know the doctrine, whether it be a god or whether I speak of myself.

But friends, people that love the Lord, this is where we begin to talk about very serious things.

I'm sure you're all aware of how I'm involved in a very serious thing right now, and I'm sure that a lot of you realize that I should be possibly scared, and hurt. There's women, children and men involved in our situation here at Mount Carmel. But I am really concerned about the lives of my brethren here, and also would be even greater concerned about the lives of all those in this world.

You know, without Christ, without Jesus, we have no hope. Why? Well, because we know that the standard of God's righteousness is law, a law of the Ten Commandments, a law of statutes and judgments that which God gave to Moses.

This is my righteousness and wisdom.

But you know, God also gave another law. A law revolving on a system called shedding of horror and innocent man's blood. But it all would break the law of God who would seek God for forgiveness and pardon...had to bring a lamb, something innocent and slay it although...never knew the real meaning of this. Nonetheless, they were commanded to do it,...the sacrifices of the turtle dove, red heifer.

It was a very sophisticated and very holistic type of worship. Of course, God had to give these people their own country and had to give them...things to be able to perform the rituals and...lamb for your sins that they sacrificed. It would definitely keep a man on guard not to sin too much, because otherwise he could lose his livestock pretty quick in the end.

Well anyway, thanksgiving to God from as far back as the year 32 all the way to Malachite. There has been other writing, writing of the prophets, writing to that Utopia...of Moses, but actually it dealt the law of Moses with an additional testimony for the same God who...mercy has not only given us a law but also a way to escape for those...souls who might fall short of the glory of God's law. Some scholars will agree that the glory of God's law is the divine perception of an old character. God's law is the divine perception of an old character. God's characters are yet the law.

Now, Christ is the only hope for a world to mend now. How do we know? Well, the prophet. The prophet died. But what if we're not familiar with the prophet? Well, were the Jews familiar with the prophet when this word of God was made flesh? When Mary, the virgin, had a baby boy, did everyone really believe that she was truly a virgin when Christ was conceived?

We search the Scriptures and we'll find the certain arguments—the Pharisees confronted Christ and said to him, "We be not sons born of fornication." So obviously, not everyone believed that he was a child of a virgin birth. If they hadn't looked back to Isaiah...and learned the mystery of Immanuel, that a virgin was conceived...then they might not really put too much consistency into the fact that that day Christ claimed to be born of a virgin.

I mean, if Isaiah the prophet was a false prophet, well then naturally they would be...having things before would be false, too.

But Christ, he didn't look...to just fulfill prophecy. He did miracles. Miracles of mercy such as healing sick, feeding the hungry, raising the dead, and we said he was seen...Matthew, Mark, Luke and John gives us a full view of the opposition and also the confinement in doing these miracles.

But sad to say, even though he had done so many miracles in his day, yet when it came right down to it, they did not believe in him. It's amazing to think that even his own disciples were slipping, except Mary Magdalene. She stayed with him to the very end, didn't she?

But we need to sit here and we need to ask ourselves the question, How come the men of that generation did not believe in Christ? In Matthew 23, Christ had to say to the Jews, "All of Jerusalem, Jerusalem, how often I would have gathered you, but you would not." Why? He tells them that they have forsaken the prophet. How does the subject of gathering Israel and the prophet combine together? Then he tells them that their house, their temple, is left in dust and that in Matthew 24 as Christ...his disciples came to him secretly to ask him concerning these things, that should be the sign of my coming, like the end of the world. Well, Christ began to tell them that no man deceives you,...and my name, and I am Christ.

A lot of Bible students think that verse refers to people coming and saying that they themselves are Christ. Well, actually if someone came claiming to be Christ, Christ covers that subject by saying...alone in the desert, believe him not...If he has a secret chamber, believe him not. But he goes on to say that as lightning strikes to the east, even to the west, will also show in...me. He goes on to add, "But wheresoever the carcass will end, there will the eagles be gathered together."

Now unless we knew what was on the mind of Christ the day he sat with his disciples...and gave instruction to them according to Matthew 24. Unless we could look into his mind, we would only have to speculate and it would only be an opinion to try to figure out what it means, "wheresoever the carcass is, the eagles." What carcass? Whose carcass? What eagle? What are the eagles?

Well, Christ tells you...in Matthew 24. He says that ye shall see the abomination of desolation, spoken of by Daniel the prophet, and the Holy Place. Of course, it says ye that read it may not understand. What kind of points are these? What is in the mind of Christ? Is Christ trying to tell us that we need to go back and study the prophet Daniel? That maybe Daniel had the inside story on abomination and desolation? Abomination is something nobody wants, especially if it makes us desolate. What do these things mean?

Well, we learned earlier in the Book of John. Christ stated, "My doctrine is not mine, but he who sent me." Now, we've got Matthew, Mark, Luke and John and everybody in the Christian world who's free. To hear these men reveal Christ, the Christ they didn't understand sometimes, the Christ they had to see cruelly mocked and beaten and ridiculed, and killed. But thanks being to God on the cross, their Jesus said, "Father forgive them, for they know not what they do." He also said, which is a point...to get into not quite yet, that "Father, in thy hand I commit my spirit."

...began to see that Christ is quite well-versed in the Scriptures. Always referring the temptation by saying, 'It is written, it is written, it is written.'

Now, what is this spirit of Christ? Well, they pierced his side and out of his side came blood and water. Again, another mystery. Which became something to do with eating his body and drinking his blood. But what do these things really mean? Well, after we've read Acts and learned of the pyro...and glowing tons of fire that came upon the apostles who by firstly knew Christ were given another chance to recover from their falling. We learned through Romans that there is a righteousness in Christ and through Corinthians...Oh, we have such a wealth of information from such intelligent men who speak sometimes very deep, mythical sayings about a God who is the form of humanity, who is the son of God, who sits at the right hand of God in the highest court in the universe, who promises that one day he will come again.

Well, the last move is possible through this great controversy. And I might add, those who persecuted Christ, who would not hear him no matter what sign was given, also persecuted his disciples.

And finally, we end up in the Book of Revelation, where John, the last living disciple on the island of...being a prisoner for the word of God and for the testimony of Jesus Christ, which would probably be quite controversial to the saints and the Pharisees of the day would have to say, we're sure...on the Lord's day had a vision. It states in this vision—we should all be familiar with it hopefully, or get familiar with it—he has a messenger who comes to him and identifies himself as the Spirit, and he is told to write the seven churches of Asia of which we can see clearly in the Scriptures that they were given specific and direct messages from Christ...specifically told the churches what he would help them to do.

Now we know that Christ is the only man in the Scripture who ever kept the law of God perfectly. We know that because we've heard the rite of the apostles. But, sad to say, the religious leaders of his day and the majority of the apostles of his day didn't think so.

It's funny how that is. It's kind of like people always like to build the...and garnish their...yet they hate to kill living prophets. But nonetheless, the...churches lived to see it. For anyone to read direct counsel given, beginning with a name for church...the rest is given.

Finally, we get to the fourth chapter of Revelation, and the student of Scriptures becomes interested in the subject, which according to John says, "After these things I fall behind the road to go to heaven.

The question that every true Christian is this: Is John telling the truth, or is he lying? He knows he just gave...to the seven churches of Asia...or even of the oncoming years thereafter.

So the events of chapter four clearly explained by John that his messenger as sent to him stated that he be taken up hither, which must be hereafter.

Now what does he behold? He says he is of the spirit, immediately after the spirit was behold that a throne was set in heaven. And he states that the throne was occupied.

What sat on the throne?...A careful study of Scripture goes all the way through prophecy, to the Bible, as far back as the days of Genesis...where it says God is a rock; he is our rock.

All the prophets refer to God as a rock. He claims that there was a rainbow around the throne, that there were living beings around the throne, saying that God is holy, holy, holy, which was, is and is to come, God, who created all things, were and are.

Now these instructions emphasized that there is a God, a kingdom, a judiciary and the respect that John witnesses that there are twenty-four elders sitting on twenty-four thrones seems to imply a judgment that uniquely enough in this judgment or in this throne or in this heavenly sanctuary as we see in the rise of Paul, the apostle.

Paul talks about the heavenly things, the heavenly design. In this sanctuary we see a God, a rainbow, a throne, and this God created all things, is holy and deserves to be worshiped...the idea being this is in a book or a scroll, sealed with a seal. Notice it's written on the inside and the backside....

Well, the meaning of these things can only be speculated until we have solid proof—in other words, unless we were there ourselves to see it in detail, then what we are allowed to see in the Scripture as John also divulges, is the mighty angel.

The angel is in this little room with all these angels, thousands and thousands, and this mighty angel questions all those in heaven: "Who is the one who owns this book and the..." Clearly the Scriptures say that no man have it, neither on earth, neither under the earth.

So hey, God says in his book, at least John testified in his book that the mystery of God is sealed. Well, what happens is as we continue on in chapter five that John begins to weep until one of the others says, "Please do not, John; behold the lion in the trial of Judas...."

...to open the book and to loose the seal thereof. We know the lamb is the symbol of Christ is brought. John beheld a lamb that had been slain in the midst of the throne...Well, what's the meaning of these things?

We see that God does have a book, which must be the hereafter somewhere—cannot be before John's day.

And then John beheld a lamb in chapter six, beginning to open the...Now, I've heard a lot of statements the last couple of days from people that are versed in Scripture saying this and that about the meaning of these seals.

Now remember, we have already seen in heaven when Christ reveals the seals, he is the only one that can do so, and remember the revelation between God and Christ and the Father and how he is to reveal the seals.

...How these things be—the seven seals opened? We will begin to see the opening of the seventh seal—contains all the information for the Bible.

We have to find a key to understand these things. The only way we can do that is to have the fear of God. John sees that he beheld four angels scattered to the four corners of the earth. The living God has something that we need to know, and the seven seals have seven angels and seven trumpets.

In chapter ten, a mighty angel comes down from heaven and speeds through the clouds and the fire, and he has in his hand a little book open. He puts his right foot upon the earth...and cries and the lion roars. What do these things mean? What are we really looking at?

The revelation is the revelation of Jesus Christ that God gave to him, and remember the most fearful warning ever given to man is the warning found in Revelation 22, where Christ said, "For I testify to every man to ever hear the word of this prophecy, God shall add unto him the plague that reaps this prophecy; if any man shall take away from the words of this prophecy, God shall take away...the glance of life, the things in life of this prophecy."

Now that's spiritual. That means the book is not to be messed with or pranked with by anybody who would dare think that they can make speculations or private opinions or unlock the mystery of the seven seals and what they contain.

Remember the event of the seventh seal. Contained from the seventh chapter on, the trumpets and the information thereof, just as the sixth seal contains information thereof.

Well then, what must be hereafter, John says? A revelation of who? Who gave it to him? Who only can reveal it—who can come—what can one bring? What reward?...Will he come with a strong hand? What do these things mean?

We know in the first seal that Christ opens it and we hear the noise of thunder. One of the four kings says, come and see and behold a white horse. He that sat upon him had a bow. A crown was set upon him and he went forth to conquer.

Well, in order to understand this seal, we have to find out a secret about Christ. And to the aides of the Church of Philadelphia, we see Christ addresses them with this message; "Of he that is Holy, of he that has the key of David, he that open it and no man shut it, and shut it and no man open it"—this from chapter three of Revelation.

Well, what does this door opening and shutting mean? Isaiah 22 talks about the key of David and refers to Hilkiah. But still, what is the key of David—what does this mean?

Well, I think at the time, Christ being the root offspring of David, David was a great king of Israel. If David was an ordant of God, being a shepherd lad and to the power of God he was able to overthrow the greatest...Goliath, in his day...

Well, we see that David wrote 150 psalms that are published in most Bibles of today's modern world. Now I say that because some scholars will agree that there are other psalms, too. But as far as the King James and the books of that caliber, we have 150 psalms.

Well, our subject is the first seal. We don't want to have any opinions, though; we just want to simply find the mystery of God in the prophets.

Well, let's turn in our Bibles to Psalm 45, and let's see if we can't get some kind of hint to what the first seal is. It states here—this is the King James Version—"My heart invited a good matter. I speak of the things which I have made touching the king." What could it possibly mean? What does it mean about the king, about somebody's heart? Is our subject about a king or a person's heart? Is he talking about Solomon?

". . . therefore God blessed me forever . . . in thy majesty ride prosperously because the truth . . . and thy right hand shall teach thee terrible things . . . thy throne, oh God, is forever."

Is David saying that Solomon is God? He's probably saying that God is God. Why would a prophecy about Solomon have to do with God's throne? What could this possibly mean? Let's take a look.

Scripture says that David was made from God's own heart. Although David...by God's heart...could it be that David was used by God to write down God's messages that would one day be revealed by Christ? If Christ does have the key of David, would he not be able to reveal the heart of God?

God in heaven looks to be a rock, doesn't he? Oh God, hard rock, but wait a minute...through Christ we can see that God is not as hard as you might think he is.

Come up hither in the light of the judgment and see the Father on the throne. See the book in his right hand and watch him give it to Christ and watch him open the first seal, and let's see about the man on the white horse with a crown and a bow. Now God is the one who is ridden. My heart sank in that....Is God a maker or creator? Who is the king? Could it be Christ? Did God write a book? Does God want to talk about his son according to the book? What then, does God think about his son?

...Although I did decree this...when you see there's no...desiring, God never left us. He's found the children of men.

One, grace is poured into thy lips. I guess whatever Christ says those who hear it will find grace, won't they? Therefore God has blessed me forever.

...thy upon thy side, oh most mighty? Is Christ the

most mighty? With thy glory and thy majesty? I mean, it seems like in Revelation like all of heaven bowed before the lamb, did they not?

That's a lot of glory...power, honor, glory, riches, kingdom, might. Whoa, that's a lot of inheritance there. But in the gospel it says I've received all things of my father...

So what could this truth be? What truth in the Bible talks about riding a horse prosperously [sic] and its truth? Could it be Revelation? Could it be the first seal, maybe a truth about Christ, maybe a truth about him being a king with a crown; could it be a truth about him having a horse, riding conquering as a conqueror?

So in the cause of truth, the truth of God took the heart...and he doesn't say anything about the judgment.

You see he just gives it to the lamb, and you know the lamb...terrible thing. Ooh. So in his right hand, a sword or a book—well, what does this book teach? My arrows are sharp in the heart of the king's enemies. Surely, Solomon was he a killer? Did he kill for God? Christ, is he a killer? Did he kill for God? Will Christ ever destroy the wicked?

What kind of gospel is this? My throne, oh God, is forever and ever. Is Christ God? The scepter of thy king, the right scepter—does he deserve to rule? Why?

Does he love righteousness and hate wickedness? Therefore God is not a Christ God. My God is not his God, the Father? Is he not going to ignore him above that...above his fellows?

...All thy garments...that made me glad; I mean, should Christ ever be made glad? What is that, where did that take place?

The king's daughters were among the honorable women? What's that?...How can this be Christ? Christ is God. What would he be doing with a woman? Well, maybe she's the church. Who's the king's daughters then? Maybe there's more than one church.

Well, whatever it may be, we know in verse ten whether it's a spiritual church or a literal woman, there's one thing required. "Harken, oh daughter, and consider." Consider what? Consider God's heart...? Consider who the king is? Consider who's going to be the powerful one, who's going to win? Consider about the throne of God? Consider maybe Revelation? Who the father gives the book to?

"Incline thine end, forget...thy own people thy father's house." Well, if this was a spiritual church, it seems kind of funny for God to tell the spiritual church to forget her own people and fear the domination of the father's house and be—well, I thought her own father would be God if it were spiritual.

Now, if it was a literal girl—'Harken, oh daughter, consider, incline thy ends'—we can understand. Now if a...girl is going to marry a man, she has to uproot the one family and join to another. Not completely, but we understand what we're saying. So if she wants to listen and learn "so should the king greatly desire thy beauty, for he is thou lord, and worship thou him. And the daughter Tyre shall be with him again." Who's Tyre? Wonder what that is.

"Even the rich among thy people shall entreat thy favor." Rich people want to treat the favor of this queen? "The king's daughter is all..." How did she become the king's daughter?...what does she grow...does she have a truth or something? Is there some kind of light she has within her? "Her clothes are of raw gold. She is to be brought to the king in raiment of needlework. The virgins, her companions that follow her should be brought to thee with gladness; rejoicing they be brought. They should enter in the king's palace. Instead of my father, it shall be thy children." What does that mean?

Well let's break this down. If Christ is the son of God, if that's the case, and if we all are sons of God, if we believe in Christ, then naturally, every girl would be a daughter of God, wouldn't she? When we look up to the Father on the throne...we know that he is greater than all. And he's Christ's father and he's also everyone's father...

Hosea teaches us that we're to say, "You're not my people"; there should be said, "You're the son of the living God." So...says in the Gospels, if he calls him God then the word of God of...will not be broken.

Well, we're ruining God's word and God's Spirit. This is what makes us become born again, born by the Spirit...Well, so, a girl believes in God. So therefore God the Father has many children, doesn't he? Christ being the firstborn and all thereafter... But instead of thy father, it should be thy children.

To the person that really doesn't understand Scripture, this would seem to be a very controversial subject. I mean, Christ never had any wife. Has to be spiritual. "I'll make thy name remembered in all generations therefore, so the people praise thee forever and ever."

Well, even if it is spiritual, we know one thing: We...the spirits of God know that Psalm 45 is the very prophecy which must be hereafter according to the first seal. But just to make sure that it's going to be fulfilled, let's turn in our Bible to Revelation 19 just so we can get a better chapter of what we are really looking at.

Now remember, in the eighteenth chapter of Revelation we know that was the great call. He made all nations drink of some wine of the wrath of fornication. Then we find that something very bad happens, and then verse twenty-three of chapter eighteen, "no more at all candles will shine there...the voice of the bridegroom and the voice of the bride."

Well, the merchants of the earth...says in verse twenty-three: "And for by thy sorceries were all nations deceived."

We all know about capitalization; we know about advertisement, selling something, making something better than it really is. "For here is found the blood of prophets, saints of all who were slain upon the Earth." You see, just because people don't accept the truth of God's word does not mean it's not true. And some truth that we might teach can get us in trouble.

But anyway, in...chapter nineteen it says, "And after these things I heard a great voice...from heaven. Hallelujah. Salvation, and glory and honor and power to the Lord our God. Why?...

Isaiah 51 talks about judgments of God. Says something about hard for me to seek after righteousness, yet I seek the Lord, look to the rock..." Again, remember in Revelation, God the rock? If God is a rock, he's the only one who can make us new, right? And it says look to the pit for which you've dug in Isaiah 51. Talks about Abraham and promises of God.

"Hearken unto me, my people; and give ear unto me, O my nation. For laws are received from me and I will make my judgments rest, for a light to the people."

Now we know that the law of God commands. Now we know what God and his sons of the world—he was the law made flesh. And though he kept the law perfectly, nonetheless he also forgave based on men's ignorance. "Father, forgive for they know not what they do."

We all know on the right hand of God there's more light, more light to be known. So if God's judgment of the seven seals are righteous and true, 'cause he judges the great whore, which no doubt a whore is not a very faithful bride, is she? Absolutely not:

"Which did corrupt the earth with her fornication and revenge at the blood of his servants at her hand"? Seems like this great whore doesn't commit itself to God, herself to God, does she? She probably will be responsible for the blood of God's servants; she probably won't know where they're coming from...

I mean, she's not really very faithful when it comes to God's word, when it comes to knowing God's truth. And I think that the kind of personal thing to be with a guy and love a guy and not even know where he's coming from— that's how most whores are isn't it?

Think of how many people claim they love Jesus Christ and that there is truth and they don't even know where the seals are found in the prophecies. Huh, wonder what that could mean? And the...elders, the four thieves fell down and worshiped God instead of on a throne, and a voice came in heaven...verse five says, "Praise our God. How many, all of your servants...heard the voice of a great multitude, heard the voice of many waters, the voice of a mighty thunderings saying, 'Hallelujah,' for the Lord God omnipotent reigneth.

"Let us...and rejoice and give honor to him, for the marriage and the lamb, which the marriage and the lamb"—which we learned about in Psalm 45—is come." So here we see that in Psalm 45 the lamb only has to destroy his enemy. And who are his enemies? Those who do not believe the word of God. Now if a person never had a chance to know, you've got to forgive 'em for they don't know what they do. But should anybody dare to try to go against the truth of God and try to hurt Christ because they know not, and refuse to know, then we're talking something serious.

"Let us be glad and give honor to him, for the marriage of the lamb has come and his wife has made herself ready." How do you think that girl in Psalm 45 made herself ready? You think she made herself ready by denying God on the throne? By denying the importance of the lamb on the first seal? Do you think she made herself ready by denying that Christ had a...of David? Well, if so then Psalm 45 wouldn't mean nothing to her, would it? But anyway, it says, "To her it was granted that she should arrayed in fine linen, clean and white, for the fine linen is the righteousness of the saints."

My friends, are you right? Are you right? Don't worry about me. Are you right? Does your father sit on a throne? Does he have a book in his hands? Did he give it to the one you say you love? "Was the promise that I come...with me, was that not true? Was someone that so loved the world that give his only begotten son, do you not believe...

The question of the judgment is not whether you're doing wrong or you've done evil. The question is, who's worthy? Now, Christ doesn't come to be worthy of us. Christ comes to give you his knowledge, his righteousness. Is it not right that Psalm 45 is the same as the first seal? Is it not Revelation 19 that confirms this? Well, if she has the righteousness of saints, we as saints, do we not know rightly how to divide the word of God, line upon line,...precepts, is he here, there, and a little here and there a little? The truth of God?

He said, "Be right; blessed are they which are called to the marriage...of the lamb." And he said unto me, "Here are the true sayings of God." Well, some people may not think so.

But now notice how John wanted to fall down and worship before the seat of the angel before some of these things? He said, "Heed unto it not, round thy fellow servants and thy brethren at the testimony of Jesus." Worship God. The testimony of Jesus is the spirit of prophecy. What do you want to do? You want to learn the wrath of Christ by him riding a white horse into heaven and destroying the unbelievers? Or would you rather him just come, and teach you these things ahead of time? "And John saw him and opened and behold, a white horse. And he that sit upon him was called faithful and true. And if right...judge make war." He doesn't do it out of unrighteousness. There's a truth almost 2,000 years old called the Revelation. And men have built empires, churches, all in the name of Christ. But have they given to their people the knowledge of which only the lamb can give? No.

"His eyes were a flame of fire, the way he sees, seven eyes will be burned, and on his head were many crowns." Takes those from the kings of the Earth, you know. And he had a name written that no man knew but himself.

People don't understand what the name Koresh means. No one knows; scholars could not tell you; you look at all the courses they don't know, but it's found in Isaiah 45. It was originally a name give to a Persian king...But there's a mystery to the name Koresh. He was clothed in a...dipped in blood 'cause people don't like to learn truth that's not out of their own head, and his name is called the Word of God. That's why so many times Christ has to be rejected. For people know not the word of God, and without knowing the word of God, the book, they'll not know the seals, the...of Christ, fulfilling Isaiah, should be Matthew 24, where the carcass is, there will be eagles gathered together. Why, because Isaiah...strong hand, and what's stronger than that book of seven seals, that's the word of God, fulfilling what it says in John. "He that believeth...on me believeth not on me but on him that sent me. For my...is not my own but his that sent me. And the armies which are in Heaven follow him upon white horses.

There. That's the Armageddon here. Clothed in white linen, fine and clean. Now, Isaiah 13 will tell you more detail. Just like in Job 2...Now let me emphasize something to you again...Remember, I'm giving you a key of David now...Every time you read a psalm, like in Psalm 1, the judge is the one spoken of in Revelation 4 and 5. When you read Psalm 2, the heathens that rage, that imagine vain things, they're the one's whose thoughts are contrary to the thoughts of God, against the Lord and against his anointed, saying, "Let us break their bands asunder and cast their cords from them." You see, when the lamb comes again, there's only one way to know who he is: He has to reveal the seven seals. "That man must not be judged by the law, for all have broke the law come short of the truth...of God. That they be...but truth." But notice in Psalm 2: The heathen rage and imagine vain things; they want to stop this anointed one, 'cause, to make his bands asunder. What do you think that is, I mean bands...there are seven bands on the book.

This is happening today. He that sits in heaven— that's the father, you know, sitting on the throne. He laughs! He laughs while man began to make the worst mistake they've ever made. All the nations...were judged by a judgment and they fell when it became time for God to make them fall.

Now, yes, in Psalms 2 it says, "I will declare the decree the Lord said unto me: Thou art my Son; this day have I begotten thee." Well, aren't we all sons of God if we hear the words of God?...Absolute terrible warnings are given...

We know Christ would never want to do that. The...comes to a time when the judgment when it begins, clearly it says, now this will be why he came to the earth...

Now, ministers should show you where the seals are. I have given you a small taste. Is Psalm 45 the same as Revelation? Doesn't that make it plain?...Christ getting married...Christ having to do with the enemies who believed not God's word. Does not Psalm 1 teach us to stand in judgment? Don't receive...the scorn for the sinners.

Only God's thoughts are holy. And when God's thoughts be revealed in the seven seals, all true Christians should make that their foremost interest. In Psalm 2, why do the heathen rage, why do they have to fight the guy that's got the seals?

...How come people have to judge according to appearances and say that they won't open their eyes and ears and hear where a person's coming from? In Psalms 4, who is the one speaking there when it says, "...sons of man, how long will you turn my glory to shame? How long will you seek after leasing and love vanity?"...The Lord will hear when I call unto him. Who in the heavens has God separated from all of heaven?...The lamb wishes to judge no man as to the flesh but gives to all men a truth in fulfillment of the testimony of John.

"...You shall know the truth, and the truth shall set you free."

In Zechariah, who is that man on the red horse? Does Revelation talk about men on a red horse? How does it apply?...In the book of Hosea, who is that merchant man...that Hosea speaks of?...Is he trying to sell? I mean, what are we dealing with here? Where is the fourth seal found in the prophecies? Where is the fifth seal? The sixth seal? The importance of the seals is, if you do not listen, you are going to end up making the worst mistake you've ever made in all of your life.

We made an agreement with ATF agents that they would allow me to have national coverage of this tape that I might give to the world all...of information that I have tried so hard to share with people—that if I would do this that all the people here at the facility, compound here, which y'all call it, will give ourselves over to the world, give ourselves out to you; this is what I promised; this is what we're going to keep.

Now Revelation chapter 13 tells us very clearly what our ideology should be...and all the world that wonders that...who do they worship? Remember before I said it to you, God said it....But now in spirit and in truth, let's come up here when I come from. Let's believe in a God on the throne now, all churches...we're all brethren. But let's get into unity with one God, one truth, one lamb, one spirit, and let's receive the reward of righteousness. Thank you very much. God bless."

APPENDIX B

On April 13, 1993, the Bureau of Alcohol, Tobacco and Firearms filed an affidavit with the United States District Court of Waco, Texas, in regard to the search of the Mount Carmel compound housing David Koresh's Branch Davidians. That affidavit, which refers to Koresh by his birth name of Vernon Wayne Howell, is presented here and contains a significant amount of background information regarding the ATF's monitoring of the Davidians and their weaponry buildup at Mount Carmel. In essence, this affidavit explains the federal government's original interest in the Branch Davidian cult of David Koresh.

Attachment A

The residence of Vernon Wayne Howell, and others, described as a large two story tan structure with a light grey composition roof, several breaks in the roof line and white shutters on the windows; with a three or four story square addition to the structure near the center of the complex which appears to be an observation tower. There is a rusty cylindrical water tank at the north end of the structure which is approximately 60 feet in height. There are also numerous vehicles of various makes and models around the structure, as well as several outbuildings located on the premises which is approximately 70 to 80 acres in size. At the entrance driveway to the premises is a small frame shack.

To locate the property begin at Exit number 330, Loop 340 and Texas Highway number 6, at its intersection with Interstate Highway 35, just south of Waco, McLennan County, Texas, go east on Loop 340, which curves into a northerly direction for approximately 8.1 miles to its intersection with Texas Farm Road number 2491. Turn right, or east on Farm Road 2491, and proceed for approximately 5.6 miles to its intersection with Double EE Ranch Road/County Road number 222. Turn left, or north and proceed approximately .4 of a mile to the entrance driveway which is on the right or east side of Double EE Ranch Road. At the entrance to the property is one small mailbox and one large mailbox accompanied by a Waco Tribune Herald delivery box which is yellow in color with black printing upon it. Affiant and other authorized agents seek to search the *entire* 70-80 acre compound, including all buildings, vehicles and structures on the premises located both above and below the ground.

Property List

Gunsmithing materials, equipment and tools

Firearms

Clothing

Blood

Shell casings

Bullets

Bullet fragments

Fingerprints

Handwriting

Typewritten documents

Typewriters

Computers including their hard drives, disks, printers and all information stored thereon

Audio tapes

Video tapes

Photographs

Walls, ceilings, floors and parts thereof and other parts of the building structure

Locks, keys and any security devices, both fixed and portable

Human bodies and body parts

Animal carcasses

Telephones, cellular phones, radios, walkie-talkies, scanners, address books, travel documents, including but not limited to passports, visas and maps

Documents identifying individuals residing in the compound and documents evidencing the day-to-day management of the compound, financial control over the compound and similar documents pertaining to the "MAG-BAG" location

Vehicles and vehicle parts

Other evidence and other items of an evidentiary nature

Affidavit

Affiant alleges the following grounds for search and seizure:

I and other agents, have for many months been investigating a case involving federal firearms and explosive violations believed to be committed by Vernon Howell, also known as David Koresh, and numerous other members of a "cult-type" group living in a compound located on approximately 70-80 acres described above. The investigation showed that members of the group had been receiving substantial quantities of firearms and components to create destructive devices. Attached hereto is the affidavit of Davy Aguilera supporting the issuance of a federal search warrant on the said premises. It is incorporated herein. Agents were keenly aware of the dangerous nature of the search warrant to be executed. Several years ago, Howell and others, many of whom are still with the group, were involved in a fierce gun battle at the area of the compound with a former or rival cult member.

Affiant has spoken with many agents who were involved with the attempted execution of the search warrant and has learned many of the details of that attempt. At approximately 10:00 a.m. on February 28, 1993, ATF agents attempted to execute the previously ordered search warrant on the Howell compound. As agents entered the premises, they received a heavy barrage of gun fire including large caliber machinegun fire. During this time, they also witnessed several hand grenades being thrown from the structure. Four ATF agents were killed and approximately sixteen were injured by gun fire coming from the compound.

On March 2, 1993, I spoke with Special Agent Charles Meyer of the ATF, Austin, Texas, with whom I have worked for some 17 years. Agent Meyer explained to me that he has within the past 48 hours spoken at length with agents who were involved in the attempt to enter the compound in their attempt to execute the search warrant. Special Agent Dale Littleton (Special Agent with ATF for some 20 years) stated to Agent Meyer that as Littleton and others began their attempt to enter the compound, they received heavy machinegun fire from, he believed, every window of the compound building. Further, Agent Littleton stated that as they approached the front door of the main compound, and after announcing themselves as a federal agent with the search warrant, an unknown individual closed the door and there was gunfire coming through the door and adjoining walls. Agent Meyer also spoke personally with Special Agent Clair Rayburn of the Austin ATF office who was involved in the attempt to enter the compound building to execute the search warrant. Special Agent Rayburn related as she exited the rear of the trailer she saw gunfire coming from virtually every window of the compound. Agent Rayburn was injured by the gunfire coming from the compound. Members of the ATF Search Warrant Execution Team from New Orleans, Louisiana Division were assigned the task of climbing upon the roof of the structure and entering an upstairs window. These agents have related to me that they received fire which came up through the roof as well as through the walls of the compound. From this fire and other fire whose direction I do not know at this time, at least two agents from New Orleans Division were killed (according to the attached hospital reports) and at least three were injured. Physicians have stated that bullets or fragments thereof were located in bodies of the injured. Additionally, agents with whom I have spoken who evacuated dead and wounded agents stated that they appeared to have gunshot type wounds. I know from my experience that the path or trajectory of bullets can be extremely important in determining the direction of fire. In this case it may be that entire ceilings or parts of walls or other parts of the structure of the building would reflect bullet trajectory. Therefore, permission is sought to photograph and seize walls, ceilings and other parts of the structure of the building which may reflect the path of bullets fired.

When ammunition cartridges are chambered in a firearm and fired, markings unique to that particular firearm are made on both the projectile and the cartridge casings. In particular, markings on the projectile are made by lands and grooves of the rifling in the barrel. Firing pin markings are made in the primer of the cartridge casing when indented by the firing pin. Extractor markings also appear on cartridge casings. Therefore, permission is sought to seize these casings and other related evidence so that comparisons may be made by laboratory personnel to determine from which firearms bullets were fired and from which firearms the casings were ejected. Special Agent Davy Aguilera, ATF Austin, who acted as the Affiant in the original search warrant in this case involving the compound, has learned through his investigation and has related to me that a number of the firearms that are believed to be in the compound that were used against the agents were purchased from various federal firearms dealers and therefore ATF Forms 4473 which should bear handwriting of the purchaser and possible fingerprints should exist. I therefore seek by this search warrant affidavit permission to search for and seize documents which may contain handwriting of individuals in the compound who may have purchased weapons or used weapons against the agents. Prior to the making of this affidavit, I have spoken with Special Agent Robert Blossman of the United States Secret Service. Special Agent Blossman has been with the Secret Service for some 17 years and has extensive experience in investigations which involve handwriting as its principle form of evidence. Agent Blossman has been trained by Secret Service handwriting experts as to the significance of "unsolicited handwriting." Unsolicited handwriting is handwriting that is from a normal course of business writing with no outside influence which no attention has been drawn to the writing. These types of handwriting examples are important because no attempts to disguise or alter the handwriting have been made. Therefore, permission is sought to seize all of these items which may bear handwriting so that comparisons may be made by laboratory personnel relating the firearms receipts and purchases to specific individuals in the compound. Special Agent Aguilera further related to Affiant that Howell espouses certain doctrine hostile to law enforcement and particularly the ATF. Often times, according to Aguilera, Howell would reduce to writing his theories or sermons. Further, Special Agent Robert Rodriguez who personally spoke with Howell during the investigation learned that Howell had video tapes and other commercially produced material which are critical of firearms law enforcement and particularly the Bureau of Alcohol, Tobacco and Firearms (ATF). I therefore intend to search and seize video tapes, writings, and other materials which evidence Howell and other cult members' motive for wanting to shoot and kill ATF

Agents. Typewriters, computers (including disks, hard drives and printers) and other items used to draft writings are sought. Howell is known to agents investigating the case to record songs and possibly other messages espousing his doctrine, therefore audio tapes and audio tapemaking equipment is sought. Further, I know that often times persons who violate firearms laws take or cause to be taken photographs of themselves displaying their weapons and sometimes static display these weapons and ammunition for photographs. These photographs are sought.

Earl Dunagan, Special Agent
Bureau of ATF

Subscribed and sworn to before me this 13th day of April,1993.

Dennis G. Green
United States Magistrate Judge
Western District of Texas - Waco

This warrant, affidavit and all accompanying papers are hereby sealed by order of this court.

Signed by me this 13th day of April, 1993.

Dennis G. Green,
United States Magistrate Judge
Western District of Texas - Waco

Affadavit
Affiant alleges the following grounds for search and seizure:

I, Davy Aguilera, being duly sworn, depose and state that:

I am a Special Agent with the U. S. Treasury Department, Bureau of Alcohol, Tobacco and Firearms, Austin, Texas, and I have been so employed for approximately 5 years. This affidavit is based on my own investigation as well as information furnished to me by other law enforcement officers and concerned citizens.

As a result of my training and experience as a Special Agent for the Bureau of Alcohol, Tobacco and Firearms, I am familiar with the Federal firearm and explosive laws and know that it is unlawful for a person to manufacture, possess, transfer, or to transport or ship in interstate commerce machineguns, machinegun conversion parts, or explosives which are classified, by Federal law, as machine guns, and/or destructive devices, including any combination of parts either designed or intended for use in converting any firearm into a machine gun, or into a destructive device as defined by Federal law, and from which a destructive device may be readily assembled, without them being lawfully registered in the National Firearms Registration and Transfer Record, U. S. Treasury Department, Washington, D.C.

During my 5 years experience with the Bureau of Alcohol, Tobacco and Firearms, I have investigated persons who have unlawfully possessed, transferred or shipped in interstate or foreign commerce firearms and/or explosive devices which were not registered to them with the National Firearms Registration and Transfer Record, and have successfully participated in the prosecution of several of these individuals.

On June 4, 1992, I met with Lieutenant Gene Barber, McLennan County Sheriff's Department, Waco, Texas, who has received extensive training in explosives classification, identification and the rendering safe of explosive devices and has been recognized in Federal Court as an expert witness in this field. Lt. Barber stated that he had received information in May 1992, from an employee of United Parcel Service, Waco, Texas, that from April through June of 1992, several deliveries had been made to a place known as the "Mag-Bag", Route 7, Box 555-B, Waco, Texas, 76705, located on Farm Road number 2491, in the names of Mike Schroeder and David Koresh, which the UPS employee believed to be firearms components and explosives. Through my investigation, I know that the place known as the "Mag-Bag" is a small tract of land located at the above address which has two metal buildings located on it. The name "Mag-Bag" comes from the shipping label which is accompanied many items shipped to the above address. I and other agents have personally observed vehicles consistently over the past six months at the "Mag-Bag" location which are registered to Vernon Wayne Howell, aka: David Koresh. Lieutenant Barber further stated that the UPS employee, Larry Gilbreath, became suspicious and concerned about the deliveries, most of which were shipped Cash On Delivery, (C.O.D.) because of their frequency and because of the method used by the recipient to receive the shipments and to pay for them.

Lieutenant Barber explained that David Koresh was an alias name used by Vernon Wayne Howell who operated a religious cult commune near Waco, Texas, at a place commonly known as the Mount Carmel Center, which is one of the premises to be searched and more specifically described above. I have learned from my investigation, particularly from my discussions with former cult members that Vernon Howell adopted the name David Koresh more than a year ago. The name "David Koresh" was chosen by Howell because Howell believed that the name helped designate him as the messiah or the anointed one of God. Lieutenant Barber further related that he was told by Gilbreath that he has been making deliveries to the "Mag-Bag" and the Mount Carmel Center on Double EE Ranch Road, Waco, Texas, for several years, but he had never been suspicious of any of the deliveries until 1992. Gilbreath became concerned because he made several C.O.D. deliveries addressed to the "Mag-Bag", but when he would stop at that location that he was instructed to wait while a telephone call was made to the Mount Carmel center by the person at the "Mag-Bag", usually Woodrow Kendrick or Mike Schroeder, notifying the person who answered the phone at the Mount Carmel Center that UPS was coming there with a C.O.D. delivery, after which Gilbreath would be instructed to drive to the Mount Carmel Center to deliver the package and collect for it. That on those occasions when he was at the Mount Carmel Center to deliver and collect for the C.O.D. packages. He saw several manned operation posts, and believed that the observers were armed.

Lieutenant Barber stated that he was told by Larry Gilbreath (UPS) that in May of 1992 two cases of inert hand grenades and a quantity of black gun powder were delivered by him to the "Mag-Bag." The source of these shipments was unknown to Gilbreath.

On June 9, 1992, I was contacted by Lieutenant Barber who told me that he had learned form Larry Gilbreath that in June of 1992, the United Parcel Service delivered ninety (90) pounds of powdered aluminum metal and 30 to 40 cardboard tubes, 24 inches in length and 1 1/4 to 1 1/2 inches in diameter, which were shipped from the Fox Fire Company, Pocatella, Idaho, to "Mag-Bag." From another shipper whose identity is unknown, two parcels containing a total of sixty (60), M-16/AR-15 ammunition magazines were delivered by UPS to the "Mag-Bag" on June 8, 1992. I know based upon my training and experience that an AR-15 is a semi-automatic rifle practically identical to the M-16 rifle carried by United States Armed Forces. The AR-15 rifle fires .223 caliber ammunition and, just like the M-16, can carry magazines of ammunition ranging from 30 to 60 rounds of ammunition. I have been involved in many cases where defendants, following a relatively simple process, convert AR-15 semi-automatic rifles to fully automatic rifles of the nature of the M-16. This conversion process can often be accomplished by an individual purchasing certain parts which will quickly transform the rifle to fire fully automatic. Often times templates, milling machines, lathes and instruction guides are utilized by the converter.

Lieutenant Barber related to me the following background information about the Mount Carmel Center commune which is located at Rt. 7, Box 471-B, Waco, Texas, and consists of some seventy (70) acres of land, occupied by Vernon W. Howell, a/k/a David Koresh and others.

The property was once owned and operated by George Buchanan Roden, who once was an unannounced candidate for the office of President of the United States. Roden inherited the property sometime in the 1950's, and beginning about January 1986 established and led a religious cult group with about twenty (20) followers. He claimed to be the Prophet of the group. The property at the time was known as the "Elk Property/Mt. Carmel Center." About this same time, Roden was in jeopardy of losing the property by foreclosure due to delinquent taxes which had not been paid since 1968.

About this same time, Vernon Wayne Howell, had established a similar group in Palestine, Texas, known as the Branch Davidian Seventh-Day Adventists. Sometime in 1987, Howell, laid claim to ownership of the Mt. Carmel Center property and wanted to acquire it by any means possible. On November 3, 1987, Howell led an armed group of eight men into Roden's camp and a 45-minute gun battle ensued. Roden was shot in the finger and was the only person injured.

Eight people, including Vernon W. Howell and Paul Gordon Fatta were arrested by the McLennan County Sheriff's Department, Waco, Texas, and were indicted for attempted murder by a McLennan County Grand Jury. All eight subjects were tried in State court at Waco, Texas, and were acquitted of the charges of attempted murder by a jury.

After the armed assault by Howell and his followers, George Roden vacated the property. In 1987, the property was taken over by Howell and his cult group. The taxes owed on the Mt. Carmel Center have been paid by Howell's group. His cult has grown to about seventy (70) to eighty (80) people which includes men, women and children who now live on the Mt. Carmel Center property.

Lieutenant Barber furnished me with recently taken aerial photographs of the Mount Carmel Center which had been taken by Captain Dan Weyenberg of the McLennan County Sheriff's Department, Waco, Texas. Among the things noted in the photographs was a buried bus near the main structure and an observation tower, approximately three or four stories tall with windows on all four sides enabling a view from the structure of 360 degrees.

I was also advised by Lieutenant Barber that Robert Cervenka, a known long time McLennan County citizen, who lives near the Mount Carmel Center compound, had, on several occasions, from January through February of 1992, heard machinegun fire coming from the compound property. Mr. Cervenka offered law enforcement authorities his residence to be used as a surveillance post.

On July 21, 1992, I met with Robert L. Cervenka, Route 7, Box 103, Riesel, Texas. Mr. Cervenka farms the property surrounding the east side of the Mount Carmel property. Mr Cervenka stated that he has farmed that area since 1948. From about January and February of 1992 he has heard machinegun fire on the Vernon Howell property during the night hours. He is familiar with and knows the sound of machinegun fire because he did a tour overseas with the U.S. Army. He believes that some of the gunfire he heard was being done with 50 caliber machineguns and possibly M-16 machineguns.

On November 13, 1992, I spoke with Lieutenant Gene Barber who told me that Mr. Cervenka, whose ranch is adjacent to the Mount Carmel Property, had reported hearing bursts of gunfire from the Mount Carmel compound on November 8, 1992, at approximately 2:45 p.m.

On June 8, 1992, based on information gained from Gilbreath by Lieutenant Barber, I interviewed Dave Haupert, Olympic Arms Inc., Olympia, Washington, a company which had shipped several parcels to David Koresh at the "Mag-Bag", Route 7, Box 555-B, Waco, Texas. Mr. Haupert told me that the records of Olympic Arms Inc., indicated that approximately forty-five (45) AR-15/ M-16 rifle upper receiver units, with barrels of various calibers, had been shipped from March through April of 1992 to the Mag-Bag Corporation for a total cost of $11,107.31, cash on delivery.

On January 13, 1993, I interviewed Larry Gilbreath in Waco, Texas, and confirmed the information which had previously been related to me by Lieutenant Barber. Mr. Gilbreath told me that although he had been making deliveries at the "Mag-Bag" and the Mount Carmel Center for quite some time, his suspicion about the packages being delivered to those places never was aroused until about February 1992. At that time the invoices accompanying a number of packages reflected that they contained firearm parts and accessories as well as various chemicals. He stated that in May 1992, a package which was addressed to the "Mag Bag" accidently broke open while it was being loaded on his delivery truck. He saw that it contained three other boxes the contents of which were "pineapple" type hand grenades which he believed to be inert. He stated that there were about fifty of the grenades and that he later delivered them to the Mount Carmel Center. The Mount Carmel Center is that tract of land depicted in the photograph labeled "Attachment B", with the main residential structure being depicted in "Attachment C."

Mr. Gilbreath stated that these suspicious packages were usually addressed to the "Mag Bag" or to David Koresh. When he would stop to deliver them to the "Mag Bag", he was met most of the time by Woodrow Kendrick, and on other occasions by Steve Schneider. They would have him wait while they telephoned the Mount Carmel Center to tell them that UPS was coming with a C.O.D. package. He would be instructed to take the package(s) to the Mount Carmel Center. Upon arriving at the Mount Carmel Center, he was usually met by Perry Jones or, on occasion, by Steve Schneider, who would pay the C.O.D. charges in cash and would accept delivery of the shipments.

On this same date, June 8, 1992, I interviewed Glen Deruiter, Manager, Sarco Inc., Stirling, New Jersey, and learned from him that in May of 1992, their company shipped one M-16 parts set kit with a sling and magazine to the "Mag-Bag" in the name of David Koresh. The total value of these items was $284.95.

Also on June 8, 1992, I interviewed Cynthia Aleo, Owner/ Manager, Nesard Gun Parts Company, Barrington, Illinois, and learned from her that in May of 1992, her company shipped to the "Mag-Bag", two (2) M-16 machinegun car kits and two (2) M-16 machinegun EZ kits. These kits contain all the parts of an M-16 machinegun, except for the lower receiver unit which is the "firearm" by lawful definition. Ms. Aleo stated that the total amount of sales to the Mag-Bag was $1227.00. Within the past month, I have spoken with Curtis Bartlett, Firearms Technician with BATF and have learned that Nesard Company has been under investigation in the past by ATF for engaging in a scheme to supply parts which would enable individuals to construct illegal weapons from various component parts.

On June 9, 1992, I requested that a search of the records of the National Firearms Registration and Transfer Record, Washington, D.C., to determine if Vernon W. Howell and/or Paul G. Fatta, one of Howell's closest followers, had any machineguns or other NFA weapons registered to them. The result of the search was negative.

On this same date, June 9, 1992, I requested a search of the records of the Firearms Licensing Section of the Bureau of Alcohol, Tobacco and Firearms, Atlanta, Georgia, to determine if Howell, Fatta or the "Mag-Bag" Corporation were licensed as Firearms dealers or manufacturers. The result of this search was negative.

On June 10, 1992, I requested a search of the records of the Firearms Licensing Section of the Bureau of Alcohol, Tobacco and Firearms, Atlanta, Georgia, to determine if David Koresh, Howell's alias name, or David M. Jones, a known associate of Howell, were licensed as Firearms dealers or manufacturers. The result of this search was negative.

On June 23, 1992, I spoke with ATF compliance Inspector

Robert Souza, Seattle, Washington, who inquired about the Mag Bag Corporation, Route 7, Box 555, Waco, Texas. He had received some invoices reflecting a large quantity of upper receivers and AR-15 parts being shipped to "Mag-Bag", Waco, Texas, from Olympic Arms Inc., 624 Old Pacific Hwy., S.E. Olympia, Washington. Inspector Souza faxed me copies of invoices, reflecting purchases of twenty (20) AR-15 upper receiver units with barrels by the "Mag-Bag" on March 26th and 30th, 1992. These items are in addition to the items referred to above.

As a result of my investigation of shipments to Howell/Koresh and Mike Schroeder at the "Mag-Bag" Corporation, Waco, Texas, through the United Parcel Service, and the inspection of the firearms records of Henry McMahon, dba, Hewitt Hand Guns, Hewitt, Texas, I have learned that they acquired during 1992, the following firearms and related explosive paraphernalia:
One hundred four (104), AR-15/M-16, upper receiver groups with barrels.
Eight thousand, one hundred (8,100) rounds of 9mm and .223 caliber ammunition for AR-15/M-16.
Twenty (20), one hundred round capacity drum magazines for AK-47 rifles.
Two hundred sixty (260), M-16/AR-15, magazines.
Thirty (30) M-14, magazines.
Two (2) M-16 EZ kits.
Two (2) M-16 Car Kits.
One M-76 grenade launcher.
Two hundred (200) M-31, practice rifle grenades.
Four (4) M-16 parts set Kits "A".
Two (2) flare launchers.
Two cases, (approximately 50) inert practice grenades.

40-50 pounds of black gun powder.
Thirty (30) pounds of Potassium Nitrate.
Five (5) pounds of Magnesium metal powder.
One pound of Igniter cord. (A class C explosive)
Ninety-one (91) AR/15 lower receiver units.
Twenty-six (26) various calibers and brands of hand guns
and long guns.
90 pounds of aluminum metal powder.
30-40 cardboard tubes.

The amount of expenditures for the above listed firearm
paraphernalia, excluding the (91) AR-15 lower receiver
units and the (26) complete firearms, was in excess of
$44,300.

From my investigation, I have learned that a number of
shipments to the "Mag-Bag" have been from vendors
with questionable trade practices. One is presently under
investigation by the Bureau of Alcohol, Tobacco and Firearms, for violations of the National Firearms Act, which
prohibits unlawful possession of machineguns, silencers,
destructive devices, and machinegun conversion kits.

Because of the sensitivity of this investigation, these vendors have not been contacted by me for copies of invoices
indicating the exact items shipped to the Mag-Bag.

On November 13, 1992, I interviewed Lieutenant Coy
Jones, McLennan County Sheriff's Department, Waco,
Texas, and learned from him that he had spoken with an
employee of the United Parcel Service, Waco, Texas, who
wished to remain anonymous. This person told Jones that
Marshall Keith Butler, a relative of the person who wishes

to remain anonymous, is a machinist by trade, and is associated with Vernon Howell.

The records of the Texas Department of Public Safety reflect that Butler has been arrested on seven (7) occasions since 1984 for unlawful possession of drugs. Two of the arrests resulted in convictions for possession of a controlled substance. Butler's latest arrest and conviction was in January 1992. Butler received a sentence of three (3) years in the Texas Department of Corrections. In April 1992 Butler was paroled to McLennan County, Texas.

On November 13, 1992, I interviewed Terry Fuller, a deputy sheriff for McLennan County Sheriff's Department, Waco, Texas, and learned from him that November 6, 1992, at approximately 1:25 p.m., while on routine patrol in the area of the Mount Carmel Center, the property controlled by Vernon Howell, he heard a loud explosion in the area of the north part of the Mount Carmel property. As he drove toward the area where he thought the explosion had occurred, he observed a large cloud of grey smoke dissipating from ground level on the north end of the Mount Carmel property.

On December 7, 1992, I spoke with Special Agent Carlos Torres, Bureau of Alcohol, Tobacco and Firearms, Houston, Texas, who had been assisting me in a portion of this investigation. He related to me the results of his interview on December 4, 1992, with Joyce Sparks, Texas Department of Human Services, Waco, Texas. Special Agent Torres told me that Ms. Sparks received a complaint from outside the State of Texas, that David Koresh was operating a commune type compound, and that he was sexually abusing young girls. Ms. Sparks stated that on February 27, 1992, she along with two other employees of the Texas Department of Human Services and two McLennan County Sheriff's Deputies responded to the complaint. They went to the Mount Carmel Center compound, located east of Waco in McLennan County. When they arrived at the compound, they were met by a lady who identified herself as Rachel Koresh, the wife of David Koresh.

Mrs. Koresh was reluctant to talk with Ms. Sparks because David Koresh was not there. She had strict orders from him not to talk with anyone unless he was present. Ms. Sparks finally was able to convince Mrs. Koresh to allow her to talk with some of the children who were present. She talked to a young boy about 7 or 8 years old. The child said that he could not wait to grow up and be a man. When Ms. Sparks asked him why he was in such a hurry to grow up, he replied that when he grew up he would get a "long gun" just like all the other men there. When Ms. Sparks pursued the subject, the boy told her that all the adults had guns and that they were always practicing with them.

Ms. Sparks also told Special Agent Torres that she was escorted through part of the building where she noted a lot of construction being performed. She also said that she could not determine how many people were in the group, but estimated about sixty (60) to seventy (70) people there including men, women and children. She stated that she saw about 15 to 20 adult males there.

Ms. Sparks also said that on April 6, 1992, she visited the compound again. On this occasion she talked with David

Koresh. She asked Koresh about the firearms which she had been told by the small child. Koresh admitted that there were a few firearms there, but said that most of the adults did not know of them, and that there were too few to be of any significance. Ms. Sparks said that when she pressed Koresh about the firearms and their location at the compound, he offered to show her around. He requested that she wait about 30 minutes until he could get the other residents out of the building so they would not see where he had the firearms stored. After a period of time, Ms. Sparks was escorted through part of the building by Koresh. She noted that there was more construction activity and the inside of the structure looked quite different from her previous visit. Each time Ms. Sparks asked Koresh about the location of the firearms, he would tell her that they were in a safe place where the children could not get to them. He then would change the subject.

Ms. Sparks said that she noticed a trap door in the floor at one end of the building. When she inquired about it, Koresh allowed her to look into the trap door. She could see a ladder leading down into a buried school bus from which all the seats had been removed. At one end of the bus she could see a very large refrigerator with numerous bullet holes. She also saw three long guns lying on the floor of the bus, however, she did not know the make or caliber of them. She stated that there was no electricity in the bus. Everything she saw was with the aid of a pen light. When questioned by Ms. Sparks, Koresh said that the bus was where he practiced his target shooting in order not to disturb his neighbors.

Ms. Sparks felt the entire walk through the compound was staged for her by Koresh. When she asked to speak with some of the children and other residents, Koresh refused, stating they were not available. She said that during her conversation with Koresh, he told her that he was the "Messenger" from God, that the world was coming to an end, and that when he "reveals" himself the riots in Los Angeles would pale in comparison to what was going to happen in Waco, Texas. Koresh stated that it would be a "military type operation" and that all the "non-believers" would have to suffer.

On December 11, 1992, I interviewed Robyn Bunds in LaVerne, California. Robyn Bunds is a former member and resident of Vernon Howell's commune in Waco, Texas. She told me that in 1988, at the age of 19, she gave birth to a son who was fathered by Vernon Howell. Her departure from the commune in 1990 was a result of Howell becoming progressively more violent and abusive.

While she was there, she and the other residents were subjected to watching extremely violent movies of the Vietnam war which Howell would refer to as training films. Howell forced members to stand guard of the commune 24 hours a day with loaded weapons. Howell always was in possession of firearms and kept one under his bed while sleeping. Robyn stated that her present residence in California belonged to her parents. For a period of several years Howell had exclusive control of the residence and used it for other members of his cult when they were in California. It was later relinquished by Howell to Robyn's mother. In June 1992, while she was cleaning one of the bedrooms of the residence she found a plastic bag containing gun parts. She showed them to her brother, David Bunds, who had some knowledge of firearms. He told her that it was a machinegun conversion kit. She stored the gun parts in her garage because she felt certain that Howell would send some of his followers to pick them up. Subsequent to her discovery of the conversion kit, Paul Fatta, Jimmy Riddle, and Neal Vaega, all members of Howell's cult and residents of the commune in Waco, came from Waco, Texas, to California and picked up the conversion kit.

On December 12, 1992, I interviewed Jeannine Bunds, the mother of Robyn and David Bunds. She told me that she was a former member of Howell's group in Waco, Texas, having left there in September 1991. She is a registered nurse and was working in that capacity at the Good Samaritan Hospital, Los Angeles, California. While at Howell's commune in Waco, she participated in live fire shooting exercises conducted by Howell. She saw several long guns there, some of which she described as AK-47 rifles. Mrs. Bunds described the weapon to me and was able to identify an AK-47 from among a number of photographs of firearms shown to her by me. I believe that she is well able to identify an AK-47. In July of 1991, she saw Howell shooting a machinegun on the back portion of the commune property. She knew it was a machinegun because it functioned with a very rapid fire and would tear up the ground when Howell shot it. Mrs. Bunds also told me that Howell had fathered at least fifteen (15) children from various women and young girls at the compound. Some of the girls who had babies fathered by Howell were as young as 12 years old. She had personally delivered seven (7) of these children.

According to Ms. Bunds, Howell annuls all marriages of couples who join his cult. He then has exclusive sexual access to the women. He also, according to Mrs. Bunds, has regular sexual relations with young girls there. The girls' ages are from eleven (11) years old to adulthood.

On January 6, 1993, I interviewed Jeannine Bunds again in Los Angeles, California. I showed her several photographs of firearms and explosives devices. She identified an AR-15 rifle and a pineapple type hand grenade as being items which she had seen at the Mount Carmel Center while she was there. She stated that she saw several of the AR-15 rifles and at least one of the hand grenades.

On January 7, 1993, I interviewed Deborah Sue Bunds in Los Angeles, California. She was the wife of David Bunds, and she had been a member of the "Branch Davidian" since birth. She stated she first met Vernon Wayne Howell in July 1980. When Howell assumed leadership of the "Branch" in Waco, Texas, in 1987, he began to change the context of their Doctrine. While she was at the Mount Carmel compound in Waco, Texas, she was assigned, under Howell's direction, to guard duty with a loaded weapon. About February 1989, she observed Howell shooting a machinegun behind the main structure of the compound. After describing the firing of this weapon to me, I believe that Ms. Bunds was describing the firing of an automatic weapon.

Mrs. Deborah Bunds also told me that during an evening meal a short time after having seen Howell shoot the machinegun, she overheard Howell and his closest associates discussing machineguns, specifically AK-47 type machineguns.

During this investigation I made inquiries of a number of law enforcement data bases for information about those commune residents who I have been able to identify. Through TECS I learned that forty (40) foreign nationals from Jamaica, United Kingdom, Israel, Australia and New Zealand have entered the United States at various times in the past and have used the address of the Mount Carmel Center, Waco, Texas, as their point of contact while here. According to INS records most of these foreign nationals have over stayed their entry permits or visas and are therefore illegally in the United States. I know that it is a violation of Title 18, United States Code, Section 922 for an illegal alien to receive a firearm.

On January 1, and January 3, 1993, Mrs. Poia Vaega of Mangere, Auckland, New Zealand, was interviewed telephonically by Resident Agent in Charge Bill Buford, Bureau of Alcohol, Tobacco and Firearms, Little Rock, Arkansas, who also is assisting me in this investigation. The results of Special Agent Buford's interview on January 1, 1993, was reduced to writing and furnished to me. Special Agent Buford's interview on January 3, 1993, was tape recorded with the permission of Poia Vaega and has since been transcribed and typewritten. Both the tape recording and the transcription was furnished to me by Special Agent Buford. Both interviews with Poia Vaega revealed a false imprisonment for a term of three and one half (3 1/2) months which began in June of 1991 and physical and sexual abuse of one of Mrs. Vaega's sisters, Doreen Saipaia. This was while she was a member of the "Branch

Davidian" at the Mount Carmel Center, Waco, Texas. The physical and sexual abuse was done by Vernon Wayne Howell and Stanley Sylvia, a close follower of Howell, on several occasions.

It was learned from Mrs. Vaega that she and her husband, Leslie, were also members of Howell's group in Waco for a short period of time in March 1990. Upon their arrival at Mount Carmel Center, she and her husband were separated and not allowed to sleep together or have any sexual contact.

According to Mrs. Vaega, all the girls and women at the compound were exclusively reserved for Howell. She stated that Howell would preach his philosophy, which did not always coincide with the Bible, for hours at a time. She and her husband left the compound after ten (10) days because her husband did not agree with Howell's doctrine, but that her two sisters stayed behind.

Mrs. Vaega also related that she was present at one of the study periods held by Howell when Howell passed his personal AK-47 machinegun around for the group to handle and look over.

On January 6, 1993, I received the results of an examination conducted by Jerry A. Taylor, Explosives Enforcement Officer, Bureau of Alcohol, Tobacco and Firearms, Walnut Creek, California, in response to a request from me to render an opinion on device design, construction, functioning, effects, and classification of explosives materials which have been accumulated by Howell and his followers. Mr. Taylor has received extensive training in

Explosives Classification, Identification and rendering safe of explosive devices and has been recognized on numerous occasions as an expert witness in Federal Court. Mr. Taylor stated that the chemicals Potassium Nitrate, Aluminum, and Magnesium, when mixed in the proper proportions, do constitute an explosive as defined by Federal law. He further stated that Igniter cord is an explosive. Also Mr. Taylor stated that the inert practice rifle grenades and hand grenades would, if modified as weapons with the parts available to Howell, become explosives devices as defined by Federal law. Finally he stated that block powder, is routinely used as the main charge when manufacturing improvised explosive weapons such as grenades and pipe bombs. I know that Title 26, United States Code, Section 5845 makes it unlawful for a person to possess any combination of parts designed or intended for use in converting any device into a destructive device. The definition of "firearm" includes any combination of parts, either designed or intended for use in converting any device into a destructive device such as a grenade, and from which a destructive device may be readily assembled. See United States v. Price, 877 F.2d 334 (5th Cir. 1989). So long as an individual possesses all of the component parts, item constitutes a destructive device even though it is not assembled, so long as it can be readily assembled. United States v. Russell, 468 F. Supp. 322 (D.C. Texas. 1979).

On January 8, 1993, I interviewed Marc Breault in Los Angeles, California. He is an American citizen who lives in Australia with his wife Elizabeth. He was once a member of the "Branch Davidian" in Waco, Texas. He lived at the Mount Carmel Center from early 1988 until September 1989. While there he participated in physical training and firearm shooting exercises conducted by Howell. He stood guard armed with a loaded weapon. Guard duty was maintained twenty-four (24) hours a day seven (7) days a week. Those who stood guard duty were instructed by Howell to "shoot to kill" anyone who attempted to come through the entrance gate of the Mount Carmel property. On one occasion, Howell told him that he wanted to obtain and/or manufacture machineguns, grenades and explosive devices. Howell stated he thought that the gun control laws were ludicrous, because an individual could easily acquire firearm and the necessary parts to convert it to a machinegun, but if a person had the gun and the parts together they would be in violation of the law. On another occasion, Howell told him that he was interested in acquiring the "Anarchist's Cook Book", which I know is a publication outlining clandestine operations to include instructions and formulas for manufacturing improvised explosive devices.

On January 12, 1993, I spoke with Special Agent Earl Dunagan, Bureau of Alcohol, Tobacco and Firearms, Austin, Texas, who is assisting me in this investigation. He related the results of his inquiry to the ATF Firearms Technology Branch, Washington, D.C., for an opinion concerning the firearms parts which have been accumulated by Howell and his group. Special Agent Dunagan stated that he had spoken with Curtis Bartlett, Firearms Enforcement Officer, Washington, D.C., and was told by Officer Bartlett that the firearms parts which Howell has received and the method by which he has received them, is consistent with activities in other ATF investigations in various parts of the United States, which have resulted in the discovery and seizure of machineguns. Mr. Bartlett stated that the firearms parts received by Howell could be used to assemble both semi-automatic firearms and machineguns. He has examined many firearms which had been assembled as machineguns which included these type parts. Mr. Bartlett also told Special Agent Dunagan that one of the vendors of supplies to Howell has been the subject of several ATF investigations in the past. ATF executed a search warrant at this Company and had seized a number of illegal machineguns and silencers.

Special Agent Dunagan told me that on January 12, 1993, he spoke with Special Agent Mark Mutz, ATF, Washington, D.C., who was the case agent on the above ongoing investigation dealing with illicit supplier who has provided gun parts to Howell. Special Agent Mutz stated that during the execution of the Federal search warrant at the company's office in South Carolina, he saw large quantities of M-16 machinegun and AK-47 machinegun parts. The company maintained their inventory of these parts as "replacement parts" so they fell easily within a loophole in the Federal law which prohibited ATF from seizing the parts. Special Agent Mutz stated that the company had all the necessary parts to convert AR-15 rifles and semi-automatic AK-47 rifles into machineguns if their customers had the upper and lower receivers for those firearms. Based on my investigation, as stated above in the description of gun parts shipped to Howell, I know that Howell possesses the upper and lower receivers for the firearms which he is apparently trying to convert to fully automatic.

Mr. Bartlett told me that another one of the vendors of supplies to Howell, Nesard Gun Parts Co., 27 W. 990

Industrial Rd., Barrington, Ill., has also been the subject of the ATF investigation. Officer of that company, Gerald Graysen Cynthia Aleo and Anthony Aleo all pled guilty to ATF charges. The Nesard Co., which owned Sendra Corporation, was shipping AR-15 receivers through the Sendra Corp., along with part kits from the Nesard Co. When these parts are assembled it resulted in the manufacture of a short barreled rifle. Even though the above subjects are convicted felons they continue to conduct business because the Nesard Gun Parts Co., distributes gun parts and not firearms.

On January 25, 1993, I interviewed David Block in Los Angeles, California. He stated that he was member of Howell's cult at the Mount Carmel Center, Waco, Texas, from March 1992, until June 13, 1992. During the time he was there, he attended two Gun Shows with Vernon Howell, Mike Schroeder, Paul Fatta, and Henry McMahon who is a Federal licensed firearms dealer. The gun shows were in Houston and San Antonio, Texas.

While at the Mount Carmel Center he saw a metal lathe and a metal milling machine which were normally operated by Donald Bunds and Jeff Little. Donald Bunds, a mechanical engineer, has the capability to fabricate firearm parts, according to Block. On one occasion at the Mount Carmel Center, he observed Bunds designing, what Bunds described as a "grease gun/sten gun" on an Auto Cad Computer located at the residence building at the compound. The computer has the capability of displaying a three dimensional rendering of objects on a computer monitor screen. The object appeared to be a cylindrical tube with a slot cut into the side of it for a bolt cocking lever. Bunds told him that Howell wanted Bunds to design a "grease gun" which they could manufacture. Mr. Block told me that on another occasion at the Mount Carmel Center he saw Donald Bunds designing a template which Bunds explained was to fit around the "grease gun" tubes indicating where the bolt lever slots were to be milled out. This was another step in manufacturing "grease guns" which had been requested by Howell. I know that a "grease gun" is a machinegun following after the design of a World War II era military weapon.

During his time at the Mount Carmel Center Mr. Block was present several occasions when Howell would ask if anyone had any knowledge about making hand grenades or converting semi-automatic rifles to machineguns. At one point he also heard discussion about a shipment of inert hand grenades and Howell's intent to reactivate them. Mr. Block stated that he observed at the compound published magazines such as, the "Shotgun News" and other related clandestine magazines. He heard extensive talk of the existence of the "Anarchist Cook Book".

Mr. Block also told me that he met James Paul Jones from Redding, California, who was visiting the Mount Carmel Center in April or May of 1992. According to Howell, Jones was a firearms and explosives expert.

On February 22, 1993, ATF Special Agent Robert Rodriguez told me that on February 21, 1993, while acting in an undercover capacity, he was contacted by David Koresh and was invited to the Mount Carmel compound. Special Agent Rodriguez accepted the invitation and met with David Koresh inside the compound. Vernon Howell, also known as David Koresh played music on a guitar for 30 minutes and then began to read the Bible to Special Agent Rodriguez. During this session, Special Agent Rodriguez was asked numerous questions about his life. After answering all the questions Special Agent Rodriguez was asked to attend a two week Bible session with David Koresh. This was for Special Agent Rodriguez to learn the 7 Seals and become a member of the group. Special Agent Rodriguez was told that by becoming a member he (Rodriguez) was going to be watched and disliked. David Koresh stated that Special Agent Rodriguez would be disliked because the Government did not consider the group religious and that he (Koresh) did not pay taxes or local taxes because he felt he did not have to. David Koresh told Special Agent Rodriguez that he believed in the right to bear arms but that the U.S. Government was going to take away that right. David Koresh asked Special Agent Rodriguez if he knew that if he (Rodriguez) purchased a drop-in-Sear for an AR-15 rifle it would not be illegal, but if he (Rodriguez) had an AR-15 rifle with the Sear that it would be against the law. David Koresh stated that the Sear could be purchased legally. David Koresh stated that the Bible gave him the right to bear arms. David Koresh then advised Special Agent Rodriguez that he had something he wanted Special Agent Rodriguez to see. At that point he showed Special Agent Rodriguez a video tape on ATF which was made by the Gun Owners Association (G.O.A.). This film portrayed ATF as an agency who violated the rights of Gun Owners by threats and lies.

I believe that Vernon Howell, also known as David Koresh and/or his followers who reside at the compound known

locally as the Mount Carmel Center are unlawfully manufacturing and possessing machineguns and explosive devices.

It has been my experience over the five years that I have
been a Special Agent for the Bureau of Alcohol, Tobacco
and Firearms, and that of other Special Agents of the
Bureau of Alcohol, Tobacco and Firearms, some of whom
have the experience of twenty (20) years or more, who
have assisted in this investigation that it is a common
practice for persons engaged in the unlawful manufacture and possession of machineguns and explosive devices to employ surreptitious methods and means to acquire the products necessary to produce such items, and
the production, use and storage of those items are usually
in a protected or secret environment. It is also my experience that persons who acquire firearms, firearm parts,
and explosive materials maintain records of receipt and
ownership of such items and instruction manuals or other
documents explaining the methods of construction of such
unlawful weaponry.

At approximately 10:00 a.m. on February 28, 1993, ATF agents
attempted to execute the previously ordered search warrant
on the Howell compound. As agents entered the premises,
they were fired upon with machineguns and other large
caliber weapons. I was personally present at the scene and
heard the machinegun fire. Four ATF agents were killed and
approximately seventeen were injured by gun fire coming
from the compound. I personally spoke with Special Agent
Bill Buford who is the Resident Agent in Charge of the Little
Rock, Arkansas ATF Office. Buford, who was one of the
agents on the assault team who were attempting to execute
the warrant, advised me that he was able to enter a portion of

the Howell compound, and upon entering he observed what he described as "an arsenal". He further told me that, "Everything that we suspected to be in there was in there". I am making this affidavit on April 13, 1993, and state to the court that although I and others have attempted to execute the warrant on the main compound location (described above), we have been unable to search the premises and retrieve evidence because of heavy armed resistance from members of the cult group living at the compound. On March 5, 1993, Special Agent Charles Meyer of the ATF Austin, Texas, Office spoke with a cooperating individual who I do not wish to name at this time because of serious concerns for the safety and well being of the said cooperating individual. Meyer and I believe that this individual is being truthful in the information given because both Meyer and I have been able to independently corroborate the information received from this individual and have found the information provided by this individual to be extremely accurate and consistent with other evidence known to investigators such as receipts for firearms and destructive device components. This individual has been personally present on numerous occasions over the past year, and as recent as late February, 1993 when Howell and others discussed the conversion of firearms from semi-automatic to machineguns. This individual stated that she/he has personally observed MAC-10 and MAC-11 firearms located within the Howell compound within the past 45 days. It appeared to this individual that over the counter hardware and equipment was being utilized to manufacture these grenades. Within that same time frame, this individual has observed firearms silencers being manufactured within the compound. It was believed by this individual that the silencers were designed for AR-15 rifles. This individual also observed approximately 100 fully automatic AR-15/M-16 machineguns within the compound during the past 45 days. Tactical vests, that is, clothing designed to carry firearms ammunition and magazines, radio equipment and other paraphernalia were observed by this individual as were police scanners in the past 45 days. Further, I know that ATF Agents attempting to execute the search warrant on February 28, 1993, have stated that they observed what appeared to be tactical bests and body armor on many of the cult members who were firing upon the agents. This individual observed that Howell was attempting to construct radio controlled aircraft which can be used to carry explosives. Parts of these aircraft were observed by this individual within the compound in the past 45 days. This individual within the past 45 days observed what he believed to be large caliber rifles built upon tri-pods. This individual believes that the weapons that were observed may be .50 caliber weapons. Further, this individual, during this time frame observed in the compound video tapes and instructional booklets and other written materials dealing with firearms and combat training. Federal Agents have been observing the compound almost constantly since February 28, 1993. During these observations, they have seen cult members utilizing counter surveillance equipment, such as spotting scopes and binoculars. Agents have been in periodic contact by telephone with Howell and others since the 28th of February, when the siege of the compound began. Howell and others have stated that they (the cult) have night vision equipment (believed by agents to be star scopes). I know that cellular phones have been used by the group located at the compound to communicate both before and during the execution of the warrant. Phone toll records indicate this.

On March 2, 1993, Katherine Matteson, DOB: 2/3/16, a

"Branch Davidian" member, who has been residing in the compound in Waco, Texas, was released from the compound. Matteson brought out with her some personal belongings, to include a notebook, which contains explicit handwritten notes, of which I have reviewed. These handwritten notes depicts various different caliber weapons and ammunition. These notes also contain instructions on how to become a proficient firearms shooter by utilizing the proper techniques. These notes are so explicit, that it describes how to utilize windage when shooting a weapon and how one should mentally prepare oneself to survive.

On March 9, 1993, through ATF Command Post, Intelligence Branch, Waco, Texas, I received information from the ATF Field Division, Charlotte, North Carolina, concerning the activities of an FFL d.b.a: Rhino/Shooters Equipment/ Armitage International, et al., Seneca, S.C. Greenville, SC. Special Agents determined that said business had made eight shipments via UPS to David Koresh, et al., Route 7, Box 555, Waco, Texas. This information was reflected in UPS activity between 3-92 through 7-92. A subpoena was subsequently served on UPS in Greenville, SC, for copies of invoices of the shipments being delivered to Vernon W. Howell. The invoices reflect such items as eight (8) FN-FAL full auto Sears; five (5) M-16 bolt carriers; one (1) M-16 selector; thirty-one (31) M-16 full auto Sears and pins, all items of which are used to convert an AR-15 semi-automatic rifle into a M-16 machinegun rifle.

On March 9, 1993, in conjunction with this on-going investigation, I was advised by the ATF Los Angeles, California Field Division, that ATF Agents from the Long

Beach, California Field Office, executed a search warrant at a residence located at 2707 White Ave., La Verne, California. This residence is owned by Vernon W. Howell and or the Branch Davidians, and occupied by Branch Davidian members. As a result of this search, the following items were taken into ATF custody:

1. Correspondence to and from the compound in Waco, Texas.
2. Fifteen (15) audio cassette tapes, which contain predisposition toward violence.
3. Five (5) audio cassette tapes, which also contain predisposition toward violence.

On the following day, March 10, 1993, I was also advised that a consent to search the garage of the residence located at 2707 White Ave., La Verne, California was obtained by ATF Agents. As a result of this search, the following components for improvised explosives were recovered and taken into ATF custody:

1. Sulfuric acid.
2. Nitric acid.
3. Baking soda.
4. Saw dust, mixed with aluminum powder.
5. Six plastic baggies containing, what appear to be dirt.

On March 23, 1993, ATF Special Agent's Mike Taylor, Dale Littleton and I, interviewed Henry Stanley McMahon Jr., a Federal Firearms License Dealer, who at one time did business at 909 Rosedale, Hewitt, Texas. During this interview, McMahon stated that Vernon W. Howell had told him that in the Spring or early summer of 1992, he had observed the "ATF S.W.A.T. Team" training at a vacant house approximately 500 yards toward the compound next to the "Mag Bag". McMahon further stated that Howell had told him that this was training conducted by ATF to assault the compound/Mount Carmel property. Howell had stated to McMahon that ATF is so arrogant that there conducting their training right in front of us because ATF wants to send us a message of what they're going to do to the cult members. This training exercise, described by Howell that took place in the Spring of 1992, was confirmed by ATF with Police Officer Monroe Kelinske, Waco Police Department, as taking place from March 5 through March 9, 1992. This vacant house was being utilized by the Waco Police Department and other Police Departments as a training facility to execute warrants.

On April 2, 1993, Joyce Sparks, Investigation Supervisor, Department of Human Services, Waco, Texas, provided me with a narrative, concerning an interview she had with a former cult member, who will be referred to as the source. The source stated that she became a part of the cult when she was about three or four years old. She also stated that when she was ten years old, she was taken out of the compound to a motel room in the Waco, Texas area by her mother, where Vernon W. Howell, A/K/A: David Koresh was waiting in bed for her with no pants on. She stated that, while in the motel room, Howell sexually molested her. When asked how she was feeling when this happened, she responded "scared" but "privileged". She was asked if she knew what was going to happen to her when she was left in the motel room by her mother. She said that she knew it would happen "one of those times". She explained that they didn't talk about this because they didn't have to. It was understood in the group that this is what happens. They did not need to talk about it. That was just the way it was and everyone knew it.

It was asked if she knew about any other girls who had experienced this and she said yes. She reported that she knew about Michelle Jones. When asked how she knew this, she explained that Howell had talked about having sex with Michelle when she was fourteen. He told in a Bible Study once what it was like when he had sex with Michelle.

I now seek re-issuance for the warrant for the main compound and surrounding land (entire description set forth above). Further, because an extremely dangerous situation exists at this time and will likely continue to exist, agents may need to take advantage of the cover of darkness to enter the premises. Therefore, I seek permission for a nighttime (after 10:00 p.m.) warrant. I further request that this affidavit and all accompanying papers be sealed by the court to avoid further danger to agents and to avoid detection of the nature and scope of the investigation.

_____

Davy Aguilera, Special Agent
Bureau of ATF

Subscribed and sworn to before me this day_____ of_____, 1993

_____

Dennis G. Green,
United States Magistrate Judge
Western District of Texas - Waco

This warrant, affidavit and all accompanying papers are hereby sealed by order of this court.

Signed by me this day _____of_____, 1993.

_____

Dennis G. Green,
United States Magistrate Judge
Western District of Texas - Waco
ORIGINAL SIGNED BY AFFIANT

AFTERWORD

When this book went to press, authorities were still sifting through the charred remains and rubble at Mount Carmel, searching for and attempting to identify the remains of Branch Davidians. As of April 27, 1993, a partial list of the people believed to have been at the compound at the time of the April 19 fire was compiled by the *Associated Press*. That list, as well as the whereabouts of other Branch Davidians is presented here.

The first section lists people whom the FBI previously identified, and who were unaccounted for and presumed dead. Several were believed to have been killed the day the siege began, February 28, 1993. More than thirty others also were believed to have been inside.

David Koresh (nee Vernon Howell), 33, the Davidian cult's leader was presumed dead. The other sections list the people who were in the compound February 28 and were arrested that day, left subsequently or escaped the fire. Ages are listed where known. Unless a person is listed as "nationality unknown" or as some other nationality, he or she is believed to be a United States citizen.

Unaccounted For

Mary Jean Borst, 49
Pablo Cohen, 38, Israeli
Evette Fagan, 34, British
Lisa Marie Farris, 26
Dayland Gent, 3, Australian
Peter Gent, 24, Australian, killed February 28
Sandra Hardial, 27 British
Diana Henry, 28, British
Paulina Henry, 24, British
Phillip Henry, 22, British
Stephen Henry, 26, British
Vanessa Henry, 19, British
Zilla Henry, 55, British
Cyrus Howell, 8
Rachel Howell, 23
Star Howell, 6
Sherri Lynn Jewell, 23
David Michael Jones, 30
Michele Jones, 18
Perry Jones, age unknown, reportedly killed Feb. 28
Serenity Sea Jones, 4
Bobbie Lane Koresh, 16 months
Nicole Elizabeth Little (nee Gent), 24, Australia
Jeffery Little, 32
Douglas Wayne Martin, 42
Lisa Martin, 13
Sheila Martin, 15
Abigail Martinez, 11
Audrey Martinez, 13
Crystal Martinez, 3
Isaiah Martinez, 4
Joseph Martinez, 8

Juliete Santoyo Martinez, 30, nationality unknown
Jillane Matthews, age and nationality unknown
Alison Bernadette Monbelly, 31, British
Melissa Morrison, 6, British
Rosemary Morrison, 29, British
Theresa Noberega, 48, British
Judy Schneider, 41
Mayanah Schneider, 2
Steve Schneider, 43
Michael Schroeder, 29, killed February 28
Laraine B. Silva, 40, British
Floracita Sonobe, 34, Filipino
Scott Kojiro Sonobe, 35
Aisha Gyarfas Summers, 17, Australian
Gregory Allen Summers, 28
Startle Summers, 1
Hollywood Sylvia, age unknown
Lorraine Sylvia, 40
Rachel Sylvia, 13
Stanley Sylvia, age unknown
Doris Vaega, age unknown, British
Margarida Joann Vaega, 47, nationality unknown
Neal Vaega, 37
Jaydean Carnwell Wendel, age unknown
Mark H. Wendel, age unknown

Arrested February 28, 1993
Woodrow Kendrick, 63, in jail
Norman Washington Allison, Jamaican, in jail

Left Compound After February 28, 1993

Brad Branch, 35, in jail, charged with conspiracy to murder
Livingston Fagan, United Kingdom, in jail
Oliver Gyarfas, 19, Australian, in jail
Victorine Hollingsworth, 59
James Lawter, 70
Margaret Lawson, 76
Sheila Judith Martin, 46, in halfway house
Catherine Matson, 77
Gladys Ottman, 67
Anita Richards, age unknown, in halfway house
Rita Fay Riddle, 35, in halfway house
Ophelia Santoya, age unknown, in halfway house
Kathryn Schroeder, 34, in jail
Kevin Whitecliff, 31, in jail
Najara Fagan, 4, British
Renae Fagan, 6, British
Heather Jones, 9
Mark Jones, 12
Kevin Jones, 11
Christyn Mabb, 10
Jacob Mabb, 9
Scott Mabb, 11
Daniel Martin, 6
James Martin, 10
Kimberley Martin, 4
Natalie Nobrega, 11, nationality unknown
Bryan Schroeder, 3
Angelica Sonobe, 6
Crystal Sonobe, 3
Joshua Sylvia, 7
Jo Ann Vaega, 7, nationality unknown

Jaunessa Wendel, age unknown
Landon Wendel, 4
Patron Wendel, age unknown
Tamarae Wendel, 5

Survived April 19 Fire

Renos Avraam, 29, British, in jail
Jaime Castillo, 24, in jail, charged with conspiracy to murder federal agents
Graeme Leonard Craddock, 31, Australian, in jail
Clive Joseph Doyle, 52, hospitalized in good condition
Misty Ferguson, 17, hospitalized in critical condition
Derek Lloyd Lovelock, 37, British, in jail
Ruth Ellen Ottman, 29, also known as Ruth Ellen Riddle, hospitalized in good condition
Dave Thibodeau, 24, in jail
Marjorie Thomas, 30, hospitalized in critical condition

CONTACT RESOURCES

For people wanting assistance and more information about cults, these organizations and/or individuals can be contacted:

United States

Rick Ross
P. O. Box 32906
Phoenix, Arizona 85064-2906
(602) 956-0325

American Family Foundation
P. O. Box 2265
Bonita Springs, Florida 33959
(212) 249-7693

Christian Research Institute
P. O. Box 500
San Juan Capistrano,
California 92693
(714) 855-9926

Cult Awareness Network
2421 West Pratt Boulevard
Suite 1173
Chicago, Illinois 60645
(312) 267-7777

International Cult
Education Program
P. O. Box 1232
Gracie Station
New York, New York 10028
(212) 439-1550

Interfaith Coalition
of Concern About Cults
711 Third Avenue
New York, New York 10017
(212) 983-4977

Watchman Fellowship
P. O. Box 74091
Birmingham, Alabama 35253
(205) 871-3366

Canada
Cult Information Service
Calgary, Alberta
(403) 261-6754

Australia
CCG Ministries
176 Albert Street
Osborne Park,
West Australia 6017
(61) 9-344-2200

Wellspring Retreat
and Resource Center
P. O. Box 67
Albany, Ohio 45710
(614) 698-6277

England
Family Action, Information
and Rescue (FAIR)
BCM Box 3535
P. O. Box 12
London, England WC1N-3XX
(44) 1-539-3940